JN410915

Formation and Conflict of Modern Humanities Network in Northeast Asian Sea Region

Editor

Humanities Korea Plus Research Group Pukyong National University

Writers

Sehyun Cho Professor, Department of History, Pukyong National University

Sukyoung Kwak HK Research Professor, Institute for Humanities and Social Sciences, Pukyong National University

Moonkee Kim Professor, Department of History, Pukyong National University

Kwangdeok Seo HK Research Professor, Institute for Humanities and Social Sciences, Pukyong National University

Bogo Lee Professor, Division of Undeclared and Exploratory Majors, Pukyong National University

Seungwoong Ahn HK Research Professor, Institute for Humanities and Social Sciences, Pukyong National University

Minho Yang HK Research Professor, Institute for Humanities and Social Sciences, Pukyong National University

Minkyung Choi HK Professor, Institute for Humanities and Social Sciences, Pukyong National University

Mihee Kong HK Research Professor, Institute for Humanities and Social Sciences, Pukyong National University

Formation and Conflict of Modern Humanities Network in Northeast Asian Sea Region

Editor Humanities Korea Plus Research Group Pukyong National University

First Edition Date Oct 31.2019

Writers Sehyun Cho · Sukyoung Kwak · Moonkee Kim · Kwangdeok Seo · Bogo Lee · Seungwoong Ahn · Minho Yang · Minkyung Choi · Mihee Kong

Published by Somyong Publishing

15, Seocho Joongang-ro 6-gil, Seocho-gu, Seoul, Korea

Tel. 02-585-7840 Fax. 02-585-7848

somyungbooks@daum.net

http://somyong.co.kr

₩31,000

ISBN 979-11-5905-441-9 93810

This work was supported by the Ministry of Education of the Republic of Korea and the National Research Foundation of Korea (NRF-2017S1A6A3A01079869).

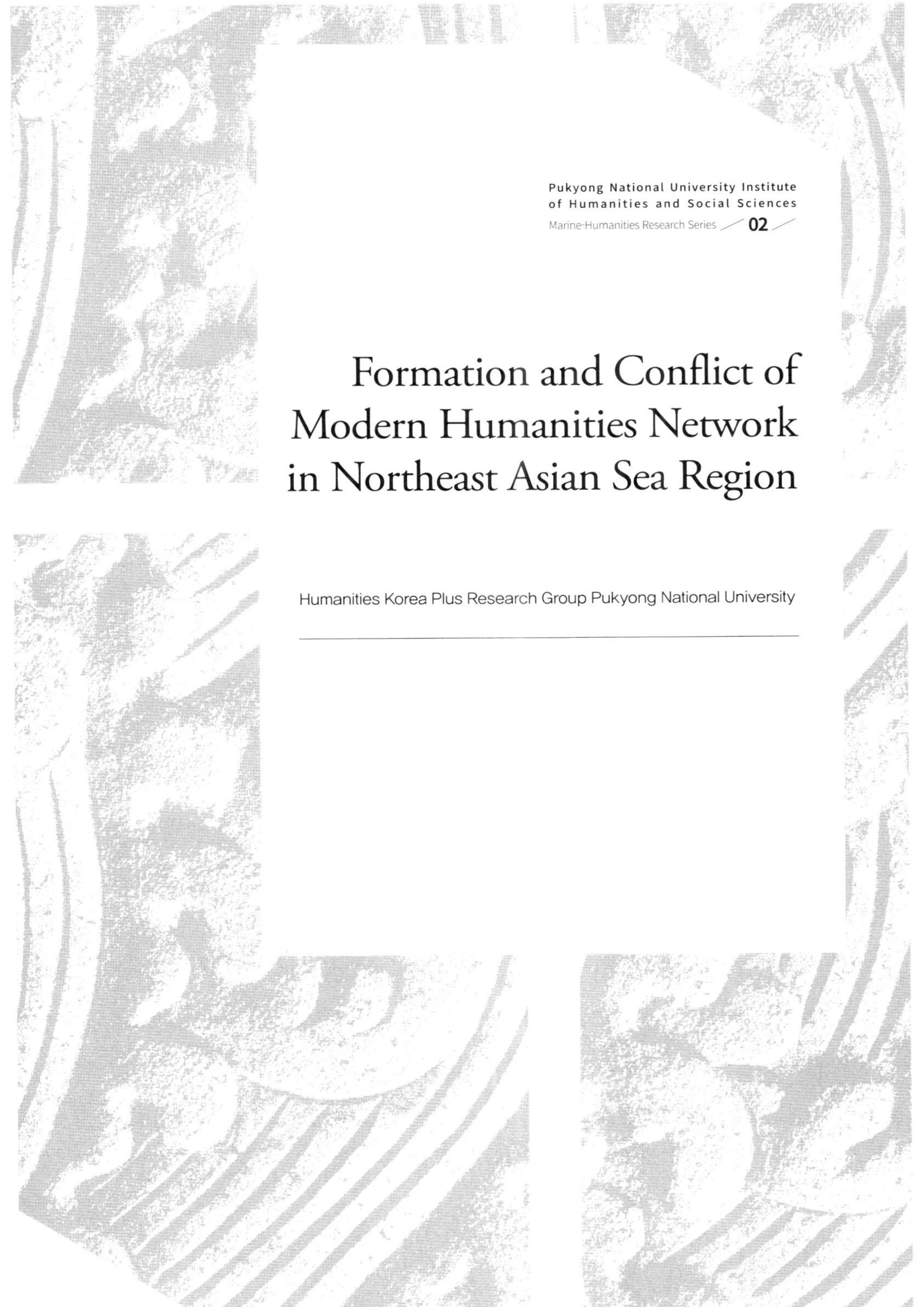

Pukyong National University Institute
of Humanities and Social Sciences
Marine-Humanities Research Series 02

Formation and Conflict of Modern Humanities Network in Northeast Asian Sea Region

Humanities Korea Plus Research Group Pukyong National University

Preface

The Institute for Humanities and the Social Science and the Institute of Marine-Humanities of Pukyong National University have pursued a holistic approach to studying human life revolving around the ocean based on the university's long tradition of maritime and fisheries education and research and the local infrastructure of Busan, the maritime capital of Korea. Land has been home to human existence for such a long time, so people have only recently started to recognize the ocean as an integral part of their lives. As people expanded their maritime activities from fishing and trading in coastal seas to the open sea, the ocean has truly become an object of study that deserves careful examination and research. The ocean used to be the realm of science/technology and ocean industries. However, with frequent navigations across the open sea and the subsequent formation of a global sea route network, similar to the Silk Road on land, the ocean has developed into a global venue for the movement of people, goods, ideologies, religions, knowledge, animals, plants, and even germs around the world.

The ocean is now as integral to human activities as land. Though humanistic approaches to examining the relationships between ocean and human beings have not been established yet, it is time to build so-called 'Ocean Humanities' since humans have become an overwhelming threat to the ocean in modern times. Ocean Humanities should squarely deal with issues relevant to humanities proper instead of simply focusing on defining the characteristics of 'maritime culture'. This is because international relations in the Northeast Asian Sea Region have become critical while conflicts and absurdities at national, societal, and individual levels have been escalating. The rise of such issues is due to more lively trade along the sea route network in modern time. Diverse human groups with distinct characters and cultures have come into contact with one another, experienced conflicts, and entered into negotiations, and this has created tensions in the ocean between the East and the West, national and transnational actors, central and local authorities.

The history of each sea region comprises the social cultures and acculturation processes driven by human groups in contact, which have cumulatively and collectively led to the current situation. Therefore, studying Northeast Asia from the perspective of the sea region can be considered a worthwhile approach to chartering a way forward by clarifying the historical processes at work in the Northeast Asian Sea Region and looking for solutions to conflicts after analyzing experiences of contacts and negotiations. 'Humanities focusing on sea regions' should be based on the idea that openness, expansibility, exchangeability, and coexistence are the focal points of marine culture and present them as assets of humanities while pursuing the externalization of marine humanities. At the same time, they should recognize sea regions as the connecting points between the ocean and land as well as the conflict-causing areas in Northeast Asia and consider practical measures to respond to existing issues of tensions and conflicts. Furthermore, they should offer new perspectives of looking at the relationships between the ocean and human beings.

All this being said, the Humanities Korea Plus Research Group of Pukyong National University focuses on "A Study on the Dynamics of Humanities Network in the Northeast Asian Sea Region" with the recognition that sea regions reflect the loose connections of land masses in an attempt to explore how history evolved in the Northeast Asian Sea Region connecting the Yellow Sea, the East Sea, the East China Sea, and the Pacific Ocean and what significance the history holds for Northeast Asians. First, this research project provides an academic approach to viewing the world in terms of sea regions rather than in terms of existing land which separates individual countries. It also promotes active discussions to solve pending issues and offer future research directions based on the historical context of Northeast Asian phenomena and its accumulated experiences. The so-called '(Northeast Asian) humanities focusing on sea regions' are a completely new area of study created by the Humanities Korea Plus Research Group of Pukyong National University. This series of publications on 'Humanities Focusing on Sea Regions' are expected to present a summary of research achievements and reveal the true nature of the new field as more books in the series are published. Finally, I hope that 'The Series of

Humanities Focusing on Sea Regions' will become a cornerstone contributing to the development of humanities which cover humans and society.

Son Dong-Ju
Director of Humanities Korea Plus Research Group,
Pukyong National University

Summary of the Series in English

The Northeast Asian Sea Region, consisting of the South China Sea, the East China Sea, the Yellow Sea, and the East Sea, has long been home to people who navigated the sea and traded goods. In this region, there have been various exchanges of human resources and goods by fishermen in the coastal waters, merchants, diplomatic delegations, naval forces carrying out aggressive wars, and pirates engaged in pillage. However, in modern times, Westerners with different historical and cultural backgrounds began to appear in this unique Northeast Asian space. Merchants and missionaries were the first Westerners who arrived in the region via the East Sea.

In early times, Western merchants traded goods with East Asian merchants whose main area of activity was the Northeast Asian Sea Region. In an effort to meet their needs and wants, they tried to procure local goods in a way that conflicted with the policies of medieval East Asian countries. At that time, seaborne trade was booming in the East Asian Sea, and the trade items were supplied from land and shipped through the waters. Thus, some specific spaces of the sea region became important, and this gave birth to ports. These ports were under the control of the country which ruled the land. So, opening ports to foreign trade became critical events whether before or after the modern times.

As more Western merchants sought opportunities to trade, trading, which used to be done freely among individual merchants, gradually increased in volume and profitability. Thus, it was deemed necessary for governments to intervene in trade and adopt a system that would secure trade deals. This heralded the emergence of a nation-state and the establishment of a global trading system based on alliances of nation states. In other words, free seaborne trade among individuals gradually turned into trade between countries. Mobilizing military power(naval forces) to secure the safety of individual trade led to terrible acts of war(naval battles) in the Northeast Asian sea region, the Opium War being a prime example. As a result, the East Asian Sea has been waters of war, not free trade. The breakout of the Opium War turned the East Asian Sea into a place of confrontation and conflicts, not a place of peace and coexistence after the modern times.

The Northeast Asian Sea Region has its dark aspects, but the significance of historical events arising from the contact of Eastern and Western cultures in the region cannot be ignored. Western merchants brought and took back various items other than trade goods, and their exotic daily life was introduced to the region as a new culture as they settled in the Northeast Asian sea region for long-term trade. As a result, the region emerged as a place of exchange and convergence of a variety of cultures. In addition, missionaries came along with

Western merchants, risking their lives to cross the sea and spread Christianity throughout the region. Starting with the Jesuit missionary Matteo Ricci, many missionaries have come to East Asia to propagate their religions, and they have brought not only the Bible and catechism books but also Western disciplines. Thanks to their efforts, new cultures have been implanted in East Asia have created a new culture in the East Asia, and locals have considered it a supreme task to embrace it as part of modern civilization as nation-states are established based on international trade.

'Formation and Conflict of Modern Humanities Network in Northeast Asian Sea Region', which is the 2nd year primary agenda of 'AStudy on the Dynamics of Humanities Network in the Northeast Asian Sea Region' covers the major confrontations and conflicts which were caused in the process of a humanities network being established in the Northeast Asian sea region, focusing on both positive and negative aspects. Indeed, it is quite natural that confrontations and conflicts arise as a result of cross-cultural contact and interaction which sometimes gave rise to war. The existing threat of war in the Northeast Asian sea region finds its originates from such historical forces.

This volume deals with how a humanities network has been established in the Northeast Asian sea region over the past 150 years, investigating the processes from the perspectives of knowledge, the private sector, and history. The first part is a collection of articles that examine Chinese modern history from an oceanic perspective, review Chinese policies to become a maritime power, and trace the spread and embracement of fish-related knowledge in the Northeast Asian sea region from a natural historical perspective. The second part consists of articles handling diverse aspects of cross-cultural exchanges in the Northeast Asian sea region based on modern history of academics and Western missionaries' travelogues. They also deal with Chinese modern writers' understanding of culture in the sea region and foreign words borrowed from the Western languages. It is hoped that the papers included in this volume will contribute to an understanding of the significance of the Northeast Asian sea region and to finding wisdom to positively address confrontations and conflicts surrounding the East Asian Sea.

Seo Kwang-Deok, Ph.D.
HK Research Professor
Humanities Korea Plus Research Group,
Pukyong National University

Contents

Preface 003
Summary of the Series in English 007

Part 1 / **Marine and East Asian Modernity**

Sehyun Cho_ A Maritime View on the Formation of Modern China __15

Sukyoung Kwak_ China's Maritime Power Strategy and Sinocentrism : With a Focus on Islands Disputes and the Maritime Silk Road __59

Moonkee Kim_ Affluence in the Little Ice Age : Natural History of Herring, Cod and Pollock __85

Part 2 / **Cultural Exchange in Northeast Asian Sea Region**

Kwangdeok Seo_ Contention Between National Studies and Regional Studies(Foreign Studies) in the Course of Formation of East Asian Modern Studies : Focusing on the Formation of Chinese Studies in Korea before Liberation __115

Bogo Lee_ Dual Position of Cross-Border Travelers in Cultural Contact Zones Viewed from "Journal of a Voyage Along the Coast of China" __145

Seungwoong Ahn_ Shen Cong Wen and Maritime Culture of Qingdao __176

Minho Yang_ A Study on the Introduction of Modern Western Languages to Japan : a Focus on Loan Words from the Dutch Language __204

Part 3 / **Hybridity of Sea Area Culture**

Minkyung Choi_ A Review of the Concept of 'Diaspora Space' and Busan – Focusing on the Beginning of a Movement __225

Sehyun Cho_ From the Chinese Concession Area(淸國租界地) to Choryang(草梁) Chinatown – History of Overseas Chinese in Busan __252

Mihee Kong_ A Consideration of the Characteristics and Historical Background of Japanese Fusion Cuisine Created Through Cross-cultural Exchanges with the West in Port Cities __284

Contributors __311

Part 1

Marine and East Asian Modernity

Sehyun Cho_

A Maritime View on the Formation of Modern China

Sukyoung Kwak_

China's Maritime Power Strategy and Sinocentrism

With a Focus on Islands Disputes and the Maritime Silk Road

Moonkee Kim_

Affluence in the Little Ice Age

Natural History of Herring, Cod and Pollock

A Maritime View on the Formation of Modern China

Sehyun Cho

1. Introduction

While the early modern period in East Asia could be characterized by the ban on maritime trade, the modern era essentially began in the sea. Accordingly, the perception of the sea during the Qing dynasty, which span across the early modern and modern periods, changed dramatically. The Qing dynasty before the nineteenth century maintained stable relations with foreign countries with the so-called Chinese world order as its basis. Maritime exchanges between the East Asian regions were restricted due to the ban on maritime trade implemented during the Ming and Qing dynasties. As a result, little maritime disputes took place, aside from several issues including piracy. When the European maritime empires, including Portugal, Spain, the

Netherlands, the British Empire, and France, set sail to East Asia, China restricted maritime trade by keeping a firm hand on the clearance for ships. As is widely known, foreign relations during the Qing dynasty were based on the order of *Huayi*(華夷) and the sea ban(海禁). Tributary trade, of course, continued by sea during the sea ban and during the period the sea ban was relaxed, maritime customs offices were operated to manage the trade and collect the tariff for private ships.

The Chinese perspective towards the sea fundamentally changed after China was invaded by the Western powers and after the Opium War. The Western powers' advances towards East Asia gathered speed in the mid-nineteenth century, as the imperialist powers, with the UK and France at the forefront, swarmed up to Northeast Asia by passing through Southeast Asia. This trend intensified as the Western powers began to compete and fight for colonies in Northeast Asia beginning in the late nineteenth century. The modern era in China essentially began when the sea ban system was disbanded by Western powers. The advent of the modern treaty system after the two Opium Wars signified the dissolution of the sea ban system. Scholars have traditionally considered modern history to begin when the sea ban policy was lifted, that is, when ports were opened and states were established. In recent years, the international relations in East Asia in the nineteenth century are explained as a conflict between the Chinese-centric tributary system and the Western-centric treaty system, which later led to the incorporation of the tributary system into the treaty system.

As the modern concept of the nation-state brought about a change in the perceptions towards the borders and territories on land, new perceptions towards the boundaries and areas in the sea also appeared. The maritime boundaries during the Qing dynasty, of course, existed and were called the external sea and the internal sea, but they were far from the modern notion of territorial waters. It is difficult to say that there were no maritime boundaries during the premodern era, but the use of such boundaries was limited to managing the fisheries of fishers and having the military jurisdiction over the coastal sea and the present notion of sovereignty hardly existed. Drastic changes, however, occurred at the end of the Qing dynasty. This paper focused on how the Chinese perception towards the sea changed from the traditional to the modern concept as China accepted the Western concept of the sea. This paper posited that if the period beginning from the Opium War to the Sino-Japanese War(mostly until the Self-Strengthening Movement) was when the maritime order was reorganized and the maritime concepts converging the existing Chinese and Western concepts were being formed, the period beginning from the Sino-Japanese War leading to the Chinese Revolution in 1911 (mostly around the late Qing Reform) was when the Western maritime concepts, such as the concept of territorial waters, were accepted in China.

2. The Formation of the Chinese and Western Convergent Maritime Concepts during the Self-Strengthening Movement(洋務運動)

1) The Signing of Trade Treaties and the Rise of the Shipping Industry

Free trade promoted by the UK in the nineteenth century could be defined as the trade order across nation-states separated by land or maritime boundaries. The UK, which established a maritime empire, pressured the Qing dynasty from the sea to transition from a traditional state to a modern nation and eventually succeeded in dissolving the sea ban system. One of the most noticeable changes that represented the dissolution of the sea ban was the collapse of the monopoly led by the Cantonese trade system and the establishment of modern maritime customs offices in a number of open ports. Later, maritime customs offices became administrative bodies affiliated with the Zongliyamen(總理衙門) and aside from collecting tariffs, managed various aspects of diplomacy during the Qing dynasty, as foreign trade or tariff duties were conducted under the management of foreign-national tax accountants.

The modern maritime customs offices played an important role in importing the new system of capitalism to China; this institution succeeded in breaking down the traditional concepts of *Hua* and *Yi* and affected Qing's foreign policy during the Self-Strengthening Movement, thereby establishing the basis for Qing's foreign relations with the world powers. Maritime customs offices also managed maritime affairs, including the collecting of fee for ships, managing the ports and the facilities at the port, lighthouses, and supervising the purchase of ships and nautical charts. The Chinese maritime customs offices were under British control for a long time and English was the language used for most tasks. As a result, the jargons used in the maritime customs officers were mostly Chinese words translated from English. The maritime customs offices were pivotal in importing the new system of capitalism to China and at the same time set the basis for the Qing dynasty relations with the UK and the Western powers.

It might be said that the Europeans were incorporated into the Asian trade network until the nineteenth century but after the mid-nineteenth century, trade took a different form by taking place in open ports through open doors and unequal treaties often incurred by wars. The Treaty of Nanking and the Treaty of the Bogue, signed between the Qing dynasty and the UK in the aftermath of the First Opium War, as well as the Treaty of Wanghia, signed between the Qing dynasty and the United States, and the Treaty of Whampoa the Qing dynasty signed with France were all treaty systems based on the law of nations, which laid the foundation to the establishment of new maritime order in various fields, including the maritime customs offices, shipping, and the navy. The articles of the treaties intended to apply the international law and domestic law on maritime affairs of the Western powers on the Chinese sea. After the Second Opium War, the Qing dynasty simultaneously signed the

Treaty of Tientsin and the Treaty of Peking with the United States, the UK, and France, which gave shape to the treaty system and brought about a reorganization of the maritime order.

The articles on shipping in the commercial treaties show that the Qing dynasty, which was unfamiliar with the sea, gave a number of rights to the Western powers by entering the treaties. As five ports were open, the representative sovereignty over waters and the right to navigate and trade in the coastal waters were all granted to the Western powers. The right to navigate the coastal waters was reflected in the treaties signed after the First Opium War by default and was extended to even the right to navigate domestic rivers, including the Yangtze River after the Second Opium War. The treaties signed after the First Opium War did not specify that foreigners could sell and transport domestic goods in the Chinese coastal waters. However, the Western powers interpreted that as long as it was not prohibited, it could be done. As China experienced the Second Opium War, the Western powers officially legalized the transport of both Western goods and Chinese goods to commercial ports. In terms of sailing, the right to guide sea routes, that is, the navigational rights, was violated. Prior to the Opium War, the guides in China's coastal waters were all Chinese. However, directly after the First Opium War, the Western powers, discontent with the Chinese guides, made it consecutively easier for them to hire guides themselves through the Treaty of the Bogue, which was signed between the Qing dynasty and the UK, the Treaty of Xiamen between the Qing dynasty and the United States, and through the

Treaty of Whampoa between the Qing and France. This was also stipulated in the Treaty of Tientsin, which was signed after the Second Opium War, and Robert Hart, the Inspector-General of China's maritime customs office, separately established the center for water navigations and had foreign employees take over the open ports in China.

Furthermore, in regards to the navy-related articles in the treaties, the Western powers, including the UK and the United States which came to China by sea, were extremely interested in sea rescue operations from the beginning. Articles on sea rescue operations were, therefore, included in treaties signed after the First Opium war and were specified after the Second Opium War. Through such measures, the traditional policy of repatriating castaways was abrogated. Another interesting item, which was added after the Second Opium War in tandem with the sea rescue operations, was on the apprehension of pirates. The British Navy was especially proactive in apprehending pirates and succeeded in suppressing them with the cooperation from the Qing dynasty. The treaties stipulated that China would be aiding British warships should they be engaged in any military activities. Rescue operations and the suppression of pirates helped the Western powers and the Qing dynasty to improve their relations. The article allowing Western powers to dock their warships in Chinese harbors was one of the representative navy-related privileges the Western powers enjoyed. As a special ship, the warship had extraterritoriality in the territorial waters of any country. The docking of foreign warships in Chinese harbors, therefore, was a politically sensitive issue. While the Treaty of the Bogue, which was signed after the First Opium War, used a vague expression, "official ship"(官船), the Xiamen Treaty between the United States and the Qing dynasty set a more detailed article on warships in China. The Treaty of Tientsin, which was signed as a result of the Second Opium War between the Qing dynasty, the UK, and the United States, included a wider definition on warship docking and enabled the warships to be docked for any purpose. The fact that foreign warships could roam freely in China's seas and could be anchored long-term in its harbors and wield a nearly limitless authority left great and long-lasting repercussions on the Chinese society.

As the ports were opened after the signing of commercial treaties at the end of the Qing dynasty, the maritime order was reorganized. The traditional sailing boat industry went into decline and the steamship industry began to flourish. There was a change in the traditional maritime concepts in the modern age as China began to acknowledgment its navigational rights through its competition with the West. Shipping traditionally implied the task of moving the grain, which was collected as tax, to the capital by waterways, but in the modern age, its range widened to include the moving of travelers and goods. Existing research on the modern shipping industry focused on the shipping competition between China and the Western powers, the infiltration of foreign shipping companies into China, and the development of the Chinese shipping industry, including the founding of China Merchants Steam Navigation Company(輪船招商局). During this period, the shipping industry was developed, initially through the competition between Chinese and foreign sailboats, which was followed by the mutual competition between sailboats and steamboats, and finally through the competition between Chinese and foreign steamboats. It is generally accepted that the foreign steamboats appeared as there was an increase in foreign trade and that the traditional Chinese sailboat trade went into decline as the foreign steamboats dominated the shipping industry. The pirates made frequent appearances and were suppressed during this process.

After the Qing Navy was annihilated by the British Navy during the First Opium War, pirates began to appear in the Southeast coastal waters. From approximately 1840 to 1860, piracy was the biggest obstacle preventing domestic and international trade by sea. Foreigners, including the British, Dutch, and Portuguese, therefore, defended the port by using armed ships and collected protection fees from merchant ships, fishing boats visiting the ports and the ships navigating the coastal waters. During this period, only the British Navy was allowed to protect its national trade gains by force in the Chinese waters. The British Navy succeeded in crushing the pirates after a few decades of effort and took initiative in protecting all the merchant ships. After a new treaty was signed in the wake of the Second Opium War, the Qing dynasty officially stated that it will wipe away the pirates with the help from the Western forces, including the UK. Under this context, it is worth noting that the rise of pirates had huge influences over the sailboat industry in the Chinese coastal waters.

In response to the expansion of foreign shipping companies, China's sailboat industry was also active in the Southern coastal areas, especially in Fujian and Guangdong while the Qing's maritime policy repeatedly issued and lifted the sea ban. China finally opened its doors when the sailboats were replaced with steamboats. The early 1860s was the heyday of the high-speed clipper ships since they were the most common variety among foreign ships. However, drastic changes took place in international trade between the East and West after the opening of the Suez Canal. Foreign shipping industries came into China and their new steamboats overpowered Chinese sailboats in their competitiveness. Sailboats were no match to steamboats, which were fast and stable in speed and could sail in any season or in the face of any wind. Foreign merchants established large steamboat companies, including Russell & Company, Butterfield & Swire and Jardine, and began to do business in not only Shanghai but also the coastal ports and even in the rivers, including the Yangtze. Thrown out of the competition with the foreign companies, a majority of the traditional Chinese shipping companies went bankrupt and the rise of the shipping industry expedited the collapse of the inland canal networks.

In relation to the beginning of the Chinese shipping industry, the shipping method of the grain collected as tax also went through change at the end of the Qing dynasty, as they were shipped by the sea instead of being shipped by the Grand Canal. This was because the canal networks collapsed due to a number of natural disasters and popular uprisings, which made it much more efficient to ship the grain by sea. However, as China's navigation rights were violated after the two consecutive Opium Wars, the profits from China's rivers and the sea began to be taken by foreigners. Chinse ships and Western steamboats engaged in fierce competitions not only over the shipping of grains but also of pisolites and salt. Around this period, the *Yangwu*(洋務) officials, including Li Hongzhang, used China's monopoly over the grain shipping industry to establish the China Merchants Steam Navigation Company, which became one of the representative companies of the Self-Strengthening Movement, in order to compete with the West. Although the China Merchants Steam Navigation Company was not established for the shipping of grains, grain shipping was the main reason and economic background behind its establishment. The success of the China Merchants Steam Navigation Company broke down the monopoly of foreign steamboat companies and made room for competition, precipitating progress in China's modern shipping industry.

2) The Adoption of the Law of Nations(萬國公法) and the Modern Maritime Dispute in Northeast Asia

When explaining the international relations in East Asia, the transition from the traditional era to the modern era is often called "the transition from the tributary system to the international law system". The replacement of the tributary system, which had continued for thousands of years in the East Asian society, by the modern European international law order in the nineteenth century through the so-called Western shock, was a significant event. "The law of nations", in this context, is the title of the book in a narrow sense but also another name for "international law". *Elements of International Law* which was written by the American international law scholar Henry Wheaton(Chinese name 惠頓) and translated by the American missionary W. A. P. Martin(Chinese name 丁韙良) was the most recognized book which represented the modern order of the Western world.

Three hundred copies of *Elements of International Law* were first printed at the Tongwen guan(同文館), the School of Combined Learning, in 1864(Year 1 of the Tongzhi era) but the supply ran short of the demand from the provincial officials. Considering the fact that there was an official document requesting the reprint of *The Elements of International Law*, this book may have been reprinted by the Zongliyamen. After the initial year of its publication, *The Elements of International Law* was also introduced to Japan and became one of the two top bestsellers at the end of the shogunate, along with *Seiyo jijo*(西洋事情) by Fukuzawa Yukichi. Although the publication of *Elements of International Law* did not garner a national interest as it had in Japan, the Chinese translation became the first book on international law to be published in East Asia.

The adoption of international law during the late Qing dynasty could be divided into two phases. The first phase was from 1864 to the end of the nineteenth century and was signified with the translation of the *Elements of International Law*. The second phase was from the early twentieth century until the fall of the Qing dynasty when the Chinese students studying abroad in

Japan translated Japan's international law and introduced it to China. After the first year of Emperor Guangxi's reign, the Qing dynasty translated over 16 different books on Western international law, which is significant considering that the only one book, *Elements of International Law*, was published during the reign of the former emperor Tongzhi(from 1862 to 1874). The fact that international law was commonly called "law of nations" or the "law of ten thousand nations", which was the Chinese title to *Elements of International Law*, shows the great influence of the publication of this book in 1864. As the modern notion of the nation-state was introduced to China through the signing of treaties and the adoption of international law, the Chinese experienced a change in perception toward national borders and territories. A paradigm shift occurred in the perception of the sea as new ideas on the maritime borders and territorial waters.

Freedom of the seas, a principle established since the seventeenth century, is the broad principle of traditional international law and could also be found in the *Elements of International Law*, which was published in the mid-nineteenth century. *Elements of International Law*, which was translated by Martin, discusses marine-related issues in detail. The *Elements of International Law*, in fact, begins with definitions of territorial waters and high waters and goes on to explain the prohibition of pirates and persecuting maritime crimes, rules to seizing ships on the sea. It further provides details on the issues of building military ships and fostering the navy. It accurately reflects the major legal issues related to maritime affairs that it could be called a book of international maritime law. Contrary to modern society, where the perception towards the sea is becoming increasingly exclusive, the book reflects the notion of the freedom of the seas during the era. The parts on pirates or the existence of the license to seize private ships show the characteristics of the Western world in modern times, whereas the chapters on occupation and conquest fully display imperialistic characteristics. The concepts of territorial and high seas, as well as the detailed description of maritime war, shocked its Chinese readers, especially in regards to their maritime rights. *Elements of International Law* showed how the modern nation-states in the Western world took control and ruled the sea. The translation of this book was also used by Chinese in their maritime disputes and served as a momentum for them to gain a fresh viewpoint and come to a new realization towards the sea.

International law, which was called the "law of nations" during the Self-Strengthening Movement, was closely related to the early maritime disputes. When joining the international law system, the Qing dynasty focused on the fact that the Western powers had a new perception of and defense system in the sea, which served as the main gateway to imperialism. At the end of the Qing dynasty, the Western powers raised issues on castaways and shipwrecks or conducted illegal surveys on the sea to invade the Chinese territorial waters. The Qing dynasty realized the importance of international law by using the freshly translated *Elements of International Law* to resolve the Dagukou boat incident which arose between Prussia and Denmark.

The Dagukou(大沽口) boat incident was an event in which Prussia seized a

Danish ship in the mouth of Tientsin Harbor. In early 1864, the Prussian Chancellor O. von Bismarck was allying with Austria in a war against Denmark over the Schleswig-Holstein Attribution and Problems. G. von Rehfues, who was newly instated as the Prussian Minister to China during the war, was expected to arrive in Beijing via Tientsin in a Gazelle navy ship. However, on his way from Dagukou to Tientsin, he found three Danish ships anchored in the sea and seized them. This incident triggered diplomatic friction between the Qing dynasty and Prussia, which was effectively resolved by the Zongliyamen, by implicitly adopting some of the content from the *Elements of International Law*. The Dagukou incident was the first time international law was used to resolve a maritime dispute.

The notion of international law spread widely as news on Alabama Claims, which were made during the American Civil War, was publicized. The CSS *Alabama*, which was built in England, was used as a warship for the Confederate army to commit piracy on not only the Union states' ships but on ships around the world, but was later sunk by a Union warship. This went to the international court as the American government argued that the UK committed a violation of neutrality and filed in a claim for the compensation of damages. Although Alabama Claims was a maritime dispute between the UK and the US and was not directly related to China, it was nevertheless an extremely well-known case in the history of international law during the nineteenth century which had a huge influence in spreading the notion of international law. The Chinese learned about Alabama Claims not through *Elements of Interna-*

tional Law but through other translations of books on international law, *Introduction to the Study of International Law*(公法便覽) and *Modern International Law*(公法會通).

While the Qing dynasty defended its own profits by using international law during the Tongzhi era, it did not completely adopt Western international law theories. The Zongliyamen merely used international law on a practical level in diplomatic negotiations. The mixed usage of traditional concepts and imported theories was also apparent in the altercation between China's tributary system and the Western world's treaty system.

The first breakdown in the Qing dynasty's tributary system took place in its subordinate relationship with the Ryukyuan people. What triggered this breakdown was the "Mudan(牧丹) incident of 1871, during which shipwrecked Ryukyuan sailors were massacred. Citing the massacre of the Ryukyuan sailors by the local Taiwanese people as the reason for the attack, the Japanese army invaded Taiwan in 1874 through the sea and attacked the indigenous tribes including the Mudan community. This came as a shock to the Qing dynasty, which held discussions on a large-scale liberation and eventually decided to create the Taiwan province. The Ganghwa Island incident, which took place in Joseon in 1875, was also closely related to maritime issues. The Japanese vessel *Unyo* approached the Joseon coastal waters to survey sea routes to China and was engaged in armed conflict with the Joseon army. This incident became an international issue and led to talks between China and Japan and resulted in the signing of the Korea-Japan Treaty of 1876. In the process of managing the maritime disputes which arose in China's subordinate relations with Ryukyu and Joseon, the Zongliyamen and Li Hongzhang alternately chose the traditional option and the modern option to avert the crises. Ryukyu and Joseon also used their traditional subordinate relations with China and made an effort to gain independent status in international law.

Not long after accepting the law of nations, the Chinese began to consider it as the ideal international law and order. They perceived it as an axiom. One of such people was Li Hongzhang. He was well-read in international law and in his own way, tried to observe the law of war at sea and prevent the spread of maritime war. He, however, overlooked the fact that international law during the era was far from being unified and could be arbitrarily interpreted in favor of the powerful.

3) The Formation of the Navy and International Law Cases on Maritime Law

The invasion of China by the Western powers basically began with their navies. To reinforce their coastal waters(海防), it was essential for the Qing dynasty to form a navy as well. In modern China, the navy was not only an armed force but also a military institution with concentrated science and technological knowledge, and its formation accelerated China's modernization. The establishment of a navy presupposes modern scientific, industrial and technological progress, especially in terms of navigation, communication, shipbuilding, the development of fuel, the management of ports, as well as the manufacturing of engines and firearms. Such progress should be supported by personnel who are well trained with such technology and by a society-wide development in scientific technology. The history of the Chinese navy, therefore, provides an understanding of China's steps to modernization.

One of the characteristics which separate modern navy from the ancient navy was that both had completely different types of battleships and guns, as well as different types of fuel, power, weapons, and methods of attack. Ancient battleships were made of wood, sailed by using wind and manpower and were armed with personal weapons, such as swords and bows, and close-range cannons. One of the representative methods of attack was to collide with the enemy ship, which was why the bows of the ships were reinforced with thick metal and were used in attacking the sides of enemy ships to sink them. The modern navy, on the contrary, used steam engines to generate power and were equipped with large cannons and its operations and military tactics was fundamentally different from its ancient counterpart. The navy is a product and microcosm of the modern industry. It truly is a floating factory in the sea.

The nineteenth century was the period when the traditional navy was modernized and was also when states struggled for sea power. Metal ships replaced wooden ships, the steam engine replaced oars and the wind energy and the explosive bombs replaced empty shells. Beginning from the 1860s, the navy entered the age of ironclad warships. The warships, however, were slow due to their heavy weight and were protected by the relatively faster and lighter cruisers. The development of torpedoes and torpedo boats put an end to the faith people had placed in existing naval strategies and fundamentally changed maritime war. Such revolutionary changes in the navy and maritime wars were directly reflected in China when it in the process of learning about Western modernism.

From the Opium Wars to the Russo-Japanese War, wars in Modern China frequently took place in the sea. As threats from the sea came from the UK, France, and Japan, the importance of naval defense, rather than land defense, was continuously raised and led to the reinforcement of the navy. In accordance with such changes, the passive maritime defense policy of defending harbors and suppressing pirate activities changed to a more proactive defense policy as ports began to open in the aftermath of the Opium Wars. The traditional navy changed into the modern navy under the same context. In the early days, the Qing dynasty either manufactured replicas of Western battleships and cannons or purchased them by paying a huge fortune with the help of foreigners who were living in China. However, due to the limited perception towards maritime affairs, the ships and cannons fell short of the court's expectation and aggravated the crisis the Qing dynasty was facing. To make up for this, the Qing court began to purchase new battleships directly from foreign countries. The Qing Dynasty built battleships, naval ports, and dockyards and fostered navy personnel. Japan's invasion of Taiwan (also called the Mudan incident) in 1874 was a particularly shocking event for the Qing dynasty, which then decided that "the defense of the sea cannot be delayed any further" and began forming the modern navy troops.

The transformation of the traditional navy to the modern version is closely related to the formation of modern maritime concepts. The establishment of the navy in the late Qing dynasty began when the Qing court attempted to purchase foreign-made vessels, built a dockyard and ships in the early 1860s. The purchase of foreign vessels and cannons during the Self-Strengthening Movement could largely be divided into three phases.

The first phase began after the crisis caused by the Taiping Rebellion, when the Qing dynasty formed a modern fleet and tried to suppress the navy of the rebel forces. For this, the Qing court attempted to import eight British battleships and ships to create a small-scale navy. This plan, however, did not come to fruition as the British personnel in charge, Captain S. Osborn, insisted on taking the right to command the fleet and was in a disagreement with the royal court. The Anglo-Chinese Fleet incident was the Qing dynasty's first attempt to create a modern navy and its failure caused a setback in its plan to form a modern navy. This experience, however, helped the Qing dynasty create shipyards, such as the Fuzhou Shipbuilding Bureau(福州船政局), and to produce its own vessels.

The second phase was induced by the Taiwan incident in 1847, which took place about 10 years after the Chinese Fleet incident, and the outcome of the first dispute on defending the sea. Qing China began to form its navy earnestly after Japan's invasion of Taiwan and its annexation of the Ryukyu Kingdom. With the help of Hart, Li Hongzhang purchased four British vessels called gunboats, which were delivered to China in 1876 and were each named *Longxiang, Huwei, Feiting*, and *Chidian*. In 1878, Qing China, again through Hart, purchased four additional gunboats, which were respectively named *Zhendong, Zhenxi, Zhennan*, and *Zhenbei*. The eight gunboats purchased through Hart had much left to desire as battleships. These boats had large guns in small vessels, which made them better fitted for the coastal areas, rather than the deep sea.

The third phase was before and after the Sino-French War when the Beiyang Fleet ordered two cruisers from the UK, the *Chaoyong*(超勇) and *Yangwei*(揚威). Then in the late 1880s and the summer of 1881, Li Hongzhang ordered two armored battleships, *Dingyuan*(定遠) and Zhenyuan(鎮遠). These armored battleships were delivered after the Sino-French War due to the interference from France. From 1885 to 1888, the Beiyang Fleet also ordered four cruisers—*Jiyuan, Zhiyuan, Jingyuan*, and *Laiyuan*—in addition to armored battleships. The battleships purchased during this era were not the best in terms of quality but were nonetheless well-made enough to be used in the ocean for operations. The Qing dynasty's fleet finally became modern after the Beiyang naval forces were formally established in 1888.

The three wars—the Taiwan Incident in 1874, the Sino-French War from 1883 to 1885, and the Sino-Japanese War from 1894 to 1895—were all fought by the modern navy. The Taiwan Incident broke out due to Japan's unilateral invasion and the Qing China, shocked to acknowledge the fact that it was unable to respond to the attack at all, began to form a navy. The formation of a modern naval force was one of the objectives of the military modernization during the Self-Strengthening movement. Afterward, large-scale naval battles took place in the Sino-French and Sino-Japanese Wars. The Battle of Fuzhou between the Qing China and France, was a one-sided defeat of the Fujian Fleet by the French fleet but was significant in that it was China's first modern maritime war experience. A number of international law cases related to maritime affairs arose in this war and deepened China's understanding of maritime affairs. In the Sino-Japanese War, which took place ten years later, a number of armored battleships and cruisers were used in the Battle of the Yellow Sea, which became known as one of the most famous battles in the history of naval warfare. There were international law disputes even during this sea battle, which Qing China waged without assistance from the Western powers.

Both wars began with maritime disputes. In the Sino-French War, the Qing dynasty actively employed international law to evade the war, which led to a number of international law disputes, including the Battle of Fuzhou, the blocking of the Taiwan Strait, and the neutrality of third powers. The Battle of Fuzhou, which broke out as France violated international law, became the prelude to the modern maritime warfare in China. During the war, the French fleet violated the international law, which bans "the reckless blocking of ports", and forcefully blocked the port to Taiwan. This was an infringement not only on Qing China's sovereign rights but also on its right to have normal relations with other countries. There also were numerous disputes in regards to the neutrality of third powers, which encompassed the provision of coal, purchasing of weaponry, repairing vessels, communications support, and the cooperation from the foreign coast pilots. Conflicts also aroused on issues such as external promotion, the protection of foreign residents, the demand for states to remain neutral, and issues regarding the prisoners of war.

After the Fujian Fleet went into decline in the aftermath of the Sino-French War, the Beiyang Fleet rose to become the largest navy troop in Qing China. Japan was the fleet's virtual enemy. There were also a number of international law disputes during the Sino-Japanese war, which took place ten years later. One of which included the Kowshing(高陞號) Incident, an incident closely related to the beginning of the Sino-Japanese War. The British vessel *Kowshing* was employed by the Qing dynasty for carrying military personnel and supplies to Joseon. The Japanese, however, viewed that they had a right to stop this ship from sailing towards its destination. The British captain of the *Kowshing* tried to follow Japan's order but the Qing navy took away the captain's control of the ship and refused to surrender, which led to an altercation between the Qing and Japanese naval forces. It, however, was a violation of international law for the two states to sink a ship owned by a neutral state without declaring war. The massacre of the prisoners of war or civilians in Port Author, which was the Beiyang Fleet's military base, as well as the civilian massacre in the Battle of Weihaiwei were the other international law cases related to maritime affairs. The issue of third power neutrality also arose during this war. Losing the Sino-Japanese War eventually led to the fall of the Beiyang Fleet, which was the symbol of the Self-Strengthening Movement. As a result, major Chinese ports became leased territories occupied by the Western powers.

If the Qing court made frequent mistakes during the Taiwan Incident, which heralded the formation of the Qing navy, out of ignorance, it was its over-dependence on international law and its attempts to directly apply the legal clauses, which led it to be in the Sino-French Maritime War. The Qing dynasty did not blindly rely on international law after the two incidents but its brutal defeat in the Sino-Japanese War was a realpolitik reminder that "weak countries do not have diplomatic options". The Beiyang Fleet may have looked like a modern navy fleet, but it was internally limited by being a product of Sino-Western convergence. Qing China accepted the natural law by the media of Confucian moral values . In the early days of adopting the law of nations. But as it entered the era of imperialism in the late nineteenth century, it began to interpret international law in the context of the theory of social evolution, of the law being centered on the law of the jungle and the survival of the fittest.

3. The Adoption of the Western Maritime Concepts at the Last Qing Dynasty(清末新政)

1) The Birth of Territorial Waters

Although the inner sea was a traditional term similar to territorial waters, it had a different meaning. China's interest seems to have been focused on the ruling territory called *haijiang*(海疆), which was a broader concept than territorial waters and could be likened to coastal zones. The term haijiang became a proper noun in the Ming dynasty, especially as the attacks from Japan increased. The term haijiang can easily be found in official documents issued by the Qing court, including the famous phrase that "there have been many issues in the haijiang since the Daoguang and Xianfeng era which worried the Qing dynasty". According to one scholar, "the haijiang during the era(Qing dynasty) indicated mostly the southeastern coastal area, which encompassed the provinces in the southeast coasts, Haikou and its neighboring coasts and islands. The concept of territorial waters in the sense of maritime history was not formed until the end of the Qing dynasty". A closer look into the traditional concept of sea boundaries and the modern concept of territorial waters is also necessary. In fact, it took a long time for the Chinese to accept the concept of territorial waters as a system.

It is by no means easy to trace the formation of the Chinese perception of territorial waters, which is a symbolic process of a state that transitions from the traditional to the modern. The birth of the concept of territorial waters cannot be clearly defined by a certain point of time or event and should be considered broadly in a historical context.

First, the perception of the Qing dynasty towards maritime borders, in terms of its national border treaties, was as follows. Among the many national border treaties signed by the Qing court, the states which had maritime borders were Russia in the north, Japan in the east, and France in the south. The UK and Portugal were also involved because of Hong Kong and Macau and Joseon and Vietnam were neighboring states. In the process of signing a national border treaty with France, the maritime border issue between islands in the Beibu Gulf area became a topic of contention. Moreover, in the process of signing the treaty with Russia, the navigation rights in Tumen River arose as an issue. Such disputes, however, were not strictly modern and territorial disputes but either concerned the profits from fisheries trade or were in line with the territorial disputes on the coastal lands. It is highly likely that the concept of territorial waters was introduced to China as the law of nations was adopted during the Self-Strengthening Movement and the concept seems to have been used by the Qing dynasty in maritime disputes. Nevertheless, considering that territorial waters were not fully instated in written law even in European societies until the late nineteenth century, it is highly unlikely that the Chinese had a clear perception of territorial waters.

Maritime borders garnered attention in Modern China through the series of lease treaties signed with the world powers directly after the Sino-Japanese

War. The leased territories have not been formally conquered but were more closer to ceded territories, which not only included the land but also the nearby coastal areas. Considering that it was depredation of land, there was a possibility of an island dispute or territorial sea dispute. The areas of leased territories were at least hundreds of square miles and larger than any other existing leased territories. Germany seized the Kiautschou Bay and used Shandong as its base while Russia leased Lushun and Dalian and used Manchuria as its basis. Aside from its leased land, the UK used the extensive Yangtze area as its basis and France leased the Guangzhou Bay and used the Guangdong, Guangxi, and Yunnan Provinces as its basis. Japan also made use of the Fujian Province as its base. As a result, all the bay areas in China, aside the Tientsin area in the Zhili Province were under the control of foreign states. It is worth noting the fact that the foreign powers, including Germany, Russia, the UK, and France, paid close attention to their rights in the sea when signing the leasing treaties with China.

As foreign powers attempted to fully open the Chinese coastal areas and as China signed new trade treaties and accepted the idea of maritime rights, China experienced an enhanced perception towards maritime rights and the concept of territorial waters. In fact, a clause on territorial waters could be found in a trade treaty signed with the Qing dynasty and Mexico. This treaty was signed in the point of intersection between the nineteenth century and the twentieth century and when the notion of territorial waters gained the de facto status of international law with the support from the UK and the US, which were maritime empires. Moreover, at the end of the Qing dynasty, international law from Japan was introduced to China by Chinese students studying in Japan and Chinese officials began to use the term territorial waters around the Sino-Russian War. As can be inferred from several maritime disputes, a detailed perception of territorial waters suddenly began to appear. By seizing the coastal waters of China, the foreign powers not only secured the military and trade gains but also the profits from fisheries. Corresponding to such changes, the Chinese, who had transitioned from the traditional concept of the inner sea to the modern concept of territorial waters, began to get a clearer perception of maritime borders.

2) The Participation in International Conferences on Maritime Affairs and the Signing of International Treaties

The treaties system was initially established through the series of treaties signed in the aftermath of the First Opium War and its structure was formed through the Tientsin Treaty signed after the Second Opium War. Through this process, China, which had maintained the traditional tianxia(天下) world order", was incorporated into international and capitalist "nation-state order". Nevertheless, the order of *Huayi*, promulgated by the Qing dynasty, which prided itself for being the dynasty of the heavens, did not change in a short period. Even after the Second Opium War, the Xianfeng Emperor considered the Western powers to be dangerous and threatening and was displeased with the fact that foreigners resided in Beijing. Although the decisions were made reluctantly, the Qing dynasty created the Zonglǐ Yámén to be in charge of the diplomacy with the foreign powers, sent young men to study abroad and simultaneously dispatched envoys for a closer observation of the Western states. Scholars generally consider such changes to be the starting point for the Qing dynasty's active participation in international society.

As the Western powers expanded their capitalist colonies as well as their influence around the globe during the last 20 years of the nineteenth century, the so-called "international community" swiftly took form. Because of the many conflicts and breakup between the world powers during this era, the world powers had to resolve the newly raised issues and maintain the balance of powers through international cooperation. With their own interests in mind, the world powers called for international conferences and created unions and signed treaties to manage international issues. The fact that the Qing dynasty participated in such international conferences at this point in time is an indication that it was dissolve the China-centered tributary system in East Asia and taking part in the modern international order created by the Western states. Moreover, the Qing dynasty was signing treaties with the international community by joining international organizations. For the Qing dynasty, which was enmeshed in a number of unequal treaties with clauses on the most-favored-nation treatments, consular jurisdiction, leasing of lands, and the right to navigate inner rivers, as well as conventional tariff, to join international organizations was to actively attempt to improve or overthrow its unequal relations with foreign powers. By taking part in international treaties, the Qing dynasty also had hidden hopes to regain its position as a world power. China first approached international conferences during the Self-Strengthening Movement and began to participate in international conferences in the 1880s. It gained a deeper understanding of international treaties directly after the Sino-Japanese War. At the end of the Qing dynasty, China was an active participant in international conferences and signed about 10 international treaties during this period.

The steps the Qing dynasty took to actively participate in maritime-related international conferences and sign international treaties were as follows. Western diplomats began living in Beijing in the 1860s during the Self-Strengthening Movement and the Qing court dispatched Chinese envoys overseas in from the 1870s to the 1880s, which displayed Qing dynasty's active participation in international society. Nevertheless, the Chinese and Western convergent concept was prevalent during this era so it would be more accurate to consider that China entered the international society in earnest after its defeat in the Sino-Japanese War and the collapse of its traditional tributary system. The fact that the Qing dynasty joined in international treaties and organizations could be interpreted as an attempt to transition into a modern nation-state. Since the signatories of international treaties joined them on equal footing, China's participation helped it free itself from the unequal treaties in the long run. While China's demands were publicized as the Qing dynasty participated in international conferences, the treaty privilege which is a part of the international law became an obstacle which prevented China from participating in international conferences.

The Qing dynasty made particular effort to join international treaties on maritime issues. China referred to the international regulations for preventing collisions at sea that were instated by the European states and was early in adopting similar regulations, which were mostly implemented in its ports in the rivers or coastal waters. The Qing dynasty also joined the International Regulations for Preventing Collisions at Sea when it was signed in the International Marine Conference held in Washington D.C. in 1889. The treaty signed in this conference was the first international regulations for preventing collisions at sea and after becoming a signatory, China endeavored to observe its duty and continued to revise its own domestic regulations. China simultaneously aimed to support the interests of Chinese sailors and fishermen. Although it may not have received as much attention as other international events such as The Hague Peace Conference or the Geneva Convention, this treaty was the most important treaty among the international conferences joined by the Qing dynasty.

Discussions on international issues finally took place and the Hague Convention on war regulations were formed through the two Hague Peace Conferences respectively held in the late nineteenth century and the early twentieth century. In the first Hague Peace Conference held in 1899, three treaties, that is, the "Convention with respect to the Convention for the Adaptation to Maritime Warfare of the Principles of the Geneva Convention of 1864, the Convention with respect to the Laws and Customs of War on

Land and the Convention for the Pacific Settlement of International Disputes", along with three other declarations on reducing the damages from war, entered into force. China intended to sign these conventions as well, but after many events, was only able to ratify the treaties officially during the Russo-Japanese War in 1904. In the second Hague Peace Conference, China ratified the conventions related to naval war, including the "Convention for the Adaptation to Maritime Warfare of the Principles of the Geneva Convention, Convention relative to the Legal Position of Enemy Merchant Ships at the Start of Hostilities, Convention relative to the Laying of Automatic Submarine Contact Mines, Convention relative to the Establishment of an International Prize Court, Convention concerning Bombardment by Naval Forces in Time of War, Convention relative to the Conversion of Merchant Ships into War-ships, Convention relative to Certain Restrictions with regard to the Exercise of the Right of Capture in Naval War, and the Convention concerning the Rights and Duties of Neutral Powers in Naval War", as well as one declaration. The few wars with the Western powers in the late nineteenth century, and especially the experience of the Russo-Japanese war in the early twentieth century motivated the Qing dynasty to actively participate in The Hague Peace Conferences.

Just as conventions on naval wars took the significant portion of The Hague Conventions, a country's naval force represented its military might at the turn of the twentieth century. The Western powers thus strived to strengthen their naval power and China was no exception.

3) The Reconstruction of the Navy and the Heightened Perception of Sea Power(海權)

If one should take a broader view of the modern history of China's navy, the first phase would begin from the establishment of the modern navy during the Self-Strengthening Movement until the collapse of the Beiyang Fleet in the naval battle between the Qing dynasty and Japan. The second phase would start from the aftermath of the Sino-Japanese War when the navy was reconstructed until the early days of the Republic of China. Efforts have been made to reestablish the navy during the 10 years from the end of the Sino-Japanese War and until the fall of the Qing dynasty through the Chinese Revolution. In fact, the Qing dynasty strived to reestablish its navy despite its worsening political and economic circumstances, by purchasing warships, reorganizing fleets, organizing military bodies and fostering military personnel, until its final moment. A systematic revival of the navy was attempted during the Xuantong era. The size of the Qing navy, however, did not become close as it was before the Sino-Japanese War and the pace of its growth was also relatively slow.

The reconstruction of the navy forces at the end of the Qing dynasty could, once again, be divided into the late Guangxi era and the Xuantong era. After its defeat in the Sino-Japanese War, the Qing dynasty abolished the navy yamen, which had been the central agency for the navy for a decade, and disbanded the Beiyang Fleet. After the end of the war, the Qing dynasty was busy taking control of its disorganized navy. As many naval ports became leased territories of the Western powers, the Qing navy could hardly find any ports it could use. In the turn of the century, there were several navy-related events, such as when Italy attempted to lease Sammun Bay, the Eight-Nation Alliance's occupation of Beijing, and the Russo-Japanese War. The plan to reconstruct the navy suffered a setback for quite a while due to the national financial crisis brought up by the reparations for the Boxer Rebellion. The Qing navy, nevertheless, was steadily recovering.

The navy went through reform when the government offices were reorganized at the end of the Qing dynasty. The Nanyang and Beiyang Fleets were merged in 1906 and the next year, the Bingbu(兵部) was changed into the Department of the Army and an office of the navy was temporarily established in the Department. After the new policies were implemented and the financial crisis gradually alleviated the Qing court began to purchase more foreign warships. The Qing dynasty, for instance, purchased about 10 warships from Japan from 1906 to 1907 and four torpedo boats from Germany. One characteristic of naval reconstruction during this era was that the Western-centered naval schools were relocated to Japan. Japan's influence increased in many fields as the Qing dynasty imported ships from Japan and dispatched naval students to Japan, invited naval instructors from Japan and adopted Japan's naval system. Yao Xiguang, when devising the plan for reviving the navy in 1907, stressed that creating cruiser fleets was the most important task to establish the Chinese navy. Yao argued that China cannot take control of the coastal waters unless they could advance to the deep waters and that the distant-water fleets could be a tool to advance into the far sea.

Beginning in the first year of the reign of Emperor Xuantong(1909), the Qing dynasty established the "Seven-Year Plan to Reorganize the Navy" to reconstruct the Navy and conducted a research on the old-type naval ships, purchased cruisers for the Nanyang and Beiyang Fleets, conducted research on naval ports, expanded the navy school, and reconstructed shipyards during the first year. The navy system also went through reform and the first independent central commission for the navy, the Chouban Haijun Shiwuchu, was established in July 1909 to prepare for the separation of the army and navy. The Nanyang and Beiyang fleets were formally integrated and divided into the Cruiser Squadron and the Yangtze Squadron. In the following winter, the navy commission was reorganized and a new department of the navy was established with Zaixun as the Navy Minister. Zaixun and Sazhenbing actively searched for ways to reconstruct the navy by embarking on inspections overseas two times during this period.

One interesting phenomenon, which took place in the process of reconstructing the Qing navy after the Sino-Japanese War, was the heightened perception of sea power(海權). The maritime defense policy at the end of the Qing dynasty had a military objective to create a navy for coastal defense rather than an economic objective. However, the defects of the existing maritime defense policy became evident after the defeat of the Beiyang Fleet in the naval war between China and Japan and this led to a fundamental change in the

Chinese maritime perception during the Self-Strengthening Movement. The acceptance of the concept of sea power at the end of the Qing dynasty had a significant effect on the establishment of the navy. There were calls for establishing new ideologies for maritime conquest by reforming the traditional Chinese ideologies of farming outweighing trading(重農輕商) and land being more important than the sea(重陸輕海). Some argued that the Chinese navy should be established vigorously in order to gain sea power. The notion of the sea being the route to the world and to the economic development of national trade and the idea that the sea is strategically important and that the enemies' sea boundaries should be controlled for one state to safely trade overseas did not exist before the Western concept of sea power was introduced to China. "The country that rules the sea rules international trade. The country that controls international trade controls global wealth. This is the way to rule over the world" was the basic stance towards sea power in the late nineteenth and early twentieth century.

It is generally accepted that there was no true ideology on sea power in China until the Sino-Japanese war and that China lost the very war because of its lack of perception of sea power. The fall of the Beiyang Fleets instilled the notion of modern sea power into the Chinese people and was linked with the argument for reconstructing the navy. The reconstruction process of the navy after the Sino-Japanese War, in fact, was in tandem with the Chinese realizing the importance of sea power. The Chinese perception of sea power, which gradually changed from a sentimental view to a logical point of view during the

Self-Strengthening Movement, changed in the early twentieth century as China accepted the notion of sea power proposed by Alfred Thayer Mahan and aimed to reinforce its naval power and gain control of the sea.

4) Fisheries, Sea Borders, Island Disputes and the Change in the Perception of the Sea

The introduction and spread of motorboats and dragnets which began in the Western world in the late nineteenth century dramatically improved the fishing capacity. As a result, the traditional notion that there is an infinite amount of marine resources was soon to be abolished. Circummarine states began to demand the managing rights and control over not only their own coastal waters but of fisheries in certain parts of the far sea. States began to make plans to compartmentalize fishing areas and create marine protected areas, ban the fishing activities of foreign fishing boats and to have foreign fishing boats oblige to the controls set by the circummarine states. As the number of people working in the deep-sea fisher increased dramatically in the early twentieth century, the number of conflicts between states increased and the management of fisheries became an important issue. The management of marine resources became closely related to disputes on sea borders from this period since one of the main functions of territorial waters was to protect marine resources. A number of treaties related to territorial waters were signed because of fisheries issues and conflicts on fisheries, at times, resulted in wars.

The conflicts between nations on fisheries, which arose as the traditional fishing industry was expanded to the far sea, were closely related to the issue of sea borders. One representative fisheries dispute between the Qing court and Japan in the late Qing dynasty was the Bohaiwan fisheries dispute. After Lushun and Dalian were leased to Japan, Japanese fishing boats were frequently spotted in Bohaiwan. A murder even occurred after the conflict between the Japanese deep-sea fishing cooperatives and the Chinese Bongcheon public fisheries cooperation and fisheries disputes arose between the Chinese and Japanese fishermen at Xiongyuecheng as well. During a negotiation to resolve such a dispute, from 1906 to 1907, Japan proposed the three-mile zone principle to China and argued that the Japanese fishermen caught fish in international waters, objecting to acknowledge the Bohaiwan as Chinese territorial waters. This incident prompted the Qing dynasty to acknowledge the necessity of the territorial waters system. In the meantime, Japan attempted to legalize its fishing activities not only in Bohaiwan but also in the Yellow Sea and in the Shandong Province.

The Tatsumaru(二辰丸) incident, a dispute between the Qing dynasty and Japan which broke out in 1908, is one well-known example of a case which used the law on territorial waters act the negotiation. The Tatsumaru incident was a diplomatic dispute between the Qing dynasty and Japan caused by the smuggling of the Japanese vessel *Tatsumaru* in the coast near Macau. During the negotiation for this incident, Japan brought up several issues, including whether *Tatsumaru* was captured in territorial waters, whether *Tatsumaru* smuggled weapons, and whether the Japanese national flag was insulted in the process. Portugal used this incident to raise an old sea border issue that the Qing dynasty invaded the territorial waters of Macau. The Qing dynasty, however, used the law on territorial waters in the negotiations with Portugal. Moreover, although it was raised by a local authority, the Qing dynasty mentioned the three-mile zone principle and argued for its sovereignty over its territorial waters. After this event, the Qing dynasty officially focused on sea border issues and prepared to establish a territorial water system for the last few years of the dynasty. By this time, the general public in China also began to take interest in territorial sovereignty in the sea.

In 1908, when the Qing dynasty and Portugal were busy negotiating on the sea borders in Macau, the Qing dynasty and Japan were involved in yet another island dispute on the sovereignty of the Pratas Islands. A Japanese merchant named Nishijawa Yoshiji came into conflict with Chinese fishermen in the process of developing the Pratas Islands, which, according to Nishijawa were ownerless. Due to China's active response during the negotiations, Japan acknowledged that the Pratas Islands were Chinese territory and concluded this incident by getting back Nishijawa's investment from China. The Qing dynasty was active in responding to this incident, in diplomatic negotiations and by dispatching navy ships for inspection, threatened by the possibility that its coastal islands could be taken away by foreign powers. The Pratas Island incident shows how serious the Qing dynasty considered the sovereignty of its islands, which it had ignored as peripheries in the past. This incident also led to fierce controversy among the public and led to a rise in patriotism, which was momentum for the birth of modern Chinese citizen. The management of Paracel Islands also became an issue by this time.

As can be inferred from the three examples of island disputes, most of the island disputes which broke out at the end of the Qing dynasty were instigated by Japan. Japan's advance to the coastal waters of China motivated the Chinese to change their perception towards the sea. These maritime disputes were covered in detail by the local and central media and gentlemen and commoners who were influenced by such coverage started nationalistic public movements on a national level. Unlike in the past, the Qing court actively stepped up to resolve the disputes and the notion of territorial waters was widely introduced during the process. The disputes on territorial waters which broke out during this era formed the basis of the maritime disputes which remain unresolved in the present day.

4. Conclusion

After being defeated in the two Opium Wars, China was forced to lift its sea ban and open its sea. Relinquishing its sea ban policy signified the beginning of modern China. A new maritime environment also led to the advent of new concepts. New maritime concepts were intensively introduced during two periods in China's history. While the traditional concepts of sea ban, sea defense, and *haijiang* were introduced due to the influence of the Japanese raiders in the sixteenth century, these terms gradually gave way to the modern maritime concepts of the navy, territorial waters, sea power, as the Western power invaded China.

In the first half, this paper introduced the maritime-related clauses in trade treaties signed during the period starting from the Opium War until the Sino-Japanese War (mostly around the Self-Strengthening Movement), the rise of the modern steamboat transportation industry, the maritime law articles found in *Elements of International law*, the law of nations and the early Northeast Asian maritime disputes, the transition of the traditional navy to the modern navy, and the international law incidents related to maritime issues during the Sino-French War and the Sino-Japanese War. The characteristics of the aforementioned events were as follows. First, the Western and modern maritime order was widely covered in trade treaties but the Qing dynasty, which entered into these treaties, were busy making arbitrary interpretations rather than attempting to understand their content. The Qing dynasty was also passive in dealing with the Western powers' advance into the Chinese sea via the transportation industry. Second, when the *Elements of International Law* was first translated, the Qing officials merely used the translations for internal reference. Even after acknowledging the importance of the book, they merely used it selectively in diplomatic disputes concerning the tributary system. The same applied to the maritime law explained in the *Elements of International*

Law. Japanese society, on the other hand, explored the *Elements of International Law* seriously. Third, although the Qing dynasty constructed modern navy troops such as the Beiyang Fleet, it was defeated in nearly all the naval battles. This indicates that the Qing navy did not become an actual modern navy. This is also evident in the fact that the Qing court attempted to interpret the maritime war-related regulations in the *Elements of International Law* to the letter even during warfare, considering the regulations to be based on ideal international law. In that sense, the Self-Strengthening Movement could be understood as "the period when the Chinese and Western convergent perception of the sea was formed". It was a period during which the Chinese interpreted the modern perception of the sea by associating it with the traditional ideas.

The birth of territorial waters in terms of the treaties signed between China and foreign states from the Sino-Japanese War to the Chinese Revolution in 1911 (mostly at the late Qing Reform), the Qing dynasty's participation in international conferences on maritime issues and joining in international treaties, the reconstruction of the Qing navy and the enhanced perception towards sea power, and the change in the Chinese perception towards the sea in regards to the island disputes on fisheries were briefly introduced in the latter half of this paper. The characteristics of the aforementioned events were as follows. First, the formation of the concept of territorial waters, which is one of the indicators of the state transitioning from the traditional to the modern, was not clear-cut nor could it be easily identified. However, the trade treaties and lease treaties suggested that the territorial waters were formed in about the early twentieth century. Second, China's progress from self-strengthening to diplomacy or from the nation of laws to international law could be inferred from the Qing dynasty's active participation in international conferences on maritime affairs or its entering into international treaties. Third, the process of reconstructing the disintegrated navy after the Sino-Japanese War showed that although the Qing dynasty was unable to reconstruct the navy to its original size before the war, the Chinese perception of sea power did improve from being sentimental to being logical. The island dispute cases concerning fisheries and sea borders displayed the change in perception of the sea. The end of the Qing dynasty, when compared to the Self-Strengthening Movement period, could be understood as "the period when the acceptance of Western maritime concepts". The acceptance of Western maritime perception, however, did not mean that the perception was embraced by Chinese society. That required much more time.

The change in the status of the sea, which had been abandoned by the traditional dynasties and was open (or closed) to everyone, into a territory in the modern nation-state may not have been such a positive one. In fact, the tensions in the East Asian sea mounted as the sea was territorialized as states scrambled to acquire sea transport routes and marine resources. Just as the sea in East Asia was territorialized in the turn of the twentieth century, the East Asian sea is now encountering new threats in the age of globalization at the end of the twentieth and the beginning of the twenty-first century. The future of East Asia could be peaceful or be fraught with conflicts depending on the resolutions of the complicated island disputes and territorial waters disputes. In response to such a circumstance, scholars should depart from the excessively nationalistic viewpoint found in existing research on marine history and conduct research and present future outlooks with a universal view towards history.

China's Maritime Power Strategy and Sinocentrism

With a Focus on Islands Disputes and the Maritime Silk Road

Sukyoung Kwak

1. From a Continental State to a Maritime Power

China is "a quintessential continental state situated in the vast area in the East of the Eurasian continent and sharing borders with 14 countries along its 22,000 kilometers of its land border, making it the country with the highest number of bordering countries. At the same time, China has the geographic traits of a maritime state, with its fourth longest coastline in the world which is 18,000 kilometers long, three million square kilometers of the coastal area, and approximately 6,500 islands". Nevertheless, China has historically focused on expanding its land territories from its central plains. Although Zheng He's seven expeditions to the southern seas, which well surpassed Columbus' voyages, introduced China to the global waters, it issued a sea ban policy and shut itself out from the sea, which was why China has identified itself as a continental state for a long time and was considered as a continental state worldwide.

However, as China had to kneel down in the face of the Western powers which came from the sea in the modern era, the Chinese leaders were inevitably confronted with the maritime issues. China's complicated and distinctive modern history, nevertheless, prevented it to focus on the sea. China finally embarked on managing its waters after its reform and open-door policy and has caused military conflicts with neighboring states on islands disputes. The term maritime power, which has been mentioned for some time, was also announced by Hu Jintao in the 18th National Congress of the Communist Party of China in 2012 and created tension in the world. Hu Jintao's announcement to be come a maritime power is being implemented by his successor Xi Jinping through the Twenty-first Century Maritime Silk Road Project, which is a part of Xi's the Belt and Road Initiative.

This paper posited that China's efforts to become a maritime power did not only begin from the Twenty-first Century Maritime Silk Road Project, which is a part of the recently implemented the Belt and Road Initiative but also stemmed from the previous islands disputes. That is, China is attempting to expand its maritime territories through islands disputes while securing the sea routes to the world through the Twenty-first Century Maritime Silk Road Project, thereby becoming the control tower of the global waters and to becoming a global maritime power. China's plan to become a maritime power is becoming a source of concern as it could be interpreted as the rebirth of Sinocentricism. Sinocentricism was both idealistic and realistic even from its beginning; if Sinocentricism was idealistic in that China aims to morally reform neighboring stated and incorporate them into the Chinese order, it was realistic as it was displayed through the concept of the Chinese world order in the military and political sense and the tributary order of *great friendship*. These two different Sinocentric ideas were combined so that China could subjugate barbarians, who resist to China's cultural and moral edification as the center of the world, by force and offer rewards to the countries that do their best in serving China as their liege. China is implementing two strategies - islands disputes and the Twenty-first Century Maritime Silk Road Plan — for the grand plan of seeking hegemony through the sea and shifting the center of the global order to China. The two plans involve two contrasting moves, of military occupation and economic support, the contrast of which is strikingly similar to the double-sidedness of Sinocentricism and is adding concerns to its revival.

This paper, therefore, identified the islands disputes and the Maritime Silk Road policy as the two major strategies for China to become a maritime power and aimed to examine the relation between the two policies and analyzed the policies with respect to the double-sidedness of Sinocentricism in order to predict upcoming events. In this respect, this paper is different from the previous research conducted in a number of fields, including politics, law, economics, international relations, and military studies. This paper further aimed to find implications for the Ieo Islet disputes between South Korea and China and evaluate Korea's status and future strategies, as a country excluded from China's Belt and Road Initiative.

For this, this paper first examined the maritime perceptions of modern Chinese leaders after China turned their attention toward the sea, as well as their plans for becoming a maritime power and found that the announcement on becoming a maritime power was an idea which has been passed down from a number of Chinese leaders and has finally materialized as a policy. In addition, this paper examined the two strategies — the islands disputes and the Maritime Silk Road policy — with special focus on the Disputes over the Spratly Islands in the South China Sea where the dispute is the most heated and the Twenty-first Century Maritime Silk Road from the Belt and Road Initiative for the sake of the study.

2. From Sun Wen to Xi Jinping

China, the continental state which had prided itself to be the center of the world for a long time, was under attack from the Western powers through the sea consecutively after the Opium War and was also defeated in the Sino-Japanese war. It was a result of issuing a sea ban and sealing the sea off from the Ming dynasty and failing to create the navy properly during the Qing dynasty.

The failure of creating a modern navy was even acknowledged as China's failure to become modernized. After observing the cases of Portugal, Spain, the Netherlands, the United Kingdom, the United States, and Japan, all of which used the sea from the early days and travelled from the sea, Chinese leaders acknowledged the fact that the strength of a nation derives from the sea and took active interest in the sea.

Sun Wen, who established the basis of a modern nation-state and made plans for a stronger state and nation, despaired the collapse of the Qing dynasty followed by the defeat of its navy while he was visiting the Fuzhou Ship-Building Bureau after resigning from the post of provisional president in April 1912. Sun Wen lamented that "after the two defeats in the Jiashen and Jiawu years, most of the warships have been destroyed. The Qing government failed to equip itself and failed again to reorganize after, later failing to regain its footing forever and continued to become corrupt (……) We should manage marine transport properly and expand our navy so that the Republic's Navy could take rank with the Western powers and become the strongest nation in the world". The beginning of the perception of maritime power could already be found in Sun Wen's statement. After witnessing his country being humiliated as the Western powers used the sea to create colonies and expand their powers and China's vast territories were attacked and invaded from its shores, Sun Wen would have deeply felt the fact that his country's survival depends on the sea and would have regretted that China had not strengthened its sea power sooner. Rather than stopping at regretting past events, Sun Wen further contemplated on specific plans for China to foster the navy, drive out the Western powers, and, once again, become a powerful nation.

Sun Wen proposed various plans for the sea on fostering the navy and developing strategic ports and wrote about his understanding of sea power and his accurate future predictions on the flow of sea power in his book *The International Development of China*. He argued that the flow of sea power will move from the Mediterranean to the Atlantic Ocean, and then to the Pacific Ocean and posited that because China is at the center, sea power was decisive in the survival and fate of China, commenting that "the rise and fall of a nation's power is not at the land but at the sea. The state with the stronger sea power becomes the stronger state".

Sun Wen's views were shared by the people in New China and the People's Republic of China actively reinforced its navy after the state was founded. In the first issue of the *Newspaper of the People's Navy*, published in New Year's Day in 1950, Mao Zedong wrote a congratulatory message that "we must foster the navy. The Navy could defend our waters and effectively prevent the imperialistic invasions". In February 1953, Mao inspected the *Changjiang* and said that "the imperialistic invasions of China in the past 100 years mostly came from the sea. China has long shorelines and should foster a strong navy". Per the minister's request, Mao further added that "a strong navy should be fostered to object to any imperialistic invasions". Such visits and remarks show that Mao Zedong implemented policies with the understanding that a stronger navy force is needed to prevent foreign invasions from the sea. Mao

Zedong has, in fact, written a letter to Stalin himself to sign an agreement on the purchasing of navy equipment and purchased the necessary equipment. In 1958, when China exchanged firefight with Taiwan in Jinmen Island, Mao Zedong confirmed the width of China's territorial waters to be 12 nautical miles and announced that foreign vessels which travel in Chinese territorial waters should abide by related regulations set by the Chinese government. Mao Zedong acknowledged the importance of fostering a strong navy and the concepts of territorial waters and sea borders and codified such concepts to make them official.

However, it was difficult to foster the navy and reinforce the naval power during Mao Zedong's rule due to domestic political issues in China. The ensuing economic reform required China to continuously reinforce its naval power and for the sea to become the springboard for economic development. Deng Xiaoping's economic reforms were directly related to the sea as the international exchanges and foreign trade began in coastal cities. As the sea was utilized more actively, the perception on islands and the coast was also enhanced, which led to an increase in the number of collisions China had with its neighbors at sea as well as islands disputes. Deng Xiaoping initially took a firm stand on such incidents and employed military forces but later changed his stance and took a practical approach to "postpone conflict and embark on joint development projects". This was because economic development through international relations and cooperation was a pressing matter for Deng Xiaoping and island disputes were not matters which could be resolved simply by using military force, considering China's relations with the international community. He, nevertheless, clearly affirmed that the "Spratly Islands has always been considered to be Chinese territory in the map of the world and is a part of China", showing that he had not given up on the islands. Deng Xiaoping's maritime policy of using the sea to develop China's economy was the first economic implementation of Sun Wen's idea that China's wealth lies in the sea.

As mentioned above, Mao Zedong aspired for a strong navy and Deng Xiaoping aimed for a wealthy sea through exchanges. The maritime policies implemented by their successors became more complex and detailed and were executed more thoroughly. This becomes clearer in Jiang Zemin's comments that "the ocean should be developed and effort should be made to become a maritime power" (Report in the Sixteenth National Party Congress in 2002) or to "promote the marine industry and flourish the economy" (congratulatory message commemorating the thirtieth anniversary of the State Oceanic Administration) and Hu Jintao's announcement that China should "improve its ability to develop marine resources, develop its marine economy, protect its marine ecological environment and its marine interests and become a maritime power" (18th National Congress of the Communist Party of China). Xi Jinping, who is the success or of Hu Jintao and is implementing Hu's announcement made in the National Congress, stressed in the 8th group study of the Politburo of the Communist Party of China in 2013 that China should "take more interest in the ocean and perceive and manage the sea so that new progress could be continuously made to become an established maritime power". Considering that the Politburo group study sessions consist of lectures given by experts and group discussions on certain topics before they become major policies, they also serve as important indicators of the policy directions of the party leadership in China.

To sum up the Chinese leaders' maritime perception and policy directions, Mao Zedong took a military interest of the sea while Deng Xiaoping had an economic interest and utilized the sea. Moreover, whereas Deng Xiaoping used the sea to attract foreign capital and began international trade to accomplish economic development, Jiang Zemin emphasized ocean development and Hu Jintao the development of marine resources, both aiming to use the sea in a more specific manner. Xi Jinping, on the other hand, embraced all the former strategies and is aiming to realize their ambitions of becoming a maritime power. The different approaches taken by each leader were not because of the competition among them nor were they outcomes of the leaders' efforts for distinction; the leaders gave shape to and complemented their predecessors' policies to make them more realistic and to go one step further to the policies' fruition.

The announcement on becoming a maritime power, which was made in the 2012 18th National Congress of the Communist Party of China, was, as mentioned above, a product of the continuous and consistent supplementations made to the plans and policies of the Chinese leadership since China went through its economic reform. That is, China's announcement was not, as argued by some scholars, a sudden reaction to the "pivot to Asia" strategy proposed by the U.S. but was a phased preparation of China's ambition to accomplish economic development, regain its past glory and to become the center of the world again. The announcement, on the other hand, could also be understood as an expression of self-confidence that China is at the stage to be able to officially announce its ambition. Now that China has become one of the G2 nations, with the help of its dramatic economic development, it intends to push the US aside and reshuffle and lead the world order through the sea. This is precisely why a number of nations including the Western states have been prompt and sensitive toward China's announcement on becoming a maritime power and have raised concerns dissecting the hidden intentions behind China's announcement, in spite of China's ongoing emphasis on the coexistence, cooperation, and peace with the world.

Under such circumstances, China is expected to implement more proactive, aggressive and extensive maritime policies by time. This is why South Korea, which shares the sea and is closely related to China, should have an accurate account of the formation and characteristics of China's maritime strategies.

3. The Territorial Dispute on the Spratly Islands

Because China shares borders with many countries and experienced multiple territorial disputes, due to its vast territory, it emphasized its land border issues in the past. Nowadays, China is sharing the sea with South Korea and Japan in the Northeast and the Southeast Asian states in the Southeast and as the United Nations Convention on the Law of the Sea took effect in 1994, islands became the demarcations for territorial waters and maritime boundaries, all of which is leading to an increase in islands disputes between China and its neighboring states. With South Korea, China is facing the issue of demarcating the exclusive economic zone within the Socotra Rock area. Territorial disputes are underway with Japan over the Diaoyu Islands (called Senkaku Islands in Japan), with Vietnam over the Paracel Islands, and with Vietnam, the Philippines, Malaysia, Taiwan, and Brunei over the Spratly Islands. This paper focuses on the most complicating and heated territorial dispute, the dispute over the Spratly Islands to examine China's overall response in the island disputes, the significance, and implication in China's plan to become a maritime power, and how Sinocentricism affects China's response.

The Spratly Islands consist of approximately 230 islands, rocks, reefs and sand islands but only 11 islands, 5 shoals, 20 rocks, and reefs are above water, which makes up only 2 square kilometers of land which could be acknowledged as island territories. The Spratly Islands, which was neglected in the seventeenth and eighteenth century, became at the center of heated dispute between six countries in the present day because of the UN Convention on the Law of the Sea, which demarcated the economic zone to 200 nautical miles and because it was discovered that the islands had a huge natural gas reservoir amounting to 35 billion tons along with mineral resources including iron, copper, manganese, tin, and phosphorus, and approximately 1,500 species of fish.

As of now, 24 islets of the Spratly Islands are occupied by Vietnam, 10 by China, 7 by the Philippines, 6 by Malaysia and one by Taiwan. Brunei has not officially declared the islands as its territory but considers some of the islands as a part of its exclusive economic zone and is arguing for its rights for the Louisa Reef. Other states have stationed their troops in each of their occupied islands and have installed airstrips for their fighter plans, authorized oil explorations and have developed each island into tourist spots to gain sovereignty over the islands. Among these stakeholders, China and Vietnam's conflicts have been the most acute which is closely followed by the conflicts between China and the Philippines. The conflicts among the states are summarized in 〈table 1〉.

China argued that according to historical records and facts, the Spratly Islands were already under the jurisdiction of China since the Han dynasty and although it was conquered by France and Japan for a while, the islands were returned to China in accordance to international law. China further argument was that neighboring countries including Vietnam and the Philippines have been occupying some of the islands and rocks using military mean and developing the resources in nearby waters and have demanded sovereignty over Chinese territory since the 1970s. As can be found in 〈Table 1〉, China has been willing to begin military conflicts to win the sovereignty of the Spratly Islands and have devised immediate and long-term plans by creating individual islands, legislating related domestic law and establishing administrative jurisdiction.

〈table 1〉

<table>
<tr><th colspan="2"></th><th>China</th><th>Vietnam</th><th>The Philippines</th></tr>
<tr><td colspan="2">Claims</td><td>—Historical grounds
—Effective occupation</td><td>—Historical grounds
—Effective occupation</td><td>—Close proximity
—Preoccupancy through discovery and acquisition by prescription</td></tr>
<tr><td rowspan="8">Major Conflicts</td><td rowspan="5">China
⇕
Vietnam</td><td colspan="3">· Vietnam incorporates 11 islands into its administrative district in September 1973 ⇔ China uses military force to occupy Yongxing Island (Woody Island) in 1974 and begins the effective occupation on the entire Spratly Islands (Beginning of conflict)</td></tr>
<tr><td colspan="3">· China occupies 6 islands in the Spratly Islands in March 1988 citing weather observation as the reason for occupation ⇔ the Vietnam navy takes military action (Actual conflict)
— Three Vietnamese vessels are hit and sunk, 72 soldiers are killed and Vietnam loses the island
— China stations navy troops in Huayang Jiao (Cuateron Reef) and Chigua Jiao (Johnson Reef) and conducts various military drills such as submarine maneuvers, joint navy-air force drills, and air defense drills</td></tr>
<tr><td colspan="3">· In 1992, China grants the oil exploration rights of the Vanguard Bank, which is claimed by Vietnam, to Crestone Energy, an American company and sparks another dispute
· China legislates the Territorial Sea Act, which incorporates the entire South China Sea to its own territory → Develops into an international law dispute</td></tr>
<tr><td colspan="3">· In May 26 2011, a Chinese patrol boat cuts a cable installed by the Binh Minh 02, a Vietnamese oil gas exploration ship, at a location within Vietnam's EEZ and 120 kilometers northeast to south-central Nha Trang</td></tr>
<tr><td colspan="3">· In June 2011, after China announces that it will be conducting military drills in the international waters of the Pacific Ocean, the Vietnam navy conducts a shooting exercise using live ammunition and issues a conscription law, which provokes China and nearly leads to a military conflict before the two states decide to talk</td></tr>
<tr><td rowspan="3">China
⇕
The Philippines</td><td colspan="3">· China installs various military facilities and stations military fleet at four points in Meiji Jiao(Mischief Reef), which was controlled by the Philippines in March 1995 ⇔ the Philippines navy protests that China's actions were violating international law and destroys the stations, which leads to military confrontation</td></tr>
<tr><td colspan="3">· The Chinese Navy and the Philippines Navy confront each other near the Panata Island and Kota Island, which was controlled by the Philippines in 1997</td></tr>
<tr><td colspan="3">· Conflicts arise between a Philippines exploration ship and a Chinese patrol boat due to Chinese fishing boats fishing at the Spratly Islands near the Philippines in 1998</td></tr>
</table>

		China	Vietnam	The Philippines
		· A Chinese navy ship threatens a Philippines navy ship in 1999, as a Chinese fishing boat sinks after a collision with the Philippines navy ship		
		· China forcefully occupies the Huangyan Islets (Scarborough Shoal), which is approximately 116 nautical miles away from the Philippines shores (446 nautical miles apart from the Chinese mainland), and captures Philippines fishing boats which were fishing in nearby waters in 2012 ⇔The Philippines sues China for building an artificial island in some of the Spratly Islands occupied by the Philippines in the Permanent Court of Arbitration (PCA) →China objects to the PCA's ruling		

Data Source : Related papers compiled by the researcher

The PCA's ruling on the Spratly Island disputes and China's attitude also need to be considered. These two points are important since they could help the international community find a middle ground on island disputes or could be used as a guideline for other island disputes which involves China. As is found in 〈Table 1〉 the Philippines sued China for several issues in regards to China building artificial islands in several islands of the Spratly Archipelago in 2013 and the PCA ruled that China's sovereignty claim over the South China Sea has no legal grounds in terms of international law on July 12, 2016. The court ruled out the nine-dash line, which was China's historical grounds for the claim, and defined the topography of where China has built the artificial islands as rocks which cannot have exclusive economic zones or continental shelves. The court further acknowledged that by reclaiming land and constructing artificial islands, China has caused serious damage to the ecosystem and violated of the marine environment protection article in the Convention. The court further ruled that China also violated the international regulation in the Prevention of Collision at Sea Act and the Safety of Life at Sea

Convention against the Philippines ships and sailors.

China officially denied the entire process from the filing of the lawsuit to the ruling of the court. China claimed that the PCA had no jurisdiction and that the Philippines' lawsuit itself was a scheme devised by the United States and Japan to impede China becoming a maritime power and China's claims were followed by tough remarks and military response. In this way, China refused to come to court for the PCA trial and refused to accept the ruling and stated its firm position that it would only discuss the issues bilaterally and without the intervention of a third party. What could be confirmed at this point is that islands disputes cannot be resolved through PCA ruling and that PCA rulings do not always benefit the plaintiff. It is difficult to decide whether the object of the dispute is an island, whether the historical grounds are accurate as well as the effective occupation, owner, discovery, the related domestic law and international law and administrative jurisdiction of the disputed land. The sovereignty of some of the areas in East Asia, in particular, is unclear due to the Western occupations in modern history as well as the ambiguous articles in the handover treaties. The fact that the interests of third parties intervene and affect the decisions also makes the sovereignty issue even more unclear. In fact, not only the parties in dispute but also Russia, the United States, Japan, India, which do not want China's influence to expand further, and the international community were aligned themselves with the remaining five states, including Vietnam and the Philippines, on the court ruling of the Spratly Islands disputes.

China, in any case, lost its international trust by ignoring international law and is currently in the dilemma of having to argue in a contrasting position with another islands dispute, especially in the dispute on Diaoyudao islands. Such ambivalent attitude could be found in recent news reports from the Chinese media which refuted Korea's complaint that a Chinese combat aircraft invaded the Korean Air Defense Identification Zone(KADIZ) in Seonam-myeon, Ieodo, while claiming its sovereignty of the Diaoyudao islands and the South China Sea and demanded a Japanese company to use a map which reflected China's sovereignty. Islands, in fact, differ from land since it is difficult to make a judgment on their sovereignty and because there could be multiple aspects in disputes on them; if countries begin applying conditions that support their claims, it would be difficult to have a consistent standard for the judgment. Consequently, it is likely that China would avoid as many international lawsuits and military confrontations as possible while finding grounds to claim for sovereignty by creating artificial islands, assigning administrative jurisdiction, exploring the sea and strengthening its military power.

As mentioned above, the Spratly Islands have various maritime resources, including natural gas and oil. For China, which may have to import 80% of its oil by 2030, this is a region it could not simply give up. The Spratly Islands are also at the southernmost area of China and is between two major naval bases at Jin Lan Bay in Vietnam and at the Subic Bay in the Philippines, which makes it a strategic point for any advances to the Pacific Ocean and the Indian

Ocean, as well as an international sea route through which ships should pass through to get from East Asia to South Asia, the Middle East, Africa, and Europe. It is an important passageway for foreign trade for China since 21 among China's 39 foreign sea routes and 60% of its trade ships routes go through this area. Since it is in the southernmost point in China, the islands could also serve as a military base to protect the southern sea. If China could incorporate the Spratly Islands and the South China Sea as its maritime territory, it would be able to acquire inexhaustible amounts of maritime resources, secure a stable sea route and establish a solid military and security basis, all of which would become the starting point of China's plan to become a maritime power.

China is expected to mobilize every possible means using its well-established economic and military power and will not concede with any issue directly related to its national interest. This could also be inferred from its declaration that while it would prioritize talks and joint development, it will not rule out the use of force if necessary. China's attitude displayed in the Spratly Islands disputes is similar to its attitude in the past when it suppressed weak nations that refused to enter the Chinese world order with force and demanded them to show their respect as China's vassals and reflects the forced and hegemonic side of Sinocentrism.

4. The Twenty-first Century Maritime Silk Road

During his official visits to Southeast Asia from September to October 2013, Xi Jinping first announced the Belt and Road Initiative. The "Belt" consists of the land trade route which begins from Xian, Shanxi Province, encompassing Ürümqi in the Xinjiang Uygur Autonomous Region and Central Asia and Turkey and connects Dusseldorf in Germany. The "Road", on the other hand, refers to the sea route which begins from Quanzhou, Fujian Province, connecting Southeast Asia and the Maldives in the Indian Ocean and ends in Africa and Europe. The Initiative would be forming an economic bloc led by China, which would be a modernized version of the Silk Road and the Maritime Silk Road of the past. China's plan is to establish a foundation of a huge economic bloc which would account for 29% of the global economy and 23.9% of global trade and connect approximately 4.4 billion people, who account for 64% of the global population, in 26 countries across Asia, Europe, and Africa.

The "Road", which was the focus of this study, is a detailed strategy with the aims to establish a maritime network with China at the center and revive the maritime Silk Road created by Zheng He, who explored the sea during the early Ming dynasty starting from the West Pacific Ocean and connected the Indian Ocean, West Asia and East Africa and even reached the Atlantic Ocean by ending at the Cape of Good Hope and encompassed all three oceans and traveled for 15,000 miles and passed through 56 major sea routes, thereby establishing an unprecedented maritime network.

Through the establishment of the "Road", China will be able to resolve the urgent issue of securing a stable transportation route. Approximately half of China's oil import and 80% of its foreign trade rely on the sea route passing through the Strait of Malacca and the Twenty-First Century Maritime Silk Road would be able to "go through the Strait of Malacca and connect the major ports in Myanmar, Sri Lanka, Ethiopia and Greece" and resolve China's sea route issue once and for all, which is precisely the reason why China cannot give up the South China Sea. There is, therefore, a double-sidedness to the islands disputes, in China's point of view as they bring about discord among the countries on the Maritime Silk Road and are obstacles to implementing their initiative but could also be the key to realizing the Maritime Silk Road if China could incorporate the islands as its own territories through the disputes.

In addition, if this initiative succeeds, China would be able to establish a global maritime network with China at the center and at the helm which aims for joint economic development and is based on cooperation. This is a point which concerns the world because it may imply the revival of Chinese hegemony. The fact that China's actions to reconstruct the world order and provide support to developing countries for basic infrastructure, under the name of constructing the Twenty-first Century Maritime Silk Road, is similar to its actions to its tributary states in the past, also adds to the concerns and suspicions. China, which considered itself the center of the world, used the tributary system as one of the ways to control its neighboring countries in the past. Under the tributary system, neighboring states treated China with respect as vassals and sent envoys with tributes to China. China, on the other hand, maintained the Chinese order by being generous to the states and providing them with imperial gifts. China's friendship and solidarity with other states and coexistence and co-prosperity were based on this Chinese world order.

Sinocentricism was in decline in the modern era but now that China has achieved a miraculous economic development after its economic reforms and became one of the G2, China's ambition and confidence to reshuffle the international order and to become the leader is evident in its plan for the Twenty-first Century Maritime Silk Road. As in the past tributary system, China is voluntarily helping the development of developing states which are included in the Maritime Silk Road and is providing support, investment, economic aid and is strengthening ties with the states. "China has provided large amounts of money and technology to the Ports in Sittwe in Myanmar, Hambantota in Sri Lanka, Gwadar in Pakistan and Bagamoyo in Tanzania in order to secure its access to the ports and establish major bases for the Twenty-first Century Maritime Silk Road. Moreover, China is currently cooperating with the Chinese living abroad in the ASEAN countries in response to the pressure from the U.S. and to expand its trade with ASEAN countries."

China's proposal could be attractive to developing countries included in the Maritime Silk Road plan, as China would provide economic aid and investment and strengthen its ties with the states to help build basic infrastructure.

However, since China's intention is to establish a new Sinocentric economic order, some of the states have raised their concern or suspicion. Some states, such as India, have publically renounced China's proposal and China has had difficulty in gaining approval from the states involved in the islands disputes in the South China Sea. The conflicts with Vietnam in the South China Sea, issues with India in the Indian Ocean, as well as China's interests with the United States and countries nearby the Strait of Malacca, all indicate that China's initiative to build the Twenty-First Maritime Silk Road would be fraught with difficulties.

Then why is China trying to invoke Zheng He, who explored the vast waters to expand the Chinese world order, and to recreate the Maritime Silk Road, in spite of the cautious eyes and defensive reactions from many countries that criticize "China's dream", which China aims to achieve through the Belt Road Initiative, as the comeback of Sinocentricism and as China's attempt to become the center of the world?

First, China is referring to the historical fact of Zheng He exploring the Southern oceans with hopes to carve the perception that this is not a new idea but an act of reconstructing, inheriting and developing China's heritage so that any friction on China becoming the leader could be minimized and be taken as granted. At the High-level Forum on the Belt and Road Initiative, which was held in Beijing in May 2017, the Russian President Vladimir Putin commented in his opening remarks that there have been exchanges between the people of the Eurasian continent since the ancient times and that the members of the Eurasian Economic Union, including Russia, actively support the Belt and Road Initiative, with the hope that such tradition and mutual trust could continue in the twenty-first century. It is likely that China is highlighting the fact that Zheng He's expeditions surpassed the expeditions made by the European explorers including Columbus, in its time, scale, the distance covered and the number of expeditions in order to invoke the superiority of China and the Chinese, give authority to China's discourse that it had been and continues to be a strong nation and to succeed in making a soft landing for the initiative.

Second, China is emphasizing that Zheng He did not invade or plunder other countries during his expedition but conducted peaceful tributary trade so as to appease countries which are critical toward the Twenty-first Century Maritime Silk Road and are concerned it could be an expansionist plan set by China. "In his speech advocating the Twenty-First Century Maritime Silk Road given in Indonesia's House of Representatives, Xi Jinping said that 'Zheng He from the Ming dynasty left a beautiful story about the friendly relations formed between the Chinese and the Indonesians as a legacy for us.' Through this remark, Xi Jinping attempted to explain that his proposal of the Twenty-first Century Maritime Silk Road had an aim to reconstruct the ancient and peaceful relationship in the globalized modern world." That being said, while Zheng he's fleet did not blatantly conquer land by force, it did use force when necessary and, in the end, its primary aim was to incorporate tributary states into the Chinese world order by pressuring them politically and economically, with a firm belief that China was the country ruled by the son of the Heavens. It was, therefore, a different form of invasion.

Third, just as the tributary trade system enabled the tribute states to receive more benefits, China could imply that the Twenty-First Century Maritime Silk Road would provide economic aid and investment to developing countries as well, thereby emphasizing China's aspect as a global power. When in fact, it is to secure the sea transportation route and turn the developing countries into markets for its exports and to take the fruits of their economic development, China is emphasizing its philanthropy to become the control tower of the global network by being at the very center.

The Twenty-first Century Maritime Silk Road is, therefore, Sinocentric from its birth and is expressed to accentuate its philanthropic aspect. This would have been impossible without China's solid economic power. In the long run, it was China's dramatic economic development which enabled China to implement its plan and ideologically revive its Sinocentricism.

5. Conclusion

This paper has so far examined the maritime perceptions and policy directions of Chinese leaders in the modern era from Xun Wen to Xi Jinping and to analyze the process which led to the announcement on China becoming a maritime power in the 18th National Congress of the Communist Party and the islands disputes and the Maritime Silk Road policy as its two major implementation strategies. This paper further identified the Sinocentric aspects in the strategies to analyze China's behavior and future prospects which resulted in the following findings.

First, although China has been classified as the representative continental state, the maritime perception and policy of China's previous leaders show that China has been interested in the sea for quite a while and such interest was officially announced in the 18th National Congress. The change in China's maritime policy shows that while the leaders had different priorities, the policy has developed by complementing each other. That is, during Mao Zedong's rule, the emphasis was on military power and the navy was fostered whereas Deng Xiaoping opened China's doors and valued the sea as the passageway for foreign trade. During Jiang Zemin's terms, marine development and during Hu Jintao's terms marine resource development were valued and Xi Jinping complied all the previous strategies and announced that China will be becoming a maritime power. As can be seen, the dream of becoming a maritime power was planned for a long time which has become a specific policy China will continue to realize.

Second, the two axes of China's maritime power strategy, that is, the islands disputes and the Maritime Silk Road Policy, can be likened to the carrot and stick approach. The two axes are individual but also in a complex relationship. It is generally accepted that the success of the Twenty-first Century Maritime

Silk Road Policy depends on whether China could acquire the sovereignty of islands and secure its sea trade routes and that the islands disputes should be resolved for the Maritime Silk Road Policy to be implemented. However, in a strategic point of view, China could gain an advantage by appealing for the success of the Twentieth Century Maritime Silk Road which would bring about growth and joint development in participating countries and arguing that China should take possession of the disputed islands to realize the Silk Road. The islands disputes are, in fact, are difficult issues to resolve and China could be able to affect the international community by placing emphasis on the common benefits and development for the international community.

Third, Sinocentricism is at the center of China becoming a maritime power as well as the strategies for the goal — the islands disputes and the Maritime Silk Road. Sinocentricism is both China-centered as a sense of national pride and also has a hegemonic aspect of suppressing others with physical force, both of which would be used at need. China has so far displayed its hegemonic aspect in islands disputes by steadfastly using force or by incorporating territories into its own administrative jurisdiction or by constructing artificial islands. On the other hand, the Twenty-first Century Maritime Silk Road is more benevolent in that it provides developing countries with economic investment and cooperation and with establishing basic infrastructure and emphasizes peace and cooperative development. This is because the construction of the Maritime Silk Road requires absolute cooperation from the relevant states but it is also a reflection of China's confidence and pride in changing the world order. In spite of such policies, one should not forget that China has declared that it would not rule out the use of force when it is necessary.

Fourth, China's attitude in the Spratly Islands disputes shows that other than using military force, China has planned continuously for its ownership by making arguments based on historical grounds, effective occupation, and international treaties and by incorporating the disputed land in its administrative jurisdiction, legislating domestic law and building artificial islands. Moreover, by rejecting the PCA lawsuit, China expressed that it wants bilateral talks between the disputing states, rather than being intervened by third parties and such attitude would likely be maintained for other islands disputes as well. Considering its status and capacity at the international level, it will be difficult for South Korea or other related states to resist China's opinion, so the relevant states should search thoroughly for countermeasures. Yet South Korea is only reacting vehemently towards the Dokdo issue and is generally ignorant and indifferent to islands and maritime issues. South Korea currently faces disputes with China on the issue of Ieodo and on Dokdo with Japan. South Korea, therefore, should not only carefully observe China's course of actions in the present and in the future but also inform its citizens on islands and maritime issues and needs to be prepared to respond on such issues on the national level.

Affluence in the Little Ice Age

Natural History of Herring, Cod and Pollock

Moonkee Kim

1. Fish We Meet in Our Seas

The world is full of names. Everything that exists testifies its own existence with its name. Fish have names, too. The names contain the basic feeling and recognition of the people who used to view the fish. As the names are transmitted and exchanged, they are changed from time to time. The fish names also have a history. Seong, Hae-eung(成海應, 1760~1839), a writer in the late Joseon Dynasty, left in his Yeongyeongjae-Junjib(研經齋全集) an interesting record about the fish in the North Sea(sea of Hamgyeong-do).

The oceans surrounding the entire globe are where fish grow, and they are shared by the entire world. However, there are fish that are found only in our

North Sea, including 'Erya(爾雅)', 'Piya(裨雅)', and 'Guangya(廣雅)', which are not found in any books. There are four fish, from which the benefit is taken only by Joseon people. Their names are Myeongtaeeo(明太魚, pollock), Daegueo(大口魚, cod), Cheongeo(靑魚, herring) and Mokeo(牧魚, sandfish), all of which are Korean names.

Among the four types of fish mentioned above, 'mokeo', written in Chinese characters as '牧魚', '木魚', '目魚', or '銀魚', refers to sandfish("dorumuk" in Korean). Seong, Hae-eung mentioned pollock, cod, herring and sandfish as the fish that are found only in the Korean seas. He stated that 'Erya', 'Piya', and 'Guangya', which were not produced from the Chinese seas, were not found in the Chinese references. They were all cold current fish species caught mainly in the East Sea. What draws our attention is the word, 'Korean names', which means that these were the fish names used only in Korea but not in China. The fish names were made in Korea.

As pointed out by Seong, Hae-eung, the fish names were Korea's own names. The more important point is that herring, cod and pollock were the representative fish in the era of Joseon Dynasty with yellow corvina, the warm current fish. They represented Joseon Dynasty both in name and reality. However, from a historical point of view, his statement that herring, cod and pollock were not produced from the seas of China was not wrong, but it was not perfectly right. The situation had already been changed in his time. From 'a certain point of time', some of the fish started to be produced from the seas of China and already had 'names.' More interesting is what happened in Japan. From 'a certain point of time', a huge number of the cold current fish emerged in Japan and resulted in the growth of new fish industry. Seong, Hae-eung stated that these fish were exclusive to Korea, but they were already important fish in the three NortheastAsian countries. What caused the change? The clue is in the names of the fish.

What are the names of herring, cod and pollock in the three Northeast Asian countries? The current names of the cold current fish in the three Northeast Asian countries are summarized in 〈table 1〉.

With regard to the official names of the fish used now, the Chinese characters corresponding to herring, cod and pollock used in Korean are different from those in Chinese and Japanese. Herring is called 'Nishin' or 'Kado' in Japan, which correspond to the Chinese characters '鰊' and '鯡', respectively. Herring is called 'Feiyu(鯡魚)' in China. Cod is called 'Tara(鱈)' in Japan and 'Xueyu(鱈魚)' in China. Pollock is called 'Suketoudara(介黨鱈・佐渡鱈)' in Japan and 'Xiaxue(狭鱈)' in China. The Chinese characters '鯡' and '鱈' are commonly used in Chinese and Japanese. However, this was because the influence of Japanese fisheries science from the modern times. The situation was totally different before according to the historical records. The Korean names, Cheongeo, Daegu and Myeongtae, affected the fish names in China and Japan. The fish names were 'selected' through competition and collision. The selection process itself is a history.

〈table 1〉 Official names of herring, cod, pollock in the languages of three Northeast Asian countries

Fish name in English	Korean	Japanese	Chinese
herring	Cheongeo (靑魚)	Nishin (鰊, 鯡)	Feiyu (鯡魚)
cod	Daegu (大口)	Tara (鱈)	Xueyu (鱈魚)
pollock	Myeongtae (明太)	Suketoudara (鯳, 介黨鱈, 佐渡鱈)	Xiaxue (狹鱈)

2. Turning from 'Fish of Joseon' and 'Fish of Northeast Asia'

1) Natural History of Herring's Name

The name 'Cheongeo(靑魚)' already existed in China, as can be known from the old story of 'Ohucheong(五侯鯖, Wuhouqing)' in the era of Earlier Han Dynasty. However, the name 'Cheong(鯖)' at that time referred to not the sea herring but a type of grass carp, which is a freshwater fish. Lee, Shi-jin(李時珍) explains the fish.

> Cheongeo lives in rivers and lakes, mostly in the south. It is sometimes found in the north. It is caught regardless of the season. It looks like a carp, but the back is natural blue. The people in the south often make a salted food with it. The people in the past used to call it Ohucheong.

Because of the authoritativeness of the book Bencao-Gangmu(本草綱目),

the description of herring mentioned above significantly affected Joseon and Japan. Many scholars of Joseon compared the herrings they enjoyed with Ohucheong. However, they did not know that the two fish were different, although the same Chinese character was used.

Heo, Jun(許浚) was the first one who raised a question about the names. In his book Dongui-bogam(東醫寶鑑), he stated that the Cheongeo mentioned in the Bencao-Gangmu was totally different from the Cheongeo of Joseon, and announced, "The Chinese Cheongeo is not our Cheongeo". He clearly understood the difference between the freshwater Cheongeo and the seawater Cheongeo. In China, 'Cheongeo' meant a freshwater fish, not the seawater herring. No Chinese character referring to the seawater herring was found in many Chinese publications. It was Korea where the seawater herring was called Cheongeo. The origin goes up to at least the end of Goryeo Dynasty. Cheongeo was one of Korea's unique fish names.

As a fish that represented the era of Joseon Dynasty, herring has many nicknames. It has widely known that the name 'Gwamegi(과메기)', usually used in Gyeongbuk(慶北), is from the name 'Gwanmok(貫目)', which refers to dried herring. The representative name of herring was 'Biut(비웃).' The book Hunmong-Jahui(訓蒙字會), published in 1527, taught that the Chinese character '鯖' should be read 'Biut Cheong.' Another name of herring was 'Byeokeo'(碧魚). The Nanjungilgi, written by Lee, Sun-shin, also referred to herring as Byeokeo. The Chinese character '碧(blue)' was used to retain the meaning of Cheongeo, which literally means 'blue fish.' Jeong, Yak-yong(丁若

鏞) stated in his book Aeon-Gakbi(雅言覺非) that the origin of the name 'Biut' was Byeokeo. He wrote that Byeokeo(碧魚) had been wrongly translated to Biyu(蜚腴), because the Chinese characters '碧魚' were pronounced 'biyu.' So, he assumed that herring had the name Biut because of the wrong translation. The name Biyu is also found in China, but it has nothing to do with seawater herring. This indicates that the hypothesis by Jeong, Yak-yong has limitations.

Huang, Pil-su(黃泌秀), who lived in the late 19th century introduced another name for 'Biut' in his book Myeongmul-Giryak(名物紀略).

> In the years of Jeongjo(正祖), one of the kings of Joseon, an order was given to the Five Districts to supply 'Byeokeo' to poor Confucian scholars, giving another name to the fish, 'Biyueo(肥儒魚)', because the fish was cheap and readily available to be a good food for poor scholars.

Referring to Myeongmulgiryak, many scholars today state that 'Biut', the name for herring, was originated from 'Biyueo', literally meaning 'a fish that fattens a Confucian scholar.' However, the name 'Biyueo' was given by King Jeongjo. Remembering that the name 'Biut' appeared in the book Hunmongjahui, published in early half of the 16th century, it contradicts the time sequence that the name 'Biyueo' was originated from 'Biut.' It may be more accurately stated that the name 'Biyu'(肥儒) was created from the name 'Biut', because the name 'Biyueo' appeared far after the emergence of the name 'Biut.'

The Chinese characters '青魚' and '鯖' were in China before, but they were not related to the seawater herring, because herrings were not in the seas of China. However, in the late 16th century, seawater herring appeared in the seas of China. That was the time when the place name 'Cheongeotan(青魚灘, Qingyutan)' appeared in Rongcheng(榮城), Shandong(山東) Province. From the 17th century, the name Cheongeo was generally used in wiring collections and local papers. Describing seawater herring, the old story of Ohucheong was often quoted also in China without examination. However, the two fish started to be differentiated in China gradually. Tongzhi Huang-Xuanzhi(同治 黄縣志) record about Cheongeo(鯖魚) was in line with the differentiation.

> Bencao-Gangmu mentioned Cheongeo(青魚), wherein the character Cheong(青) is used in some regions and the character Cheong(鯖) is used in other regions. The book described it as a fish similar to carp(鯇) with a blue back. The seawater Cheongeo(鯖魚) we see now has a sharp head, a blue back and a narrow body that is about 7 to 8 chon(寸, unit of length) long and about 2 chon wide. The seawater Cheongeo is definitely different from the Cheongeo of old China.

This shows that it was clearly recognized in China that the seawater Cheongeo was different from the 'Cheongeo' mentioned in the book Bencao-Gangmu. To avoid the confusion, the word Haecheongeo(海青魚, Haiqingyu) was made in the Liaodong(遼東) province, wherein the name literally means seawater Cheongeo that is differentiated from freshwater Cheongeo. Although the name Chengeo appeared earlier in China, the origin of the name Cheongeo referring to seawater herring was Joseon.

From the ancient times, the word Cheongeo(靑魚) or Cheong(鯖) was available also in Japan. However, the word meant mackerel, not seawater herring. Mackerel is called 'saba' in Japanese, but the Chinese character that was used to refer to mackerel was Cheongeo(靑魚) or Cheong(鯖). The origin goes up to the book Engishiki(延喜式, "Procedures of the Engi Era") published in the 10th century. In summary, all the three Northeast Asian countries had the Chinese character for Cheongeo(靑魚), the meaning was different: It meant a freshwater fish in China, seawater herring in Joseon and mackerel in Japan. Then, what was herring called in Japan? In Japanese, herring is called 'Nishin' or 'Kado', and the corresponding Chinese characters are '鯡' and '鰊.' There is a legend that the herring fishing was started in Matsumae(松前) in the middle of the 15th century, but the earliest record about herring is the word for '鯡' found in the dictionary Unbo-Irohashu(運歩色葉集) published in 1548. The interest in the seawater herring is found in the late 17th century when the Chinese characters '鯡' and '鰊' were usually used as a fish name.

However, beside the Chinese character '鯖', referring to mackerel, another name '靑魚' appeared in the botanic classic Yamato-Honzo(大和本草) published in 1709. The name referred to the same seawater herring as in Joseon. The book Yamato-Honzo used the name '靑魚' instead of '鰊' and '鯡' to refer to herring. Why did Kaibara-Ekiken(貝原益軒), who is known as the scholar who established the independent botany of Japan, abandon the Chinese characters used in Japan and employed the Chinese characters corresponding to

Cheongeo? A hint may be found in the book Kankai-Shokkyo(卷懐食鏡), which was published seven years after the publication of Yamato-Honzo.

> I observed the fish. The name is the same as the Cheongeo mentioned in Bencao-Gangmu, but they are different. The herring mentioned in Dongui-Bogam looks like sardine and is about 1 cheok(尺, 30.3 cm) long. This is what is commonly called kadonos(加登能合) in Japan. When a Joseon person visited Japan, somebody asked what they call kado, and he answered that it is called Cheongeo.

There is one word in the saying of Katsuki-Gyūzan(香月牛山) that requires attention, which is Dongui-Bogam. This means that the Japanese scholars visited the Joseon Tongsinsa(通信使, Goodwill Missions) to verify the fish with the name of Cheongeo. Ekiken abandoned the Chinese character used in Japan to refer the fish and employed the Chinese character used in Joseon because of the influence of Dongui-Bogam. The Chinese characters '鯖' and '青魚' both referring to mackerel previously started to refer to mackerel and herring, respectively. Due to the authoritativeness of Yamato-Honzo, the distinction of the Chinese characters '鯖 = mackerel' and '青魚 = herring' became a tradition and continued before the modern times.

Lee, Gwan-myeong(李觀命) who visited as an ambassador China in 1718 found herrings there and recorded, "Herring is the fish of our country. The fish was not here before. For several decades, many herrings have been caught also here. The local people didn't know the name of the fish and thus called it "the

Joseon Fish". When schools of herrings suddenly appeared in the seas after the late 16th century, the fish was firstly referred to as a 'new fish(新魚)' and then employed the name Cheongeo as used in Joseon. Japan had the Chinese characters for herring '鰊' and '鯡', but the name Cheongeo as used in Joseon replaced those Chinese characters from the 18th century to the middle of the 19th century. Cheongeo was a fish of Joseon, but it became from a certain time a fish of the Northeast Asia.

2) Natural History of Cod'a Name

With herring and pollock, cod is a representative cold current fish. Lee, Su-gwang(李睟光) wrote, "Daegueo(cod) is produced from the East Sea of our country, not produced in China. Therefore, the name is not found in Chinese books. However, Chinese people consider it as a great dish. People who return to Beijing(北京) purchase it and bring it with them". Cod was a fish that was produced only from the East Sea and the South Sea, not from the West Sea. Therefore, it was Joseon's special product that was not produced in China. In fact, cod was presented to the Emperor of China as a gift by the ambassadors visiting the country, and it was often given as a king's present to Tsushima of Japan. The scholar in the era of Ming Dynasty clearly wrote, "Daegueo(cod) is produced from Joseon". Just as herring was the fish of Joseon, cod was also a fish of Joseon.

The Korean name of cod, Daegueo(大口魚), literally means 'a big mouth fish.' Heojun presented in his book Dongui-Bogam 'Huaeo(夻魚)' as the name of cod in Chinese characters, and commented, "The fish is produced from the northeast sea, and it is commonly called Daegueo". He also presented the Chinese characters '吴魚' beside '夻魚.' The notable character is '夻', which did not exist in China. In the late 18th century, the Chinese writer Li, Diao-yuan(李調元) wrote in the book Ranxizhi(然犀志), "The character '吴' is found in books with the comment that it refers to 'a big mouth fish.' The Joseon people invented the character '夻', which looks different but has the same meaning". This record points out that the character '吴' was there in China but not the character '夻', which was a newly invented Korea's own Chinese character.

An interesting change occurred in the late Joseon Dynasty. Cod started to appear in the West Sea. Jo, Jae-sam(趙在三: 1808～1866) described in the book Songnam-Japji(松南雜識) how much Chinese people liked cod.

> The fish is referred to as '吴' in the Kangxi-Dictionary(康熙字典). The name of the fish is not found in Chinese books because it is not produced in China. We call it '大口'(Daegu). In the trade market, Chinese people make cods sold. It is said that when a cod is thrown into a room, people get into the room and just lock the door. They consider cod as a tasteful dish and eat it like flies that love the meat gravy. Recently, the fish is caught in the West Sea.

The book vividly described how fanatic the Chinese people were about cod.

The noticeable part is the comment at the end of the quotation that cod was caught in the West Sea also. The map published in the second half of King Yeongjo(英祖)'s reign, Yeojidoseo(輿地圖書), also recited 'Daegueo' as the product of Chungcheo-do(忠淸道) and Huanghae-do(黃海道) in addition to Hamgyeong-do(咸境道), Gangwon-do(江原道) and Gyeongsang-do(慶尙道). From a certain point of time, cod started to appear and be caught in the West sea. Then, why was it not produced in China?

Cod was not caught in China in the past. However, from a certain point of time, cod started to appear in China. Introducing the seawater fish that were caught much in the region of Rongcheng(榮城). Daoguang Rongcheng-Xuanzhi(道光 榮城縣志), stated, "Daegu appears latest and remains even after winter". Here, the name "Daegu" appeared. Also called "Daedueo(大頭魚)', cod was an economically important fish in the north Yellow Sea in the Qing Dynasty. The point is that the name of cod was 'Daegu', which was the name used in Joseon. This shows that the fish name used in Joseon affected that of China.

Like herring, it was the 17th century when cod was widely known in Japan. The name firstly appeared in the book Kugyou-Nitki(公卿日記, Court Noble Diary) of the late 16th century, and cod fishing became an important industry in Edo period. In Japan, cod is called 'tara.' The book Gikin-Honzo(宜禁本草) published in 1629 referred to cod as 'Seoleo(雪魚)', and the book Etpo-Shokumotsu-Honzo(閱甫食物本草) published 42 years later used the Chinese character 'seol(鱈).' Hitomi-Hitsudai(人見必大) wrote as follow in the book Honcho-Shokkan(本朝食鑑):

> The Chinese character '鱈' is pronounced as 'Seol(雪)' and means 'tara(多良).' The character '鱈', which is not found in ancient books of China, was made in Japan. However, the meaning is complementary. It is known that 'Seoleo(鱈魚)' is caught a lot after the first snow in winter. Therefore, the Chinese character includes the part '雪'(meaning 'snow').

The author explained that cod was called '雪魚' because it was caught a lot after the first snow in winter. The Chinese character 'Seol(鱈)' is the combination of the two Chinese characters. It is noteworthy that the Chinese character '鱈' was made in Japan. Just as the new Chinese character '夻' was made by combining '大口' in Joseon, the Japanese own Chinese character for cod was made in Japan.

Just like herring, the Chinese character '鱈' was used to refer to the cod of Japan until the 17th century. However, a change occurred in the fish name. In the book Nihon-Shakumyo(日本釋名), published in 1699, Ekiken employed the name '大口魚'(Daegueo) instead of '鱈.' In the book Yamato Honzo(大和本草), published 10 years later, '青魚' was adopted in replacement of '鰊' and '鯡', and '吴魚' in replacement of '鱈.' The Chinese characters used in Joseon were adopted to refer to herring and cod in Japan. Why did Ekiken adopted the fish name of Joseon '大口魚' instead of the Japan-made Chinese character '鱈'? How did they learn that 'tara(鱈)' is the '大口魚' of Joseon? Hitsudai explains the procedure of the change.

> Cod is abundantly produced in Korea. Joseon Tongsinsa visited Japan in 1682. Hong, Se-tae(洪世泰), who came as a Busabijang(副使雅將, nae of office), was rich in knowledge of many things. I asked him about '鱈魚', and he answered, "It is called Daegueo in our country. It is caught a lot in the north, and we dry it under the sun to sell it."

It was Hong, Se-tae, the entourage of the Joseon Tongshinsa of 1682, who confirmed that '鱈' of Japan is '大口' of Joseon. Hitsudai directly verified the Joseon name of 'tara(鱈)' through a man of Joseon. In Yamato-Honzo, Ekiken used '夻魚' as the official name of the fish, and commented "The common name of '夻魚' is Daegueo in Dongui-Bogam". Like herring, the Japanese name of cod was also affected by the book Dongui-Bogam. Since then, '大口魚', '吴魚' and '夻魚', the Joseon names of cod were used as the official names in the Japanese lists of plants and fish.

Joseon and Japan had to invent new Chinese characters corresponding to cod, which were '夻' and '鱈.' The scholars in Joseon also knew that the Chinese character '鱈' was invented in Japan. In Japan, '夻' was considered as '韓字'(meaning 'Chinese character of Korea'), indicating that the Japanese also knew that the character was invented in Joseon. Interestingly, the two Chinese characters competed with each other, and the competition ended with the victory of Joseon. Katsuki-Gyūzan(香月牛山) stated that '夻魚' was the representative Chinese characters and ‘鱈’ is not the official character. He adopted the Joseon-style Chinese characters ‘夻魚’ as the name for cod instead of the Japanese-style Chinese character ‘鱈.’ Ekiken also knew that ‘鱈’ was a Chinese character invented in Japan. He had a very negative view to the Japanese own Chinese characters. He said that he would use the right characters and the right meaning to correct the wrongs of the old custom. It is interesting that he chose ‘青魚’ in replacement of ‘鰊’ and ‘鯡’, and ‘夻魚’ in replacement of ‘鱈.’

Yamato-Honzo, the foundation of Japanese herbal medicine, employed the Chinese characters invented in Joseon as the official characters instead of those invented in Japan. This influence of Korean fish names continued until the 19th century.

3) Natural History of Pollock’ Name

Pollock is one of the representative cold current fish with herring and cod, but its history in the Northeast Asia is very different from that of herring and cod. Pollock is distributed in a much northern region than herring and cod. Since pollock has never entered into the West Sea, Chinese knew nothing about pollock before the modern times. Pollock was produced in Japan in the Edo period, but not considered as an important fish. It was after the modern times that China and Japan paid attention to pollock. On the contrary, pollock was one of the representative fish in the late Joseon Dynasty. That’s why Joseon is critical in the history of pollock.

In the late Joseon Dynasty, pollock was the most caught fish and supplied nationwide. Jo, Jae-sam wrote about the origin of the name Myeongtae(pollock) and its abundance.

> 'Bukeo(北魚)' is produced in Wonsan Island(元山島), Deakwon(德原) in our country. It was not caught in Myeongcheon(明川) in the past. A person whose family name is 'Tae(太)' and who lives in Myeongcheon caught during fishing Bukeo for the time, and he name it 'Myeongtae(明太)' because it was big, fatty and tasty. The fish is called 'Dongtae(冬太)' if caught in winter and 'Chuntae(春太)' if caught in spring. The egg of the fish is called 'Myeongran(明卵).' Since the fish is generally caught in a great amount, everyone can eat to their fill even in a poor village in a deep mountain.

Jo, Jae-sam stated that the name Myeongtae(明太) was born because Mr. Tae of Myeongcheon caught the fish. Yu, Hui(柳僖) wrote in the book Mulmyeonggo(物名攷) that "Bukeo refers to a small Myeongtaeeo. The fish has the name Bukeo(meaning, 'fish of the north') because it is produced in the north of the East Sea". Seo, Yu-gu(徐有榘) wrote that the fresh one is called Myeongtae and the dried one Bukeo. As the demand of pollock was great, it had many names.

When did the name 'Myeongtae' firstly appear? That was in the middle of the 17th century. The word 'Myeongtae(明太)' firstly appeared in the record in the third year of King Hyojong(1652) when it was rebuked that the Myeongtae roe was offered instead of the cod roe as an offering to the king from Gangwon-do. The origin of the pollock fishery must have been prior to the record. The pollock fishery dates back farthest to the Goryeo Dynasty and nearest to the 17th century. A hint about the origin of the pollock fishery is the name 'Mutaeeo(無泰魚).' When herring and cod were already recorded in the Sejongsilok-Jirigi(世宗實錄地理志, Geography Book in Annals of King Sejong), pollock, being also a cold current fish, was not found in the book. The name Mutaeeo, presumed to be the name for pollock, firstly appears in Sinjeung-Dongguk-Yeojiseungram(新增東國輿地勝覽, geography book) published in 1530. This shows the pollock fishery had already developed in the 16th century. However, pollocks were caught only in some regions of Hamgyeong-do. The pollock fishery was fully developed in the late 17th century. For example, Heo, Jun's book Dongui-Bogam and Heo, Gyun(許筠)'s book Seongso-Bubugo(惺所覆瓿藁), published in the first half of the 17th century, do not give any hint about pollock. This shows that pollock was not an important fish at that time. The pollock fishery started in at least 16th century, but it was rapidly developed in the middle and late 17the century to become the largest fishery of Joseon.

In contrast to herring and cod, pollock has never appeared in the seas of China. Therefore, there was not a Chinese character representing pollock in China. The name 'Myeongtae(明太)' was Joseon's own fish name. Pollock is called 'suketoudara' in Japanese, meaning that pollock was considered as a type of cod(タラ, tara). The Chinese words used in Japan to refer to pollock included 'jeo(鯺)', 'juadoseol(佐渡鱈)', 'gaedangseol(介黨鱈)' and 'jojongseol(助

宗鱈).' The word referring to pollock firstly appeared in Japan in the late 17th century. The word '鯳(スケト)' firstly appeared in a suit case in 1670 regarding cod and pollock fishery in Niikata(新潟). The pollock fishery seems to be carried out in Sado(佐渡) in the late 16th century. However, because pollock was considered as "the lowest grade fish with a small size and a bad taste", it failed to draw any attention in Japan. It was a sharp contrast to the situation in the late Joseon Dynasty when pollock was supplied to the entire country and pollock fishery became the top fishery.

Then, what made Japan pay full attention to pollock? Interestingly, Joseon played a role. With the conclusion of the Korea-Japan Trade Agreement in 1883, the seas of Hamgyeong-do, Gyeongsan-do and Jeonra-do(全羅道) were opened to Japan, and Japanese fishermen entered into Joseon. Most of the Japanese fishermen who entered into Korea were from the west of Japan, who were not familiar with the cold current fish. However, as the number of Japanese fishermen entering into Korea was increased, they started to pay attention to new fish species. What drew their attention included the cold current fish, including pollock, cod and herring. Among them, the demand for pollock in Joseon made Japanese fishermen be amazed. Japanese fishermen attempted to catch pollocks in the seas of Joseon from the Sino-Japanese War. However, the fishery started from 1901 in the full scale. The fishermen continuously attempted the fishery with the help of the fishery promotion policies of Japan, they failed to make significant accomplishment until 1910. An important change occurred rather in Japan.

The development of the pollock fishery in Japan occurred in the full scale from the 20th century. The pollock fishery started from Hokkaido(北海道) in 1899 and then developed to an exclusive job in 1903 and 1904. Why did pollock happen to be in the limelight in the 20th century, while it failed to draw attention until the Edo period? The herring fishery that had been thriving in Hokkaido was suddenly declined at that time, and pollock emerged as a fish in replacement of herring. Another notable thing is pollock roe(Myeongran, 明卵). The plain taste of pollock was what the Japanese people didn't like. However, as the pollock roe of Joseon was known to the Japanese fishermen and traders, it was newly highlighted in Japan. The pollock roe of Joseon was imported to Japan in a large amount through Higuchi-Shoten(樋口商店) established in 1907, and earned the Japanese name Mentaiko(明太子). As Japanese were fascinated by the taste of pollock roe(明太子), pollock fishery developed as the top fisher of Japan until 1977. The 'exchange of taste' between Joseon and Japan caused pollock to be in the limelight in Japan.

'Myeongtae' was the fish name invented in Joseon. In contrast to herring and cod, pollock was known to China and Japan from the modern times. Pollock was an unimportant fish in Japan, but the 'taste' of 'Myeongran(明太子)' fascinated the Japanese people. Therefore, the Korean name of pollock, 'Myeongtae(明太)', means pollock also in Japan. Pollock is called 'Xiaxue(狹鱈)' in China, but it is still called 'Mingtaiyu(明太魚)' by common people. Pollock is also called 'Mintai' in Russia. The 'taste' of pollock roe instilled the fish name of Joseon in Japan, China and Russa through the modern times.

3. Affluence in the Little Ice Age

: Emergence of Cold Current Fish

1) Exchange of Cold Current Fish Names

The Chinese fish names had a dominant influence on the fish names used in Northeast Asia. In Joseon, most of the fish produced from the West Sea(黃海), shared by China, were called with the fish names in the Chinese characters used in China. Nevertheless, the Joseon's fish names for herring, cod and pollock, the cold current fish, affected China and Japan. The fish names used in Joseon were shared in Northeast Asia. It was a conversion from 'Joseon fish' into 'Northeast Asian fish.'

Until the middle of the 19th century, the Joseon names of these cold current fish dominated Japan. In the late 19th century, however, Japan started to positively use their own fish names with the rapid development of fishery science. The Chinese character-based fish names used in Joseon, Cheongeo(青魚) and Daegu(大口), gradually disappeared in Japan. The Republican China was affected by the modern fishery science of Japan. As a result, the Japanese names for herring and cod, '鯡' and '鱈', became the official names in China in replacement of Cheongeo and Daegu. The dominance of the cold current fish names that Joseon had in the Northeast fishery from the 17th century was gradually lost.

〈table 2〉 Natural fish name history of herring, pollock and cod

Fish	Country	Fish name		
		Early modern times	Modern time	Present day
Herring	Korea	靑魚, 鯖, 肥儒魚, 碧魚	靑魚	靑魚
	Japan	鰊, 鯡, 靑魚	靑魚→鰊, 鯡	鰊, 鯡(靑魚)
	China	靑魚, 鯖, 海靑魚	靑魚→鰊, 鯡	鯡魚(靑魚)
Cod	Korea	大口魚, 夻魚, 吴魚	大口魚	大口
	Japan	鱈, 大口魚, 夻魚, 吴魚	大口魚→鱈	鱈
	China	大口魚, 大頭魚	大口魚→鱈	鱈 (大口魚)
Pollock	Korea	明太, 北魚	明太, 北魚	明太
	Japan	鯳, 介黨, 須介黨, 佐渡鱈,	鯳, 須介黨, 佐渡鱈, 明太魚	鯳, 須介黨, 佐渡鱈 (明太魚)
	China	×	明太魚	狹鱈 (明太魚)

2) Little Ice Age, Sea and Cold Current Fishery

A more fundamental reason should be found about why herring, cod and pollock, the cold current fish, started to draw attention in the three Northeast Asian countries simultaneously in the 17th century. The key is climate change. In view of the history of the global climate change, the era of Joseon Dynasty corresponds to the little ice age. With regard to the climate of the Northeast Asia, cold weather continued from the middle of the 15th century to the middle of the 19th century, as the period is even called 'Little Ice Age.' The cold weather was severe especially in the 17th century. The cold weather during the Little Ice Age lowered the seawater temperature, resulting in the fish migration. The cold current fish, herring, cod and pollock, migrated to the south because of the cold seawater.

Herrings testified the huge change in the ocean environment in the Northeast Asia around the 17th century. Ryu, Seong-yong(柳成龍) mentioned in his book Jingbirok(懲毖錄) the appearance of the East Sea fish in the West Sea as a sign of Imjinwoeran(the Japanese Invasion to Korea in 1592):

> The East Sea fish were found in the West Sea and even in Han River. Cheong-eo(herring) was produced in Haeju(海州), but it was not caught in the last decade. It is now caught in the sea of Liaodong. The Liaodong people called it a 'new fish.'

Ryu, Seong-yong pointed out that many cold current fish, originally produced in the East Sea, were produced in the West Sea, and the herring that was used to be caught in the West Sea of Joseon migrated to the Liaodong region of China. Lee, Su-guang also wrote in about 1570 that the herring of the West Sea was caught in the sea of Shandong. These records indicate that a huge change in the marine environment in the late 16th century caused the cold current fish of the East Sea to migrate to the West Sea. This continued until the early half of the 18th century.

According to Ryu, Seong-yong and Lee, Su-guang, the herrings of the West Sea migrated in a large scale to the seas of Liaodong and Shandong regions of China in the late 16th century. The fact that the Liaodong people called herring a 'new fish' well illustrates their embarrassment. That was the time when the word 'Cheoneotan(qingyutan, 青魚灘)', referring to the sea herring, firstly appeared in China. The word 'Haecheongeo(haiqingyu, 海青魚)' was used in the

Liaodong region in order to distinguish the unfamiliar 'new fish' from the freshwater herring. Afterward, the herring fishery in China was brilliantly developed. Hao, Yi-hang(郝懿行) wrote, "Tens of million nets were used, and people who purchased the fish considered it as inferior". Song, Wan wrote that the people in the coastal areas ate the fish for their meals, calling it 'Cheongeo-juk(qingyuzhou, 靑魚鬻).' The 'unfamiliar fish' that started to appear in the late 16th century fed the Chinese for three hundred years since then.

The herring fishery in Japan was more brilliant. It was in the 17th century that the herring fishery began in the full scale when it was started in Matsumae, Hokkaido. In the 18th century, with the expansion of the herring fishery the entire Hokkaido, herrings were sold all over Japan through the nationwide distribution network. The herring egg(kadonoko, カドノコ) was an expensive food supplied to the nobles, but the other parts of herrings were too common to be used as the food for the people of the lowest class or cats. In particular, the fish fertilizer that was distributed nationwide through Kitamaebune(北前船) resulted in the agricultural revolution in the early modern times in Japan. The huge trade network between Hokkaido and Osaka(大阪) played an essential role in the development of commerce in the Edo period. That was the 'benefit' that the Little Ice Age brought to the people of that time, who couldn't recognize the source of the benefit.

Then, why did cod not go through such a change? Cod was the fish that was only caught in the East Sea and the South Sea before the early Joseon Dynasty. Cod started to appear in the West Sea from a 'certain time.' The 'Woedaegu(矮

大口)', the small cods that used to be caught in the West Sea, is a mystery to the fishery science of today. The record in the book Jingbirok is worth to pay attention. Ryu, Seong-yong mentioned that the cold current fish of the East Sea migrated to the West Sea. Did cod also migrate to the West Sea at the same time? Go, Sang-an(高尙顔), who was a contemporary of Ryu, Seong-yong, left the following record of interest:

> Daegu is produced from the East Sea. Since a hundred years before, it has been gradually produced from the South Sea, too. It started to be caught also in the West Sea in five or six decades ago. However, the size gradually became smaller than that of the East Sea.

Go, Sang-an wrote that cod, which used to be produced from only the East Sea, started to be produced from the South Sea from a hundred years before and from the West Sea from 50 to 60 years before. The cod of the East Sea gradually migrated to the South Sea and then to the West Sea. This indicates that schools of cods migrated to the West Sea in the late 16th century. That was the origin of 'Woedaegu(倭大口)'.

The migration of cods to the West Sea around the 17th century is also verified by the record by Heo, gyun. He wrote, "Cod is produced all from the East Sea, South Sea and West Sea. Cods produced from the North Sea are largest in size, yellow in color, and thick. Cods produced from the East Sea are red and small, and most favored by Chinese people. Those produced from the West

Sea are even smaller". The lowering of the seawater temperature during the Little Ice Age made schools of cods to migrate from the East Sea to the West Sea. Since cod was not produced in China before, there was not even a name for cod in China. After the large-scale migration of cods to the West Sea around the 17th century, cod fishery was started in China at a certain time point. The fish name 'Dakou(大口)' appeared in the local papers of China in the early 19th century at the latest. Cods that used to be attainable only in Joseon could now be caught in China.

The cod fishery in Japan also developed in the full scale only in the 17th century like the herring fishery. Hitsutai wrote, "Cods are not found in the seas of the east, west and south, but in the coastal regions of the North Sea in abundance". The development of the cod fishery was triggered by the southward migration of the cods from their main habitat around the Hokkaido to the east of the Honshu(本州) in the Edo period. Cods were offered to shoguns as winter specialty in Kaga(加賀) and Fukui(福井). In the late 17th century, daimyos of the northern lands competitively offered cods to the palace. The Edo people enjoyed the light and plain taste of cods in the banquets held in the first month of the year.

Although being the same cold current fish, pollock has a history that is different from that of herring and cod. As pollocks were distributed in a region that was more northern than that of herrings and cods, pollocks did not migrate to the West Sea even when the cold current was strong. A noteworthy fact is that the region of distribution of pollock was shifted to the south in the East

Sea during the Little Ice Age. Pollocks were produced only in the Gyeongseong(鏡城) and Myeongcheon(明川) of Hamgyeong-do in the early Joseon Dynasty, but they migrated to Gangwon-do from the 17th century. The emergence of the name Myeongtae in the 17th century reflects the change of the marine environment. Seo, Yu-gu stated, "Pollocks can be caught in four seasons all the year around". He also added, "Together with herrings, pollocks are circulated all over Korea most abundantly". The cold current fish, pollock and herring, could become the most important fish in the late Joseon Dynasty because of the climate change during the Little Ice Age.

4. In front of Global warming

It is significant in view of the Little Ice Age that the cold current fish became important in the Northeast Asia from the 17th century. The cooling of the region during the Little Ice Age caused 'a global crisis.' On the other hand, the cold weather brought about increased production cold current fish. These fish enabled even the poor people living in rural areas to feed themselves abundantly. The 'crisis' of the Little Ice Age enriched the Northeast Asia with the cold current fish. China and Japan used the fishing names of Joseon, such as Cheongeo, Daegu and Myeongtae, because they wanted to obtain important information from Joseon where the fish were known well from early years.

However, as warming of the region has continued since the late 19th century, herring, cod, pollock and sandfish, which Seong, Hae-eung mentioned as those produced only the North Sea of Korea, gradually disappeared in the seas of Korea in the late 20th century. The northward migration of cold current fish is distinctively found in the seas of China and Japan. The supply of the cold current fish is now dependent upon the Bering Sea, which is far northern from the seas of Northeast Asia. One of the major causes of the drastic decrease of herring, cod and pollock population is overfishing. However, from a more macroscopic point of view, the past migration of the fish to the Northeast Asian seas and the present migration of the fish out of the seas reflects the global climate change. The fish name history of herring, cod and pollock shows the history of the climate. These fish are truly the 'silent witnesses' of the global climate change.

Part 2

Cultural Exchange in Northeast Asian Sea Region

Kwangdeok Seo_

Contention Between National Studies and Regional Studies(Foreign Studies) in the Course of Formation of East Asian Modern Studies

Focusing on the Formation of Chinese Studies in Korea before Liberation

Bogo Lee_

Dual Position of Cross-Border Travelers in Cultural Contact Zones Viewed from "Journal of a Voyage Along the Coast of China"

Seungwoong Ahn_

Shen Cong Wen and Maritime Culture of Qingdao

Minho Yang_

A Study on the Introduction of Modern Western Languages to Japan

a Focus on Loan Words from the Dutch Language

Contention Between National Studies and Regional Studies(Foreign Studies) in the Course of Formation of East Asian Modern Studies

Focusing on the Formation of Chinese Studies in Korea before Liberation

Kwangdeok Seo

1. Introduction

One of the significant features of Chinese scholarly society connected to China's emergence in the 21th century is the attention and consolidating of the 'foreign Hanhak' and connecting it to the Gukhak(國學, national studies) of China after moderntimes and advocating the integrated study 'International Hanhak(漢學, Chinese Studies)'. As seen in an International Hanhak scholars' conference(*Gim Hyejun* 2009), international Hanhak is not just a Hanhak of the past which is humanities centered Chinese Studies. It is found in magazines and publications on foreign Hanhak beyond the introduction of scholarly works and scholar's academic essays regarding humanities related Chinese Studies, they introduce the outcome of Chinese Studies in a social science field which is called 'Chinese research'. In this way, international Hanhak is likely to merge the humanitarian and social science Chinese research which were once separated in the past Chinese history. It can be interpreted that this is an attempt to establish international Hanhak as a universal study through the re-interpretation of both Hanhak, the universal study of the East Asia region before the modern times, and new studies formed by adopting western studies after moderntimes . With the recent enthusiasm for China's Gukhak and the globalization of Chinese Studies, how sinologists in Korea would deal with the situation has been an issue. Coping with the change in academic condition from China is important, but it is much more essential to review the change in internal conditions, as Korea's Chinese studies have been originally formed in Korea. Therefore, it is important to have answers to questions such as, "why was Chinese study done in Korea? How has it been studied so far? What is its history? How can the country China be studied in Korea by a scholar?" etc. These questions should be asked and it should naturally be connected to the review of overall scholarship in Korea's modern times, especially the Hangukhak(Korean Studies).

This internal and external problem is a critical factor for reviewing the history of Chinese Studies in Korea since these Studies cannot be established without the modern birth of Hakji(學知, academic knowledge). The learning of Chinese Studies in both Korea and in Japan initiated Hangukhak(韓國學)'s birth.

It is because Chinese Studies has historically existed as a traditional study of ancient dynasties under the Chinese sphere of influence including the Chosun dynasties before modern times. As a result, Chosun studies had the task of establishing the relationship of Hanhak to Korea's history. This was an essential process for a modern birth of Gukhak.

With the So-called establishment of modern study after the adoption of western studies combined with the Gukhak (movement) initially aimed to emerge from the past study of (Hanhak). At the same time learning and wiping out from the tradition is a process to determine which viewpoint and methodology will be develop in the future.

Due to the modern establishment of separate disciplines, the existing Hanhak was confined to a single study, and was an element which reinforced the nation to establish nation-state. As a result, Chinese Study, as a modern foreign study, was ready to be born at the early stage of moderntimes, when Gukhak was first emerging. To summarize, Chinese Studies in Korea is the fruit of a modern branch of study which has a close relationship with Korean Studies, and has been influenced by the Chinese Studies of the west, Japan, as well as other countries. Whether or not the study of Chinese Studies can be conducted and improved upon in the future still remains uncertain.

With this sense of awareness, the development of Chinese Studies in Korea was will be summarized historically. Also, the composition of 'Foreign (regional) Studies and national studies', 'Nation and regionalism' and the viewpoint of 'sea region' (This geographically means the area in which it is connected with the sea but in the context, it is described as a transitional space centering on the sea beyond the conventional regional awareness in the past. To view it in this theoretical definition, it can be used as a postmodern awareness) will be used for examination.

2. Hanhak and Bukhak in Chosun
: Humanities and Regional Studies

Generally, Korean Studies and Chinese Studies have characteristics of regional studies when viewed by modern academia. Additionally, these names and the integration they had couldn't be maintained under the subspecialized academic system after the modern era. However, national or foreign studies in an academic form under the nation-state global system has always existed consciously. In particular, Chinese Studies in the East Asia region has a historicity as a universal study based on ancient East Asia's universal humanities tradition.

Given this, Chinese studies was on the boundary of universal study above the nation's study and nation's study itself. The exact time when the nation's study crossed borders was when nation states emerged and when the America-centered regional studies appeared. Also, Europe's "Sinology" was a new interpretation added to the East-Asia universal study Hanhak. This sinology was adopted by Japan and East Asian countries shaking the traditional foundation of Hanhak. Maintaining the identity as a universal study was not easy due to China's status after "modern times" as well.

The establishment of Chinese Studies in Korea is not irrelevant to this sort of world background. The different characteristics of Chinese Studies in Korea as well as Japan is underlined by the fact that traditional Korean society used Chinese characters as one of pillars of culture and it has studied and the research of Chinese cultural ideology and social regulation cannot be separated. This is why there is a huge difference conceptually between Hanhak in East Asia and the "Sinology" of Western countries.

In traditional Korea society, the research and study of Hanhak is not to understand China as a foreign place but through social regulation and cultural ideology. It was traditional Korea in East Asia where traditional Hanhak had been followed and fully developed with the aim to research and study all things China. In short, it was not only for researching and understanding China, but also for utilizing its culture, system, and tradition with the help of Hanhak.

The tradition of Hanhak, its solid foundation, can be attributed to Lee Tweo-Kye(李退溪) and Lee Yul-Gok(李栗谷) who have been revered, until now, as the Korean representative scholars in the field of Neo-Confucianism due to the discovery of their research. In addition, they have also been revered pioneers of Kukhak, the most representative study of Korea. This means that Hanhak was localized/transformed as Kukhak in Korean traditional society, a remarkable outcome derived from Korean society studying China. In the course of the development of Hanhak, studies focusing on regions of China, which have the characteristics of a regional study, emerged. Representative examples include Cheonghak(淸學) and Bukhak(北學) from Chosun study before the modern era.

The concept of Cheonghak and Bukhak is that it is a study to understand emigrants not the Chinese nation. It can also be interpreted as a product of the times away from the Hanhak's mainstream climate. After mid-Chosun, there was Cheonghak(Bukhak) that emerged from mainstream Hanhak. As this type of study directly or indirectly opened the import of foreign culture, the study Silhak(實學, realism) emerged.

Traditional Hanhak was based on the humanities centered on the Confucianism and the goal of Silhak's was to change the entire society and comprehension of Confucianism. Silhak represented by Dasan(茶山) Jung Yak-yong (丁若鏞) and Choi Han-gi(崔漢綺) arose from the process of escaping from the ideology of Chinese Studies, distinguishing internal and external problems of Chosun and establishing an alternative. In this respect, the study of Silhak at its point of origin is the beginning of Gukhak. On the other hand, it is the beginning of self-understanding of China. In this process, when looking at the Bukhak School's effort from the "sea region" viewpoint, we could integrate traditional Chinese Studies by including a variety of different perspectives and scholarship from the actual study of Qing dynasty and accept the book of that time. Of course, we must admit that Japanese Hanhak is not only an imitation of ancient Chinese Studies but also that traditional Korean Hanhak is the product of the acceptance and transformation based on Korean foundation of Confucianism. Therefore, the Korean Hanhak formation has been a part of Korean culture. In this regard, the Korean Studies which has emerged since the modern era, naturally came up with the question of how to proceed from Korean hanhak, which is part of traditional Korean Studies. It was inseparable from the question of how to establish modern Chinese Studies.

It is notable that this academic movement which had begun between the 17th century and 18th century appeared in the process of reformation of Chosun. Namely, it was one of the scholastic efforts for Silhak which developed with Bukhak Group(Theory of Northern Conquest) to adopt Qing's advanced studies critically. The representatives are Yu Hyeong-won(柳馨遠), Lee ik(李瀷), Jeong Yak-yong and others. Jeong Yak-yong who was also called Da-san can be regarded as a scholar who compiled the overall Silhak. He asserted to build Leeyonggam(利用鑑) to adopt practicalbenefit critically. In the modern context, it was an argument to build a kind of Chinese local study laboratory. However, such result could not be achieved due to bureaucrats who insisted on traditional Huayiguan(華夷觀). Park Ji-won(朴趾源)'s *Yeolha Ilgi* was regulated as a banned book. Park Je-ga was exiled.

Bukhak scholars developed their Bukhak Group(Theory of Northern Studies) as one branch of Silhak based on the logic to learn the civilizations of Qing Dynasty and promote public welfare. It was also an argument against Bukbulron(北伐論), a discourse of punishing Qing, stressed by Confucian scholars who worshipped the Ming dynasty. Hong Dae-yong(洪大容) and Park Ji-won developed Bukhakron(北學論) and it reached a climax with Park Jae-ga (朴齊家). They tried to reform Chosun society through writings by watching and learning the social constructs of the time personally by visiting the present capital of Beijing, namely Yanjing, at that time. Hong Dae-yong's book Damheon yeongi(湛軒燕記), Park Ji-won's Yeolha Ilgi(熱河日記), and Park Je-ga's Bukhakui(北學議) are the representative works. Bukhakui is the work of Park Je-ga who amalgamated the content of Bukhakron in 1786 and Bukhakui in 1798 introduced and compared Chinese culture to Chosun's after his visit to China. He mentioned the external ignorance of Chosun society. He asserted that all kinds of Chinese culture should be imported, trades and commerce should be developed and to improve the people's lives and finance status of the country. From the view point of the sea region, it is the study on Silhak or Bukhak and of course China. On the other hand, it is an adaptation to the western studies of China. In this process of work, there is a limitation in the18th century's Chosun modernization interpretation in that it was considered as a new study of China intended for Chosun's reform without western generalization.

Therefore, the Bukhak School(Northern Studies)'s argument was important from the view point of promotion and welfare unlike the theory of government officials emphasizing the Saseosamgyeong(Four Books and Three Classics) or the Bukbulron(theory of northern conquest) which neglected the Manchu tribe 'Qing.' However, it is also important from the view point of the history of Korea's Chinese Studies, since it was a Chinese approach that attempt to understand 'China' in a wider range. After the destruction of Myeong of the Han dynasty, the authenticity of Chinese culture(the core is Confucian culture) was brought from Chosun society where it a source of pride and was inherited from the Chosun to non-Han people.

This fresh new way of thought intended to change society. The Chinese historian Baek Yeong-seo said, from the view point of the Chosun scholar's reality who never stepped on land China and never saw Chinese people, their scholarly position which produced the knowledge of China's reality to introduce the Qing's culture is connected with the Chinese study led by today's social scientists. At the same time, they interpreted Chinese classics in a new way and reconstructed values and a world view prioritizing the whole of society and can be called a pioneering work of integrated Chinese study. At that time, regardless of how much the Bukhak scholars were out of Confucianism order based on the discipline of neo-Confucian, their knowledge production was for a minority of people among mainstream intellectual society. However, it confronted their society with a new 'Chinese order'. It cracked the mainstream scholarship in relation to China and created an opportunity to reconstruct the Chosun society at that time.

To sum up, it can be explained that Hanhak centered on Confucianism at the end of the Chosun is period. It was still the mainstream and a kind of Cheonghak(Bukhak). Namely, a regional study in a modern expression that has emerged from the internal reformation. In addition, it is necessary to take a closer look at the previous evaluation that it can be regarded as a 'critical approach to Chinese Studies.' However, it seems to be meaningful that there was an attempt to escape from the mainstream study of Hanhak that was equal rather than as a mirror to look back upon itself at that time. It still has a limit in that it was not able to escape from the framework of Hanhak. Also, it tried to relate to China and did not widen the horizon of recognition of the international situation surrounding Korea by consciously incorporating viewpoints of Western studies on the Cheonghak(淸學). Of course, the flow of Chinese Studies in its attempt to understand China has an evaluation as a fuse after the late Chosun dynasty enlightenment movement(*Im HyeongTaek* 1999). Next, we will closely look at how the goal of the "Establishment of a modern nation-state" was set up from the later 19th century to 20th century and look how the Hanhak, Bukhak, Western understanding and Gukhak changes and took place in the process of modern studies.

3. Establishment of the Modern National state and Chinese Studies : National and Foreign Studies

Bukhak School(Silhak) which had begun to gradually reveal their subjective self-awareness from the traditional Chinese order became aware of the world by studying China at that time. The publication of Jeong Yak-yong, Park Ji-won and other Silhak groups at the time of enlightenment proves it. Especially, the inflow of Western art including Western culture was a driving force that made intellects in the enlightenment time become interested in writings by Park Ji-won and others from the late Chosun Dynasty who were influenced by western culture. However, as can be seen from the beginning of the flowering period beginning from the civilian justice army campaign and the patriotic enlightenment movement, the first modern sense of national consciousness, a new education for nurturing the people and a theology for new education were born. Here, new studies of the new education for the people's cultivation which was part of the patriotic enlightenment movement. So what of the new studies? Of course, they were based on Western studies but it was not imitating western studies intently. The theology of Enlightenment eventually accepted western studies and Silhak studies and focused on educating the people at the root of it and it naturally became a prelude to the birth of the Gukhak. National crises similar in scale to China coupled with efforts to respond to the modern world by replacing the national sovereignty with the "Korean Empire" and increasing the status of the nation. There are some cases where the terminology 'Bongukhak(本國學)' is used, although it has not been pronounced as 'Gukhak' as it is in China and some scholarly flow oriented toward Gukhak was formed. In the argument "The foundation of the nation lies in the people, and the foundation of the people is in scholarship"(*Lee Sung-hwan* 1906), we can find full intention. Shin Chae-ho(申采浩, 1880~1936) presupposes that if the old theory or idea is not destroyed, the new usage and system will not be constructed. He emphasized the corrosion of Guksu(國粹, characteristics of a country) in a radical but a clear tone. "Guksu means 'the nation's traditional religion, customs, language, history, all habits of outstanding lessons.' Thus, destruction does not mean destroying Guksu. Destroying bad habit is planting the root of Guksu.(Dam-chong, 談叢 1910) It was an attempt to establish a new study as a study of national self-confirmation while insisting on the revolutionary transition to a new study(*Im HyeongTaek* 2004).

As Arif Dirlik pointed out, East Asian "Gukhak" in the 20th century was an academic movement of the nation-state, which eventually emerged in an area that was invaded and dominated by imperialism at that time. The content of the study ultimately focused on two objects: securing the homogeneity of people, and spreading the knowledge of the world. If the latter was to translate modern western knowledge and to teach through modern inter disciplines, the former was to rearrange and educate tradition by realistic demands and scientific methods. Here, the former was to reorganize traditional disciplines under the name of 'Gukhak.' In this way, in Korea's time of enlightenment, 'Gukhak' is established through the relationship between Western studies, Hanhak and Silhak. However, this "Gukhak " movement became colonized by Japan in 1910 and it was frustrated before its bloom. In addition, traditional Confucian scholars that inherited Hanhak had survived in each area. However, though their scholarship succeeded under colonialism the establishment of modern scholarship by Western scholarship and national scholarship could not be accomplished. In other words, national (ethnic) consciousness toward independence had sprouted from Korea's independence movement in 1919, but it mainly developed in fields such as literature (creation). In the academic field, it was essential to establish modern scholarship but it was difficult to establish an independent study through this because it could not establish education and research institutes such as universities. Therefore, old school texts were abandoned and the texts of new studies were absent during this period of panic.

Chinese Studies in Korea could not become a modern studies under such circumstances. Then, how was the transition from traditional Hanhak or Silhak to modern Chinese Studies? As mentioned earlier, the study of the Silhak scholarship played a role in promoting the change of Chosun studies through the understanding of China as it was reexamined during the enlightenment. However, traditional Hanhak was still accepted as culture for Koreans so the awareness did not change that much. A recollection reflects such perception well through the fact that a Korean student who first applied to Keijo Imperial University Department of Literature did not consider Chinese literature as a foreign literature. However, there is a need for further examination as to whether or not we can ignore 'Chosun Hanhak' as an outdated old scholarship.

As will be mentioned later, even when the Keijo(京城) Imperial University was established, Japan's Chinese Studies was replacing Chosun's Chinese Studies, efforts of Korean scholars were also made. They played a role of interpreting classical China, a universal civilization, which is the source of the Korean national culture, as a means of preserving its identity outside Keijo Imperial University, and spreading it widely. For example, Jeong In-bo(鄭寅普), an encyclopedic scholar of literature, not only showed the possibility of joining modern scholarship methods by a separate discipline, but also tried to criticize the Juja(朱子) scholars bound to private interest and Chineseness. He revealed the spirit of Wang Yangming(王陽明)'s philosophy to solve the task of the Chosun people recovering their national rights(*Baek Yeongseo* 2012).

In this interpretation of Hanhak, it may be posed as an important component of the studies of the Chosun Dynasty which will be later developed with the study of Silhak. However, this type of Hanhak and Silhak were spurned as unscientific scholarship. It did not changed throughout the entire colonial period but it was finally spotlighted after the liberation. Here we can find why Chinese Studies is seen from the standpoint of the Gukhak. In other words, Japan's Chinese Studies were introduced without being organized properly in a situation when it had to deploy the Gukhak movement as a National nation's study because it fell down to colony. Also, the past study that was excluded from Japan's modern interdisciplinary approach had to be organized through efforts to transform into independent studies and develop an identity of Chosun outside the institution. In other words, it had to take the characteristic of Gukhak. The fate of Hanhak and Silhak of Chosun in the colonial period might very well be decided in that circumstance. It is the reason to restore and re-evaluate the scholars who have conducted their scholarship silently in examining the history of Chinese Study in modern Korea. Since the beginning of the modern age, when it is said that foreign studies is raised from the necessity of the interpretation of the world in terms of its own and its people, the establishment of the national studies and the establishment of foreign studies are two sides of the same coin. After the enlightenment period, Chinese Studies, which lasted along with the flow of Kukhak out of the system, came to be accepted in the system of Japan's Chinese Studies and Chinese scholars, who studied these, began to appear.

4. Chinese Studies as Modern Studies

It should be noted, however, that the conditions for the establishment of modern Chinese Studies are not formed only by the modern transformation of traditional *Hanhak*, but also the necessity of understanding about China at that time. As you can see in the Cheonghak(Bukhak) in the Chosun Dynasty, it is about the formation of the opportunity to view itself in scholarly terms through Chinese understanding not just as a country influenced by China. It was done rather by intellectuals who worked abroad, especially in China or Manchuria for the independence movement of the country that was under colonial rule. They did not make academic achievements because they exchanged with Chinese intellectuals through scholarly exercise. They sought for the liberation and future of Chosun through learning of the reality in China. However, from the viewpoint of establishing Korea's Chinese Studies, their progress should be examined specifically. Next, we shall look at how Chinese Studies in the colonial period developed Chosun studies.

1) Acceptance of Japan's Chinese Studies and the Establishment of Chosun Studies

After Colonized by Japan, Chosun was not able to pursue independent modernization. Especially in the field of education and research, the establishment of universities, the center of modern interdisciplinary education was not approved. However, in 1924, Japan established Keijo Imperial University which is an imitation of Japan's imperial college established for colonial management and continental invasion. In this university, the department of Literature and the department of oriental History in relation to Chinese Studies were established. At that time, it began to transplant the Chinese Studies of Japan into the Chosun dynasty. Although Japan's Chinese Studies is not free from the criticism that it played a role in promoting the contempt of Chinese, its relevance to Japanese imperialism at the time is undeniable. This is because it plays a role of accumulating a variety of knowledge and information about China and Manchuria rather than being ideological. This means that since the end of the 19th century, as the Chinese order has collapsed in East Asia and has been transformed into an order of national civil law, and China has also been deployed as one of those countries, thus exploring various aspects of China was essential for Japan at the time. These were done by the Japan's Chinese scholars(There is a possibility of an error when it is evaluated as a whole since Chinese scholars all have different situations and their purpose was not handled here. However, in this paper it means tendency in a broad way).

Chinese researchers at the imperial college of Japan since the Meiji(明治) restoration pointed out that the traditional Hanhak is a different name for Confucianism and it is not a true academy because it is learning China's within the boundary of China. They also institutionalized Chinese Studies which analyzing and criticizing the Chinese culture from a free scholarship perspective. There are two trends in the so-called scientific Chinese Studies; one is focused on empirically studying the data of the classical language by Chinese scholars, the other is studying documents written in modern language and the products of chinese civilization created by China researchers. Chinese Studies in the fields of literature, history, and philosophy belong to the former. It is not a study of contemporary China's reality, but it is the result of the traditional analysis of Chinese traditional culture. It can be said that the former, after the tradition of "Hanhak" in Japan fell into the world of pure academism and it was a study aimed at culture and thought of classical Chinese in the past, away from the reality of Japan and the reality of China at that time. The latter or the contemporary studies were conducted mainly by graduates of foreign language schools. The major organizations were the national research institutes such as the Mancheol(滿鐵) Institute of Investigation and the East Asia Research Institute. In addition, these two groups of researchers were at odds with each other, especially the former which ignored the latter. In order to overcome these problems, they gradually realized an overall study of 'old China' and 'present China' should be done. Here, it is important to raise the interest in the reality of China to an academic level.

Since then, Japan's Chinese Studies centered on Kyoto(京都) University focused on the former and embraced European Sinology as a methodology. Nobukuni Koyasu explained the nature of this study. One is an academic discourse that responds to the position of 'imperialist Chinese management' where Japan forms a modern nation more quickly than a stagnant vigilant state and enters the group of Western imperialism countries and presents prescriptions from outside China. The other is that the Japanese researchers who are external observers of the research subject, systematically analyze using Western 'scientific methods.' The methodology of Japan's Chinese Studies of this character is literary criticism. As one European scholar said, Japanese researchers regard ancient Chinese literature as foreign literature from the standpoint of outside observers and exposes it as an unreliable "uncertain compilation" through the method of literary criticism and on the other hand said researcher tried to reconstruct(well-form) a reliable text. This was done in each department and scholarship including history, philosophy, and literature(*Nobukuni Koyasu* 2003). It was to consider the culturally familiar ancient Chinese literature as a strange foreign document and to reconstruct it using "scientific methods"(here, Western and Western literary method). This interpretation of the ancient Chinese literature in a way that mobilized various texts that have been transferred from the tradition of Chinese literature(including scholarship and historically related literature hermeneutics) tradition and compares them and "restores" the original meaning of the text in the process of reinterpreting these old documents. At times the interpretation is quite different from the original. This criticism of literature in modern Japan became the basis of Chinese Studies or oriental studies(A bibliography method is not limited only to Chinese Studies. At that time, bibliography was widely used at the point of Japanese studies and Hanhak, *Choi Jeongseop* 2016). The reason why Japanese oriental studies(Chinese Studies) was accused of later interlocking with Japanese imperialism is also based on the ideological tendency that this interpretation can produce. This was also linked to the ideology of the Great East Asia in the 1940s and the discussion of 'modern superstition.'

Chinese Studies was established through this progress and has been introduced to Chosun studies as an academic system of Keijo Imperial University. From that, Chosun's research in China was carried out in a discrete manner within modern disciplines such as literature, history, and philosophy. Also, the flow of traditional knowledge production, including Bukhak, was used as Hanhak and it gradually became identified with Confucianism. As a result, Hanhak which was excluded from modern scholarship changed its character to become a Confucian culture study and education indicator and introduced into the private sector outside the modern education system. In the colonial situation where it was difficult to develop a modern Korean national movement, or to establish foreign studies evolving by its own demands, the establishment of Gukhak and foreign studies was still conducted in private, not in an institutional aspect as mentioned before.

Therefore, it can be said that the Chinese Studies of the colonial Chosun eventually coexisted with two streams. One is the Japan's Chinese Studies centered on Keijo Imperial University mentioned above and the other one is Hanhak through interpretation and coordination of traditional Chinese Studies including Silhak, and personal study and research on the afore-mentioned real China.

The latter traditional Chinese studies, personal study, and research should take into consideration the boom of Chosun studies that began in the 1930s. Reasons for this are limited, but there was an attempt by intellectuals who had studied the uniqueness of Chosun studies in the late Chosun Dynasty under the universality of Sino-centrism. The pursuit of the original of Chosun studies, in spite of Sino-centrism, was continued and it appears that this process could enable Chinese Studies as modern Foreign Studies, compared to Kukhak, to be formed.

The Gukhak movement is eventually a relativization of the past scholarship Hanhak and its two sides of the coin. However, unlike in the early 19th century, Japanese nationalism which began from the Meiji period was developed as a process of separating from traditional Hanhak by using documentary methods, and there was a movement to excavate Japanese objects with strong religious connotations symboliozing the unity of the nation. The boom of Chosun Studies, which emerged in the 1930s, had a limit in that it could not compose the contents of the Gukhak in time.

More importantly, as the Hiroshi Miyajima pointed out, the entire Chosun studies is not an ideological movement or intellectual movement that started from the Anti-Confucianism, or Anti-Buddhism that seek to grasp Japan's original identity. In other words, if we talk about it from the standpoint of Japanese nationalism, Chosun Studies was compelled to discover unique ideas and objects from Chosun studies and give religious meaning to it. Although it needed plenty of time to discuss in order to establish Gukhak in Chosun studies where Neo-Confucianism, the foundation of Hanhak, is influential, it was impossible due to the time constraints, as mentioned earlier. In colonial Chosun, which was much later than China and Japan, the Chosun movement was strongly anti-Japanese, not only politically but also culturally. At the beginning, the movement was limited by time constraints that hindered sufficiently organizing the content of Gukhak, and at the same time, various factors were complicated by so-called nationalism, socialism and the Japanese external Chosun Studies due to the specific historical conditions.

2) Chinese Studies of Jeong In-bo and Kim Tae-jun

As we can see, one dictionary defined Gukhak as a Silhak of the Chosun, which still contains traditional study in some form. Besides, Jeong In-bo was a figure who had base of the Chinese Studies. He was the first man who advocated the Chosun studies movement in the 1930s. Jeong In-Bo tried to renovate Confucianism by eliminating the problems left by the interpretation of Zhu xi school through study of Yangming school's inwardness, truth, and sincerity. In the process, he found "uniqueness" and especially mentioned about the nation, "Even if our identity is irrelevant, when we leave this, we cannot exist together". Uniqueness is universally held by everyone. If it cannot be discovered and protected, it will lose its significance. It is expressed to Jeong In-bo as true mind－Silhak－truth－verity－spirit and others. The universal nature of the uniqueness encompasses all from the individual to all the heaven and earth, and in the "Five thousand years of the Chosun's spirit", "I am as far as I am from one race to the whole human race(all mankind)". He did not give a special explanation but he was still concentrating on the ethnic unit. As one can imagine, the reason of coming up with logic of all things and at one point and marking with a side dot in the ethnic unit identity is because of the awareness of colonial era. Enduring the colonial era and reviewing Confucianism, which constitutes medieval universalism of East Asia, created the momentum to form a national identity. Jeong In-bo's Chosun Study consists of two components : understanding Yangmingism without the harmful effects of Neo-Confucianism, and of Chosun's pursuit of its own identity independent from Sino-centrism. The religious aspect of the Japanese's national study is the modern product derived from Sonno(尊皇) ideology to strengthen the power of Japanese emperor. Jeong In-bo replaced Three Sovereigns and Five Emperors in the dimension of medieval rationalism with Dangoon in nationalism. He emphasized Sim(heart), and Eol(spirit) which needs to be reviewed to see if it can be interpreted in the religious context, which also can be notional(*Gim Jingyun* 2013).

Kim Tae-jun(金台俊) was one of the leading scholars of Chosun studies who took the lead in criticizing Jeong In-bo. Kim Tae-jun is seen as a fair figure behind the times in modern standards. Kim Tae-jun, a graduate student of Keijo Imperial University and the Department of Chinese Studies, denied traditional Hanhak and its methodology, he advocates scientific research on Chosun. Here, the question of the unity of the national science and the individuality of the modern discipline emerges which is so called Chosun studies. Just as Jeong In-bo made a claim by stating 'the spirit of Chosun', the question of the unity and fundamentality that makes it possible to capture Chosun as a single entity or a representative whole is what Korean Studies is pursuing. This ideology of the national study(one country's own studies) is basically geographical and geopolitical and in this aspect; internal contradiction and instability are inherent. On one hand, there is a tendency to control these individualizations when the totality of national study is constantly individualized into sub-disciplines and academic knowledge. On the other hand, there is a contradiction with mutual collision that hinders integration due to the independence of individual area which is a reasonable point(Ryu Junpil 2014) This is due to the above-mentioned characteristics of the concept of Chosun Studies, as well as those who stand on different positions and ideologies in relation to Chosun Studies in the 1930s and submitted opposing views. Eventually, the fact that the most central thesis of the Chosun Studies movement was the language(Korean language) movement by Choi Hyun-bae(崔鉉培), Ju Si-gyeong(周時經), and others might have reflected this aspect.

However, from the viewpoint of Chinese Studies, it is necessary to pay attention to the fact that the continuity of Chosun academic history could not be ensured by excluding the Confucianism and Chinese literature which are traditionally symbols of foreign culture in the atmosphere of Chosun scholarship. This is because Chosun Studies cannot be established by excluding the description of Confucianism and Buddhism in the past academic tradition and the one described in Chinese characters. It is attempted by Kim Tae-jun from Keijo Imperial University and the literature department to focus on the process of the formation of modern China and the cultural changes including modern Chinese literature. The way he took it is that he avoids the blindness of the unity of nationalism and the individuality of the modern discipline, which I have already explained, and applies it in the Chosun Studies(the study of modern Korean literature). Kim Tae-jun shows his attempt to extract Chinese literature in Hanhak as a tool in modern Korean literature and history(1931). In addition, it was excluded from the mainstream traditional Chinese literature, but it is restored as an important part of undergraduate literature from the standpoint of the people and describes "Chosun Novels History"(1933). The result of this scholarship is related to the fact that he came from Keijo Imperial University or the literature department. Kim Tae-jun did not deny that the background of this attempt was the guidance of Japanese scholars such as Shiono-On(鹽谷溫). He accepts the classical Chinese Studies of Imperial University, extended from Shiono-On, and expands novels, plays and poems that were difficult to deal with in the habit of familiar Chinese literature. Through this, it becomes a foreign literature as national literature which can read the flow of the national spirit of classics and can be historicized. However, there is another moment for Kim Tae-jun, which is the discovery of contemporary 'modern China' cultural movement attempting at a 'literary revolution.'

Kim Tae-jun targeted China while studying in the Department of Chinese Literature. In other words, Chinese literature became a foreign literature. As a result, this foreign literature became a foreign literature as an opportunity to reflect what is lacking in Korean literature not a foreign literature which should be imported. "The country Han, Dang, Song, Myeong that have been imported for last thousands of years in the past" are subject to the question of Chinese literature related to ancient China and the "Hanhak of Chosun". The study of Chinese literature as a foreign literature is also a reflection of the Chinese literary problem of Chosun studies which is kind of structured and still exists as a reality . In addition to structuring ancient China as a method of literary history, discovering the modern Chinese literary movement was also a process of rediscovering China and naming 'China.' At the same time, however, it was also a process of historically structuring Chosun literature, such as the history of Korean literature, the history of Chosun Novels History(Kim Tae-jun), and the history of Chosun literature(Lee Myung Sun). Kim Tae-jun considers that when a Korean scholar neglects "science", he confuses the idea of "Chinese, Chosun, Oriental literature" and "Chinese ancient literature". It was also considered that civilian Chosun scholars who had considered themselves as "Chinese Studies scholars" missed the consciousness of how to deal with the problems of modern academism, such as the relocation of modern

Chinese Studies, the Japanese oriental studies, and the academism of Japan's Chinese Studies.

Indeed, the "Hanhak" of Jeong In-bo style in Chosun studies can indeed deal with the oriental studies of imperial academism such as Naga Michiyo(那珂通世), Naito Konan(內藤湖南) and so on. Kim Tae-jun's history consciousness of literature is the logic of organizing Chosun literature, but it also exposed the problem of the modernity of a Korean culture that considers the reality logic of Han(漢) culture in Chosun studies through the discovery of 'China.' However, the consciousness of this problem is not disputed but it is stitched, which is because the problem of Chinese Studies is limited to the problem of 'Chinese characteristic' as writing characters(Cheon Jin 2010).

From the viewpoint of Chinese Studies, it can be interpreted that Chinese Studies as foreign studies that self-internalize throughout differentiating China and the research of China was set ideologically for Kim Tae-jun. Of course, there was no research results related to Chinese Studies and most of them are an attempted in separate disciplines labelled under(Korean) "literature". In addition, it is interesting that Kim Tae-jun's main activity in the last decade of his life was at the Myeong-ryun(明倫) Academy. It is ironic that he who severely criticized Jeong In-bo as a Confucian organization worked where the Confucian group were gathering. Of course, it might have been a type of organizational activity as a revolutionary but as a scholar studying Chinese Studies, he collected ancient literature travelling around the country. This record reflecting the 10 years states that the Confucian group was still recognized as powerful in Korean society has implications in understanding Chinese Studies in Korea. This creates the need to examine the changes of traditional Korean Studies in Korean society since the modern period more in depth.

It is significant that the Korean research boom of the 1930s (Also, known as Chosun Studies) was raised as one of the general catalysts of the formation of Korean Studies in East Asia, and that Chosun Studies or modern scholarship began to be formed at the point where it crossed from the inside to the outside of Chosun studies. The point was that the former Empire of China and the present Empire of Japan were opposed to Chosun studies in a relativized relationship with a single nation. In this context, the Chosun study movement is closely related to the birth of Korea's Chinese Studies as foreign studies. That they excluded the rest of traditional Hanhak by putting Jeong Yak-yong's Silhak in focus when the scholars of nationalism based on Hanhak insisted on Chosun Studies, and the nature of Gukhak in China and Japan socialist scholars referred to when they reconstructed the past by express scientific research as described above, were revealed most prominently during the transition to the Chosun(漢) literature history from Chinese literature studies by Kim Tae-jun.

However, as Kim Tae-jun's case shows, consciousness to target China during the colonial period appeared but it did not appear as a specific study. The emphasis on ethnicity in Chosun Studies in the colonial period ultimately restrains the study of various aspects of contemporary China in the study of

China. Therefore, it can be said that Chinese Studies as foreign scholarship during the Japanese colonial period did not achieve great results in academic history. However, the introduction and research on the real China has emerged as an exercise form due to the times, and this constituted a part of the colonial Chinese Studies. Examples can be found in the remarks of Kim Tae-jun who was interested in China during its invasion from Japan. In his biography, he reveals an interest in the socialist revolution, in spite of the fact that he wrote the academic history within the Japanese system. In terms of literary history, translated works by modern Chinese writers such as Lu Xun were introduced in newspapers and magazines. Also, major writings of Chinese theoreticians were introduced at the time. Of course, research and articles on modern China imported through Japan cannot be ignored. It is well known that the role of Takeshi Karashima(辛島驍) in Japan is noticed even when confined to the Lu Xun(魯迅) research in Korea. In order to see the whole Chinese Studies of the colonial period in Korea, it is important to review the pathways of various discourse and research.

5. From National Studies to Regional Studies

Although Chinese Studies in Korea is destined to begin with the establishment of modern scholarship, Chinese Studies also had to be non-subjective because the pursuit of 'modernity' itself was carried out by Japan under colonial rule. This means that the question of what China is was blocked. At that time, there were only two choices for scholars of the Chosun Studies. One was accepting the modern interdisciplinary established by Japan and carrying out colonial modernization by Japan, and the other was promoting the modernization of tradition-based scholarship while advocating nationalism. Chinese researchers were also not free from these options. Therefore, to the intellectuals of Chosun studies in the colonial period, China was accepted as the Chinese statue created by Japan, the Chinese statue pursued from the viewpoint of the national independence movement and the Chinese statue in the viewpoint of the traditional Hanhak.

In the view of the academic history, Hanhak which was interpreted and re-interpreted through traditional Chinese books in the traditional way still existed. Also, the attempt to interpret the Han Chinese in a scientific way through Western sinology formed a new flow by separate discipline in the modern school system. In this way, the methodology for interpreting Chinese Studies which developed together in civilian and institutional dimensions translating Chinese written books both in traditional and western ways. Also, the fact that should not be overlooked is that interest and research on the reality of China in a dimension of national movement for independence or personal exchange between China and the Chosun intellectual dimension, was on a similar level. One kind of a regional studies include print material such newspapers, magazines and reports, speeches has to be dealt as a Chinese Studies materials. On the other hand, there were other regional viewpoints studies related to China. The Keijo Imperial University and the department of Regional studies and the Chosun and Manchuria-related researches all had strong geographical characteristics. This is evident in the purpose of the establishment of the imperial college of Korea.

This arrangement makes Kim Tae-jun's position meaningful. He majored in law at Keijo Imperial University, majored Chinese Studies, and at the same time, he was a Chosun studies researcher. Moreover he was a socialist revolutionist. This background is an important tie for reviewing Korea's Chinese Studies especially in the colonial period. As mentioned earlier, this paper focused on the history of colonial Chinese Studies in comparison with traditional Chinese Studies or national studies focusing on how during this era of writing was ultimately created in a time when China could not be related . The forms of Chinese Studies facing the colonial period described above could not have existed independently of each other. This can be seen from the Kim Tae-jun case. In addition to the interdisciplinary of Keijo Imperial University, further research on the lecture and research is needed and it is urgently required to collect and arrange data on private Korean scholars and Chinese activists.

Dual Position of Cross-Border Travelers in Cultural Contact Zones Viewed from "Journal of a Voyage Along the Coast of China"

Bogo Lee

1. Introduction

—About Modern Travelogue as "Fair and Impartial Record"

The Chinese Repository(1832~1851), the first English journal published in the China continent, contains various types of articles including the vivid records by the protestant missionaries who travelled the Southeast Asia and the coastal regions of China in the earliest years. They contributed to the journal their essays and travelogues about the objective data, natural environment and people's lifestyle and culture of the regions they travelled as well as other articles including introductions to local religions, bibliography and translations of local writings. The journal gradually became a repository of the knowledge about the regions.

The present article analyzes their early writings, especially the essays having the features of travelogue, to reconstruct the fragments of recognition of China and Southeast Asia in the eyes of the protestant missionaries in the early 19th century. This article focuses on the forms and details of travelogue for describing and delineating travels because the travels recorded in the travelogues had a very special meaning to the modern Westerners. To the Westerners, a travel to the East Asia was not a passive act simply for individual's preference of leisure activities, but a type of practice for the cultural subjects of the Western culture to demonstrate their increase of the recognitional contact with and the knowledge of others through the direct interaction with the East Asian culture and daily life.

Mary Louise Pratt, who critically analyzed the significance of travelogues, pointed out that the conventional studies on travelogues 'overviewed in an admiring way the fearless exploitation of remote areas and the devotion to science', and that 'the scholars utilized the travel reports simply for attaining the information about the era, places and people they handled.' Mary Louise Pratt also stated from a literature point of view that the travelogues, under the influence of modernism, have been 'developed in the estheticism-based trend of studying literature in the manner of handling people who are well-known in literature in consideration of the intelligent or artistic levels or the European existential levels.' In fact, the travelogue of the time was not only a cultural capital of individuals recording the exploration of unfamiliar world by fragmentary and individualized people but also a medium to develop rhetoric in a way to increase of the authority of the knowledge that the travelers had about the regions.

This paper reviews the travelogue-type essays about Southeast Asia and China written by the missionaries and published in the early issues of The Chinese Repository, analyzes the custom of reproduction found in the genre of travelogue of the time, and identifies the rhetorical features in the inside. By investigating the characteristics of the viewpoints of the cross-border travelers included in the essays, this paper captures in a refreshing way the significance of the internal conflict and the conversational manners that the travelers had, in contrast to the evaluation of the travelers as the frontiers of the Empires in previous studies. With regard to the analysis of the genre, rather than simply defining the features of the travelogue as the condensate of the imperial viewpoints, this paper highlights the cross-over of viewpoints toward the world from their standing in a civilization or a country or from the existential standing of individuals. For this purpose, the view of travelogue that the writers of the texts had at that time was investigated.

> All the situations described in the book "A Voyage along the Coast of China to Mantchou Tartary by Gützlaff" may be different from what some people like or have liked or may have not be written in harmony with the taste of the critics. However, according to my humble opinion, a travelogue should be a very fair, abundant and impartial record of what happened and what was viewed through the writer's observation.

About writings in the form of travelogue, the author of the miscellany above took the examples of the travelogue written by Gützlaff, published in the early issues of The Chinese Repository, and specified that "a travelogue should be a very fair, abundant and impartial record of what happened and what was viewed through the writer's observation". The author argued that the essence of the travelogue narration is the accurate description of objective observations rather than subjective feelings, even though it may not be in harmony with the literal standards or norms of the critics.

However, the meaning of the "fair and impartial records" sought by the authors is confusing, if their view about travelogue is compared with the religious zeal revealed in the various articles published in The Chinese Repository. Despite the cool-headed and detailed observations included in their writings, the life and religions of the Chinese and Southeast Asian people were in the dark realm that should be brightened by their preaching and enlightening from their point of view. However, what requires more careful attention in reading their writings is their existence of the Christian organizations, churches and themselves that had to be continuously crossing over different categories, including the East India Company and the modern nation-states, in the marginal areas, rather than their sense of superiority about their own civilization and their religious zeal. Also noticed is the authors' internal division that they were conscious of the various classes of the readers and that they wanted to claim their own authority over the regions they travelled. This kind of discreet reading will allow to reconstruct the internal context more richly in comparison with the conventional context configured by using the travelogues.

For this purpose, we will pay keen interest to the procedures of cultural contact as a conceptual premise as well as the mutual changes occurring at the cultural contact surface. In the spaces and practices where two different cultures are in contact with each other, there exists not only a unidirectional propagation of culture but also the convergence of multiple cultures along the contact surface. Moreover, self-reflection of one's own identity, adjustment to the knowledge about objects and internalization of knowledge also occur. Therefore, the scope of recognition is far more extended through what happens on the cultural contact surface. The mutual contact between cultures manifested in details by various types of rhetoric included in specific articles is basically created in the process of organizing the recognition of others' culture into knowledge. This process may not be defined simply by the uniform imperial perspectives or by the fragmentary prejudice of individuals. Rather, the dynamics of the numerous people, material and intellectual networks, the collision and adjustment of the old and new knowledge, the change of the attitude toward the others' culture, and the tension between the belief and rationality may extend the layers of the text, allowing for more meaningful interpretation of the text.

2. Main Text

: Review of "Journal of a Voyage Along the Coast of China"

1) Journey for Knowledge and its Record

: The frontiers of *The Chinese Repository*

The main text of this paper analyzes the travelogues written by the early protestant missionary in 1832 and 1833, the early period of the publication of The Chinese Repository, to investigate the formation process of the knowledge related to the East Asian cultures included in thieve viewpoints revealed in the writings. In addition, the various patterns of cultural contact included in the writings were identified with the transculturality. The writers and editors of The Chinese Repository were very limited in the early years after the publication of the first issue. A small number of publication staff, including Morison, who was the first protestant missionary who entered into Southeast Asia and China, Bridgman and Gützlaff, played the roles of both writers and editors. What were their purposes for publishing the journal and writing articles for their own journal? Take a look at the preface written by Bridgman and published in the first issue of volume 1 of The Chinese Repository in May 1832.

> One of the objects of this work, then, will be to review foreign books on China, with a view to notice the changes that have occurred, and how and when they were

> bought about, and to distinguish, as far as it can well be done, between what is and what is not now true. Many of the old books while they contain much that is valuable, contain also so much that is worthless as to prevent their republication. Modern writers, too, have not always been clear and satisfactory in the statements. The accounts of the population, for example are found to vary from twenty million up to the 'mystical number' of 333 million.

Mentioning the objects of publishing the journal, the first editor of The Chinese Repository announced that they would "notice the changes that have occurred, and how and when they were bought about". This is a roundabout expression of the attitude that the protestant missionaries of the time had toward the conventional knowledge that the Western world had about China. The Jesuit missionaries, who had entered into and worked in China prior to the protestant missionaries, had an adaptationism-based attitude to the Chinese culture and already accumulated a considerable amount of understanding and knowledge from the late 16th century. In fact, it was a necessary for the Christian missionaries, before being dispatched to Southeast Asia or China, to learn about the relevant local knowledge left by the Jesuit missionaries and to study the local languages. Therefore, the Jesuit had an absolute status with regard to the authority in the knowledge about China.

In the preface of the journal for the publication, Bridgman announced that he would "review foreign books on China to distinguish, as far as it can well be done, between what is and what is not now true". The announcement may be understood as taking a very challenging attitude toward the authority of the knowledge that the Jesuit had accumulated about China and as expressing in a roundabout manner their goal to surpass the previous generations with the knowledge about China that they themselves would accumulate in the future. The announcement also shows that one of the motivations of operating the publication business is the complaint and critical mind that they had about the knowledge about Southeast Asia and China shared and consumed in Europe at that time.

The editor revealed the importance of the knowledge about China, and manifested their ambition to correct and review the incorrect or newly obtained local knowledge by themselves and to organize a new knowledge system related to the region. Mentioning "natural history", "commerce", "social relations", "moral characters", "religious characters" and others as the specific categories of the knowledge system, they stated, "We do not expect to find data of such value and authority as shall enable the wise men of the age to correct the chronology or improve the morality of Holy Writing" but "The numerous discrepancies and contradictions that stand recorded, on many a page of foreign books, will prove a strong incentive to consult, and to ascertain, as distinctly as possible, the competency and credibility of the most approved native authorities". He also stated, "We feel and shall take a very lively interest in the religions character of the people", expressing his strong will to preach the religion. Understanding these comments in relation to their self-allocated roles and self-regulation, the comments are consistent with their fundamental critical mind that the wrong parts of the information and knowledge about China and Southeast Asia, prepared in the previous generations, would be corrected by their positive actions, and the corrected knowledge would grant to them a new intelligent authority.

Interpreting their comments from the perspective of the lack and supply of more universal knowledge, the comments teach that the editors had considerable interests and concerns about the lack of knowledge inside the Chinese society, apart from the China-related knowledge circulated in Europe as well as its system. The lack of knowledge of their concern may be summarized into two things: one is the absence of religious enlightenment, which is the idol worship without the faith in the only true God, and the other is the ignorance in the modern knowledge in medicine and science. In the preface in the first issue of volume 1 of The Chinese Repository, Bridgman pointed out that "There is a most lamentable lack of knowledge among the millions inhabiting eastern Asian: yet, we do anticipate the day when all that which is most valuable to man, and now so richly enjoyed by the nations of the West, elevating and yet still more to elevate them, shall be equally enjoyed, and produce the same results, among the nations of the East", clearly revealing that the core of their critical mind was on the propagation of knowledge to the East Asian societies.

> We enter on our work unbiased, and influenced rather by considerations of duty than of reward. Every man has his purposes, the accomplishment of which is the

> highest object of his heart's desire. To spend and be spent in publishing "glad tidings" to those who had never heard the "joyful sound", and to bear the lamp of life to those who were perishing for lack of vision, a greater than the wisest of the sons of men, took an earthly tabernacle; and now, having ascended up on high, He commands man to go and teach his fellow to publish the gospel to every creature.

The quotation above shows that the propagation of knowledge of their concern was not subject simply to the modern knowledge but based on the concept of religious sacrifice for the preaching of gospel, which was mentioned as the "joyful sound". Therefore, it is hard to say that they completely lacked the basis of the recognition of reciprocity or equity. Overviewing the macroscopic viewpoints found in the previous studies about their identity, the mainstream is that the expansion of the imperialism in the 19th century was in an implicit relation of conspiracy with their "great century of mission". Considering the reciprocal attitude, represented by the statement that they wanted to "the nations of the East" to equally enjoy the 'richness' of the "nations of the West," it is an oversimplification of their internal motive to define them simply as the frontiers of the imperialism.

From this perspective, more positive interpretation is required with regard to their status around the modern knowledge, and their dual status as mediators should be reviewed. The analysis of their specific status of the time in terms of the production and circulation of knowledge shows that they had dual positions : they were producers of knowledge to correct and produce the knowledge about Southeast Asia and China that was being consumed in Europe, and they were also the suppliers of knowledge, providing modern knowledge and religious enlightenment to the region. However, it should never be neglected that, except their religions calling, they were under very poor conditions even in Europe. For example, Morison had gone through continuous conflict with the East India Company while travelling to the region. Bridgman stated in the preface, “We are desirous of receiving assistance in every way convenient; and, while we shall not shrink from, nor disregard, the criticisms of friends or strangers, we desire heartily, and will be grateful for any light that may be thrown on our path”. This statement seems to reflect their economically needy conditions as well as the situation where they were considerably shrinking or being criticized even in the European society, rather than having a high position. They had to be locally self-sufficient because they were checked by the East India Company in the process of getting on a merchant vessel or they lost economic aid. Therefore, the journal was a very important means of not only accomplishing their own calling but also surviving in the region. Hence, they were actually very sensitive to the situation where the journal was distributed in Europe and any other regions.

From the viewpoints of speech and rhetoric, many of the articles published in The Chinese Repository frequently mentioned the readers in Europe and America. Referring to those readers may have reflected their hope for the churches and missionary groups in Europe and America to pay more attention to the situations in Southeast Asia and China and to provide more assistances to them. The rhetorical exaggeration they employed to point out their accomplishments in the region and the backwardness of the region through God's parables might have been strengthened by their status as mediators. Their realistic and direct motivations of writing the articles and editing the journal might have been made in the middle of the tension and fluctuation of the intellectual authority that was formed in the process of propagating the knowledge about China and Southeast Asia to Europe and America with the cultural contact zones as the media and delivering the religious values and modern knowledge of the West to the region. The project of publishing The Chinese Repository as a complicated act of accumulating knowledge and mediating different regions was the first step of the long journey to discover "Asia" as a gigantic object, and the various articles published in the journal themselves have the significance of "travelogue" as the records of their travel to Asia.

2) Junk Ship Loaded with Tracts
: Three Times of Gützlaff's Travel Along East Coast of China

Gützlaff, a German missionary who worked in Southeast Asia and China, set out the exploration and missionary journey along the coast of China three times between 1831 and 1833. Meanwhile, he published an article with the long title, Gützlaff, Charles. "Journal of a voyage along the coast of China from the province of Canton to Leaoutung in Manchou Tartary; 1832~1833" in 2-1 of *The Chinese Repository* in May 1833. Chapter 2.2 of the present article follows up the itinerary of Gützlaff by analyzing the text of his article.

Gützlaff, born in Prytz, Prussia, studied in Halle and Berlin, and did missionary activities mainly in Southeast Asia with Robert Morison(1782~1834) and Jacob Tomlin(1793~1880). He was firstly dispatched to Java by the Netherland Missionary Society in 1826, and is known to the first protestant missionary who landed on Korea. He actively engaged in the missionary activities, since he had vivacious personality, was fluent in Chinese language, and even had some knowledge about Korean language. As mentioned above, Gützlaff travelled three times along the east coast of China like an exploration. The early part of the article introduces the three times of travel.

He embarked for the first, on board a junk at Bankok, June 3d, 1831, reached Mantchou(滿洲) Tartary in November and returned to Macao, Dec. 13th. On the second, he embarked Feb. 26th, visited several places in the provinces of Fuhkeën(福建) and Chekeäng(浙江) on his way up to Shantung(山東), and from thence he passed to Corea, and returning by the Lewchew archipelago, reached Macao, Sept. 4th, 1832. For the third, he embarked on the 20th of last Oct. and returned on the 29th ult. This last voyage, in regard to direct intercourse with the people and opportunity for observation, far exceeded either of the preceding; and the journal, though brief, affords abundant evidence that to the people of China, the "foreign barbarians(洋夷)" are no unwelcome visitors.

According to this record, Gützlaff carried out exploration of the coast of China three times, during which he explored the entire East Asia from Bangkok to

Macao, Shandong, Fujian, Zhejiang, the three Northeast provinces, Joseon(Korea), and Ryukyu areas. As a result of the three times of travel, he obtained the conclusion that the Chinese people did not oppose them, the protestant missionaries, hoping that a friendly relationship may be formed between the two. He particularly mentioned that the accomplishment of the third travel would bring about a very positive outcome in performing their missionary activities in China. The junk vessels of the time, called "Baitouchuan(白頭船)" in Chinese, were often used for the commercial activities of the countries with abundant production, such as Siam, to transport the products to the north and the south. The junk vessels of Chinese merchants departed each year from Hainan, Guandong, Amoy(Xiamen), Ningbo, Shanghai and other places and arrived in Southeast Asia in February, March and early April, and then moved back with the consumables for Chinese people and a considerable amount of gold. Gützlaff often used these junk vessels to transport and deliver Christian tracts and Bibles during his exploration. Like most of the missionaries in similar circumstances, the voyage by Gützlaff was basically a struggle with tough obstacles of the natural environment, rather than a comfortable tour. The adversity that their third journey on the fast-sailing vessel Sylph faced was none other than the climate and natural environment of the region.

After much consultation with others, and a conflict in my own mind, I embarked in the Sylph Capt. W., commander, and A. R., esquire, supercargo, Oct. 20th, 1832. The Sylph was a fast-sailing cargo, well manned and armed. She had to beat up against a strong northeast monsoon, and to encounter very boisterous weather before reaching her destination Teëntsin(天津) and Mantshou Tartary. From the moment we left Macao roads, we had to contest our whole course against wind and current. Furious gales, accompanied with rain and a tremendous sea, drove us several days along the coast, threatening destruction to our barque. But God who dwelleth on high did not forsake us; and though often engulphed in the deep, his almighty hand upheld our sinking vessel. Only one Lascar was swept away.

As described above, Gützlaff's "Journal of a Voyage Along the Coast of China" routinely and plainly described even the death of Lascar who was a sailor accompanied in the long journey. The extreme situations encountered on the voyage were often described as those that further strengthen their religious belief. In fact, the unfamiliar environmental conditions of East Asia were tremendous elements of adversity to the missionaries who sailed from Europe and Africa to East Asia. Considering the descriptions about their health conditions and the actual frequent premature deaths of young missionaries, their adaptation to the local environment must have involved difficulties far beyond the currently imaginable natural disasters. They continuously fought a hard fight with unexpected hardships with regard to the soil, food, climate and immune system, which might have further strengthened their religious belief. The Sylph used in the third journey, despite being an armed fast-sailing vessel, had to lose a sailor under the perilous marine conditions, and the sailors on board once rescued a junk vessel in the coast of China.

In addition to the struggle with the natural environment, Gützlaff's travel to the north along the east coast of China enabled him to contact more Chinese people. His travelogue starts to describe in more details his activities that could sprout the cultural exchange with the local people. The description of the scene where books were distributed to the people on small boats encountered in Namoh/Nan-aou(南奥), Fujian, points out that their purposes of the travels included not only the exploration of the natural and geographical environment of the region but also the investigation of the cultural level of the regions and the estimation of future missionary works. "Tendering a book to an intelligent looking man, he was at first surprised at the strange gift, but then turning to his countrymen he read it aloud. Their attention was instantly drawn toward him; other requests were made, and within a few minutes, the ship was surrounded by clamorous applicants. The captain was beckoning them away, and loosened the painters, but they clung to our tackle and declared, "we must have these good books, and will not move without them". Such determination had the desired effect; I gave them freely what they so earnestly craved, and they went away exulting." This description shows how the tracts, the pamphlets containing the Christian doctrines, were gradually started to be distributed in the cultural exchange with the local people. In this process, Gützlaff learned about their cultural potential and confirmed that they had an appropriate cultural level for conducting missionary works there.

However, a more in-depth analysis may be required about Gützlaff's mental state in describing the scene. The response of the local people excited him psychologically when he was delivering so-called "Word", which is the essence and basis of his mission under the tough natural conditions. The preaching work conducted to the local people made him comparable to Jesus who did the same work about eighteen hundred years ago, motivating him to tolerate the external afflictions that he had to face. On the other hand, he might have been highly aware of the readers in writing the description. The description may be an exaggeration or a narrative strategy to appeal to the readers with his conviction that the region he encountered had a great potential for missionary works and that there was an extensive area for mission. Most of the reader of The Chinese Repository were the members of the Christian mission groups in Europe, and they were potential sponsors to Gützlaff who could assist missionary works psychologically or materially. As another example, the subjective decisions about the success of their mission, including the decision that the mission would not be feasible in Siam, were considerably objectified through their actual experiences, but Gützlaff, as the author of the travelogue, could have no choice but to be aware of the readers. While reading his text, we need to keep it in our mind that a considerable mental exaggeration could be necessarily added to the description in order to draw the readers' emotional or material supports, as he shared his hardships with the members of the missionary groups in Europe and America. Consider the situation when Gützlaff traveled toward the north to arrive in Kae-chow(Gaizhou, 蓋州) and Tung-tsze-kow near the Bohai Bay.

Dec. 3d, our ship was coated inside as well as outside with solid ice. After several hours of labor, we succeeded in getting up the anchor, and took a speedy farewell of these dismal regions. At our re-entering Tung-tsze-kow bay, we saw a great number of junks at anchor. We were hailed by the kind natives, who procured for us provisions and fuel, which the mandarins had promised, but had never furnished. The absence of their rulers rendered them more friendly; they did everything in their power to oblige, and showed themselves worthy of our trust. —There is here a great field for Christian enterprise. The inhabitants show much sound understanding, and are free from that degrading superstition which reigns in southern Asia. Though every grove and high place was full of idols and images, and every eminence adorned with a temple, the people were not utterly enslaved by superstition. In their habits and behavior, they appeared very much like our peasantry: some of their farms were in excellent order, and plenty reigns everywhere. —Kae-chow city, which we visited, is situated about 10 miles in the interior, surrounded by a high wall, and thickly inhabited; it is a place of extensive trade, but the houses are low and ill-built, The Chinese colonists, which are by far the most numerous part of the population, are very industrious; whilst the Tartars live at their ease, and enjoy the emoluments of the government. I consider Mantchou Tartary as a very hopeful field for missionary enterprise, and humbly hope that it will soon attract the notice of some society.

To them, the meeting with the new world was the way of struggling each day, and what they met was on the surface the natural environment and the exclusive culture of the region. However, the places of struggle were sometimes turned into fields of reconciliation, and the differences in language and culture could be instantly overcome through trust. They were able to overcome risks in the extremely difficult natural environmental conditions with the help of the natives, because the natives, although being a different people, also had the fellow feelings and mutual trust that always exist between a person and another. In the northeast coast of China, Gützlaff had opportunities to contact the local people more freely, and the experiences he obtained there allowed him to compare the characteristics of the northeast coastal areas of China with that of the Southeast Asians. He learned that the local residents of these areas were more industrious and richer in understanding and had no multi-religious custom, judging that the areas had better conditions for the future Christian enterprise. Based on his observation that the Han people who migrated to the northeast areas were more industrious than the Manchu people and their farmhouses were better arranged, he thought that the characteristics of the areas were similar to those of the typical rural areas of Europe. Although their missionary activities were prohibited by the strict decree given by Beijing, Gützlaff experienced through the journey a lot of exchange and communication with many local people and earned a very positive prospect about the missionary works in the coastal areas of China. An analysis of Gützlaff's viewpoint shows that he invented himself within the boundary of the imagination of romanticized Europe and the religious features and then projected his invented identity to the narrative of the coast and inland areas of China. This was a typical manner of rhetoric employed by the missionaries.

In the second journey, prior to their third journey, Gützlaff arrived in the Shantung Peninsula and then went to Corea, Lewchew and Macao. They were also aware that their visits to the surroundings of China, Corea and Lewchew, could irritate the Chinese government. He assumed that such an attitude that China has toward those regions could have a justifiable reason. This shows that he already understood the international regime in the East Asia based on tribute, and they never underestimated the significance of tension that their cross-border journey could bring to the regime. The article "Miscellanies" in 1-5 of *The Chinese Repository states*, "Mr. Gützlaff found opportunity to distribute Christian books of various kinds wherever the vessel touched; in this way he was enabled to furnish the people with specifics, for their mental and spiritual, as well as for their bodily diseases" and "the books distributed in provinces of China, in Corea and among the inhabitants of Lewchew islands 'shall prosper.'" Then, the article asked back as follows.

And now, shall this enterprise be abandoned? When the breezes have borne the ships, richly laden, into the ports of the "celestial empire", shall the peaceful inhabitants, who, wishing for an interchange of commodities, eagerly throng their decks, be driven away by "barbarian cruelty?" We heartily wish that the subject of "free intercourse with China", might be put in its proper light, and urged by arguments worthy of the cause. We ask again, shall this enterprise be abandoned? (……) We would request our readers — those in particular who are still disposed to doubt the utility of such an enterprise to read attentively the following communications, which we received from a correspondent.

To the Christian missionaries dispatched to Southeast Asia and China in the early 19th century, the "barbarian cruelty" of China and Southeast Asia could be reduced to the multi-religious views and the absence of modern knowledge, which were considered by them as things that should be continuously eliminated through the contact with the local people. Logically, however, there must have existed an argument in the Christian societies in Europe and America that such a missionary enterprise was useless and thus economic support to the enterprise was unnecessary. The text above indicates that the editors of The Chinese Repository, including Gützlaff, were considerably aware of the groups of people who held a negative view about the enterprises carried by the editors. To them, the travelogue by Gützlaff was a very significant text as the elementary and cross-sectional evidence that the goal of "free intercourse with China" was sufficiently worth realizing and it would ultimately evangelize the region.

3) For Conversation with Other Civilizations

The travelogue by Gützlaff includes vivid records of the contact with the local people at that time. Many of the records are devoted to the description of religions, especially Buddhism, Buddhist temples and Buddhist monks.

When the conventional protestant mission was not very successful in the Buddhist countries, such as Siam, his interest in the status of Buddhism in China was so natural and necessary. He tried to build relationships with the native people mainly by distributing the tracts he prepared. He considered that the natives of China were more industrious than the Southeast Asians and had the ability to read. Also, he thought that the situation of idolatry was much better in China than in the Southeast Asia. Therefore, he often described in details his experience of visiting Buddhist temples after arriving in local areas of China.

> (1833) January 14th, we changed our station, and came to anchor under an island. The curiosity to see the ship was greater here than at our former place. (……) The priests had for a long time been desirous to get hold of a few Christian book, but when they could not obtain them, they almost wept for disappointments; —I had previously landed on the opposite shore, where I was surrounded by multitudes who did not cease importuning me till they had gotten every book out of my hands. There were very few individuals who could not read, so they we may entertain the well-founded hope, that even the smallest tracts will be perused to advantage. We enjoyed the society of the natives very much. Combining intelligence and cordiality, they lost no opportunity of showing their friendship, or of making pointed inquiries. What a filed for missionary exertion do they present! Their hearts are open to the impression of truth, and their doors for the reception of its messengers. We humbly trust in the wise government of God,

> (which can defeat all the restrictive laws of the most crooked policy), that the doors to these parts will be soon thrown open.
>
> When I first went on shore, the people seemed distrustful of receiving the word of salvation; some of them hinted that our books merely contained the doctrines of western barbarians, which were quite at variance with the tenets of the Chinese sages. I did not undertake to contest this point with them, but proceeded to administer relief to a poor man who was almost blind. He was affected with this unexpected kindness, and turning towards me said; "Judging from your actions, your doctrines must be excellent; therefor I beseech you, give me some of your books; though I myself cannot read, I have children who can read." — From this moment, the demand for the word of God increased, so that I could never pass a hamlet without being importuned by the people to impart to them the knowledge of divine things. In the wide excursions which I took, I daily witnessed the demand for the word of God. The greatest favor we could bestow upon the natives, was to give them a book, which as a precious relic was treasured up and kept for the perusal of all their acquaintance and friends.
>
> Having remained here seven days, we then departed for other parts of the Chusan(舟山) group. The weather during this time was generally dark and stormy. Feb. 4th, we arrived at the island Pooto(普陀). Lat. 30° 3' N., and long 121° E.

The landing by Gützlaff on Hangzhou was described with many conversations along with the psychological change of the local people in order to highlight the drastic changes. The local residents who firstly considered the 'word of salvation' as the doctrines of western barbarians were gradually changed as they were moved by his favor and the increase of understanding, even to the point of asking questions in a prospective attitude. This assured Gützlaff that genuine mission could be accomplished only by a reciprocal manner. His description of the local people puts a great emphasis on the fact that they started to have a craving for the books containing God's words during the one week he stayed in the area, revealing his hopeful prospect that the future missionary works would be very successful.

Then, what was the most important method of mission to Gützlaff? Judging from his writings, he was able to build an intimate fellowship with the local people rapidly because he effectively used conversation as a form of communication. Gützlaff had excellent linguistic capabilities, which enabled him to understand and speak Chinese including the local dialects. Based on his language skills, he had conversational manners to talk with the listeners seriously. Through the conversation, he might have been able to relax the tension with the local people and let their guard down. He even had a conversation with a high priest of a Buddhist temple, which allowed him to acquire an opportunity to distribute more tracts. "The high priest requested an interview. He was an old deaf man, who seemed to have very little authority, and his remarks were common-place enough. Though the people seemed to be greatly embarrassed at our unexpected appearance, their apprehensions gradually subsided; meanwhile we had the pleasure of seeing our ship coming to anchor in the roads.

Having therefore renewed my stock of books with a larger store, I went again on shore. At this time, the demand was much greater, and I was almost overwhelmed by the numbers of priests who ran down upon us. Earnestly begging at least a short tract, of which I was very soon stripped of all, and had to refuse numerous applications." In this way, he described how much his evangelizing works were welcomed in the local areas. In fact, when the blue-eyed people of the West spoke the Chinese language, the Chinese people must have been intrigued. The conversation in the local language could have quickly lifted their guard against foreigners.

The composite significance of Gützlaff's narrative strategy should be found from his vivid description of the situation of distributing the tracts. He provided a lively snapshot description with a positive view toward the local missionary works. This may have been because of his need to collect more sponsors from his readers, including those who were criticizing his missionary strategy inside the Western Christian society. Among their methods of missionary works, the preparation and distribution of tracks symbolically manifest the thoughts and efforts they had given in order to make the conversation between the two cultures permanent and to let the local people accept their values. Simply put, the missionary works described in Gützlaff's travelogue was a sketch of the efforts made by his missionary group to carry out their callings in the transcultural boundary between the West and the East Asia, the cultural contact zone, showing how earnestly they were exerting themselves to converse with the local people.

At a distance, the island appeared barren and scarcely habitable, but as we approached it, we observed very prominent buildings, and large glittering domes. A temple built on a projecting rock, beneath which the foaming sea dashed, gave us some idea of the genius of hit inhabitants, in thus selecting the most attractive spot to celebrate the orgies of idolatry. We were quite engaged in viewing a large building situated in a grove, when we observed some priests of Budha walking along the shore, attracted by the novel sight of a ship. Scarcely had we landed, when another party of priests in common garbs and very filthy, hastened down to us, chanting hymns. When some books were offered them, they exclaimed, "praised be to Budha", and eagerly took every volume which I had. We then ascended to a large temple surrounded by trees and bamboo. An elegant portal and magnificent gate brought us into a large court, which was surrounded with a long row of buildings — not unlike barracks, — but the dwellings of the priests. On entering it, the huge images of Budha and his disciples, the representations of Kwanyin, the Goddess of Mercy, and other deformed idols, with the spacious and well adorned halls, exhibit an imposing sight to the foreign spectator. With what feelings ought a missionary to be impressed when he sees so great a nation under the abject control of disgusting idolatry? Whilst walking here, I was strongly reminded of Paul in Athens, when he was passing among their temples and was an altar dedicated "to the unknown God". The crowds fixed their whole attention upon us. However, the major and intelligent part of them were so eagerly reading our books. The treatise which pleased them most was a dialogue between Chang and Yuen, the one a Christian, and the other an ignorant heathen. This work of

> the late, much lamented Dr. Milne, contains very pointed and just remarks, and has always been a favorite book among the Chinese readers.

This is a very realistic description of the scene where Gützlaff was visiting a Buddhist temple in a coastal island. He stated that the various Buddhist statues inside the temple were that of a typical idolatry, but he retained a very hopeful view to the response that the Buddhist priests showed to the books that he brought to them. This description showed not only the fact that he was very fluent in the local language but also his conviction and confidence that their means of missionary works, the tracts prepared in the local language, could deeply penetrate into the souls of the local people. From a rhetorical point of view, the description of the Buddhist priests gathering together to receive the tracts explaining the Christian doctrines in the local language provides a very unique and ironical scene, but the virtue of the detailed description was the biggest advantage of the genre of travelogue. Looking at the local people and Buddhist priests, who were seemingly intelligent, taking a careful look at the tracts they brought to them, Gützlaff felt a kindofprideindispensation, approached to religious enlightenment, and developed the anticipation that his religious enterprise would become successful in that manner.

3. Conclusions : "Journal of a Voyage Along the Coast of China" as Convertsation Between Civilizations

The present study was conducted to analyze the text of the Gützlaff's travelogue published in The Chinese Repository around 1832 and to investigate the transculturality and the mutuality of cultural contact revealed in the text. Early-stage studies are currently conducted about the cultural reinterpretation of Europe's encountering of East Asia, resulting from the political and economic expansion of Europe from the middle of the 18th century. From the conventional historical point of view, the criticism on the roles played by the Christian missionaries began with the definition of their practices in the local areas as the frontier works of the imperialism. In fact, such definition has concealed parts of the significance of their cultural understanding and the practices of cultural contact. Viewed from a more critical standpoint, the ideological criticism toward the imperialism neglects the various contexts of the situations in Southeast Asia and China that the missionaries encountered and coped with. Therefore, travelogue is a literary genre that requires reinterpretation of various contexts, because various contexts may be discovered and interpreted from travelogue, which is full of on-site realism. Whether it was filled with a distorted imperialistic view or a religious belief-based conscience, the mind and heart of the missionaries at that time must have not been so simple. Therefore, it is obvious that the intersections of various social positions and different layers of recognition must be 'interpreted from composite viewpoints.'

'Travel books about colonies and semi-colonies gave European reading publics a sense of ownership, entitlement and familiarity with respect to the distant parts of the world that were being explored, invaded, invested in, and colonized." "They created a sense of curiosity, excitement, adventure, and even moral fervor about European expansionism. They were one of the key instruments that made people 'at home' in Europe feel part of a planetary project; a key instrument, in other words, in creating the 'domestic subject' of empire.' The travelogues by the missionaries were in some part creating a 'domesticsubject' for the members of the empires that they were inside a certain project related to Southeast Asia and China and, at the same time, distinguished from them . To the missionaries writing a travelogue was not 'never a light task.' 'He had to be the witness of the actions and objects he reported, and master the customs and language of the inhabitant.' 'He had to interchange with people of the highest class, and frequently talk with their key administers.' 'Briefly speaking, to enable himself to talk with certainty and assurance about the wealth, beauty and power of an empire, he had to actually investigate the numerous subjects, the number and locations of cities, the scale of the castles therein, and all the rare and precious things inside the nation.' Of course, Gützlaff's travelogue was not aimed at explicit pillage, but it is undeniable that his writing partially had such a function.

However, the travelogues written in that period show that, to the eyes of the Christian missionaries, the people of Southeast Asia and China were considered those who needed to be liberated from darkness by means of religious salvation and the light of modernity, rather than the objects of indiscriminate exploitation. More than that, the missionaries continuously retained their intellectual curiosity and learning about the religious features of the local people and increased their own understanding about the religious principles of the areas. The present article focused on the fact that their increase of the knowledge about the local society, including the local religion, affected their cross-border daily living as people of cultural contact zones and deepened their knowledge system, rather than the fact that it was consistent with the religious and national goals of expansion that the already had . While the missionaries played the role of the frontiers of the Western European Christian civilization, they also had the identity as cross-border people and those who communicated with the multiple cultures. The dual identities and positions that the missionaries had caused them to have a composite viewpoint to China and the individual countries of Southeast Asia. On one hand, according to their calling, they tried to propagate the modern or Christian knowledge from their own civilization. On the other hand, they increased their local knowledge and the understanding of the local civilization in order to create an introspective and reflective viewpoint in the conventional knowledge system of Europe regarding East Asia. They allowed their own culture to perform 'in-depth reading' of the region by bidirectionally highlighting the internalized knowledge created at the cultural contact points between them and the others, not simply playing the role of knowledge mediator with a unidirectional perspective.

In this sense, Gützlaff's travelogue recording his voyage from Southeast Asia along the east coast of China to the northern waters is considered as a very vivid text that includes the significance of the substantial practices in the transcultural zones. Therefore, it is obvious that complicated contexts that should be reviewed from a new perspective are hidden in the record. The part that requires a refreshing perspective mostly is so-called 'the conversation between cultures or civilization' to compare and adjust cultural concept with each other for accurate understanding. This work may be successfully conducted not only by the simple contact with languages and living environments but also in the presence of the reflective understanding and deep affection for the local areas and the native people, the critical self-examination of one's own knowledge system, and, at least, the intrinsic viewpoint and attitude to admit that a part of an individual belongs to the world. In that sense, Gützlaff's travelogue is a text showing that there existed, whether consciously or unconsciously, a key to the 'conversation between civilizations' though not in a full scale. In addition, considering from the publication point of view the time of publication and the relationship between the writers and editors, the publication of Gützlaff's travelogue is regarded as a type of symbolical and ritual writing that declared the beginning of the journey to the huge cultural contact zone, The Chinese Repository, conducted for two decades from 1832 to 1851.

Shen Cong Wen and Maritime Culture of Qingdao

Seungwoong Ahn

1. Introduction

Beginning with his first novel "Mr. San Bei's Family Motto(三貝先生家訓)" published in 1925 and to his last novel "Biography Not Mysterious(傳奇不奇)" in 1947, Shen Cong Wen wrote over 200 novels in a few more years longer than a decade. How was he able to write such a huge number of novels in such a short period of time? The answer is closely related to the uniqueness of his time and his personal circumstances that made him write in several big cities of China, such as Beijing, Shanghai, Qingdao and Kunming.

The cities provided him with not just a base for living or topics and materials for creative works. The cities played a critical role for him to accumulate literary knowledge and form his own literary viewpoint, and they became a source of his restless zeal for creative works. The cities significantly affected Shen

Cong Wen literary works: Beijing, the old capital having a history of over 1000 years, with its cultural heritage; Shanghai, the megacity of trade, with its Western culture and publication business; and Kunming, located in the Southwest, with the primitive natural environment around the city.

Another city that must be mentioned in discussing the life of Shen Cong Wen as a writer is Qingdao, the city of maritime culture in Shandong Province. Shen Cong Wen taught the history of novel and the art of writing at Qingdao University for about two years from 1931 and 1933. According to his autobiographical prose "Water and cloud(水雲)", Qingdao was his mental resting place where he gave full scope to his literary imagination. In addition, as shown by many studies, Shen Cong Wen became more mature form his Qingdao Period.

Despite the importance of the Qingdao Period in Shen Cong Wen's literary career, almost no study has been conducted on the relation between Shen Cong Wen and Qingdao. Only Shen Cong Wen's episodes in Qingdao or the contribution of the comfortable environment of Qingdao to his creative works has been mentioned in some articles. Fortunately, the combination of the study on regions, cities and spaces and that of literature has been actively conducted in recent times, and that allows to review the significance of Qingdao in Shen Cong Wen's literature.

While space is related to an abstract and physical range as an extension of places having specific activities, objects or environment, place serves as a basis for experiential and specific activities and is related to the contextual and cultural significance. The deep intimacy that a person develops with a certain place, although existing in our unconsciousness, becomes a basic starting point to form one's own identity and live the life.

In other words, a city, after being a home of someone, becomes a certain special place beyond the passive meaning of an abstract and physical space. A city becomes a 'place' in the life of individuals, and plays a positive role in forming the identity of an individual. Being not just a physical space but also a cultural space, Qingdao might also have given a positive effect on the Shen Cong Wen's career. In particular, because Qingdao was a modern maritime city built by the earnest efforts of Germany, Japan and the Nationalist China, we need to pay attention to the city's unique 'placeness.'

The present article focuses on the 'less known fact' that the unique maritime environment and maritime culture of the maritime city Qingdao had a profound effect on the novel-writing by Shen Cong Wen. This will explain why the level of Shen Cong Wen's writings was suddenly increased from the Qingdao Period, and help the readers to have a deeper understanding of his literary works.

2. Maritime Liberal Arts Environment of Qingdao and Shen Cong Wen's Writing

Studies on regions, spaces and cities consistently focus on the active roles that a place plays in the formation of an individual's identity. For example, 'Personality is reformed in time and space, and an individual is defined through the specific spatiality of existence', and 'Humans always want to verify their own existence by asking 'Where am I?'' Based on the previous studies on Qingdao, this chapter reviews the significance of the unique maritime liberal arts environment of Qingdao in Shen Cong Wen's writing career.

1) Coastal Walkway : Refilling of Creative Energy

For about five years between December 1972, when he moved from Beijing to Shanghai, and July 1933 when he returned to Beijing, Shen Cong Wen had to move to many cities, including Nanjing, Wuhan and Qingdao. Among these cities, Shanghai, the huge commercial city with advanced publication industry, served as an excellent base for Shen Cong Wen to grow up to be a professional writer. His important collections, such as *Shen Cong Wen Novel Study Collection*(從文小說習作選), *After Raining*(雨後及其他) and *Shen Cong Wen Best Collection*(沈從文甲集), were published in Shanghai. However, the city where he planned and created his representative novels such as *Border Town*(邊城) and other high-level writings was not Shanghai but Qingdao. Shen Cong Wen recalled Qingdao as follows.

> The two years when I lived in Qingdao was the period when my creativity was the most prosperous in my entire life and my style became relatively mature. *Autobiography*(自傳), *Under the Moon*(月下小景) and many other short stories were written in this period. Most of the novels that I started to write after returning to Beijing, such as *Border Town*(邊城), were planned when I was in Qingdao("Memories of Qingdao(小憶青岛)").

Shen Cong Wen himself recalled that his literary works became more mature from the Qingdao Period. The reason for this, as guessed by many people, may be because he was working as a professor at Qingdao University, and thus he was richer in terms of money and time than in the Shanghai Period. However, like the sayings, such as "Where there is injustice there will be an outcry(不平則鳴)" and "Poems are made after becoming poor(詩窮而後工)", the economic and time affluence that he enjoyed in Qingdao along cannot provide a sufficient reason why his creativity was elevated in the period. Then, what elevated Shen Cong Wen's level of literary creativity in the Qingdao Period? To find the answer, the local uniqueness of Qingdao must be reviewed.

Qingdao was originally the name of a small island where fish boats in the Jiaozhou Bay(膠州灣) gathered together. After Germany occupied the Jiaozhou Bay in 1898 and constructed a colonized city as a bridgehead toward the interior continent, Qingdao was developed as an international maritime city. Undergoing the occupation by Japan and the rule by the Nationalist Party, Qingdao was developed as the political, economic and cultural center of Shandong(山東) Province. The surroundings that Shen Cong Wen experienced in Qingdao in early 1930s were closely related to the cultural purpose of Germany which had built Qingdao in 1898.

> Firstly, the Qingdao's colonized urban space constructed by the German Empire was designed as a strategic maritime city where the harbor and transportation were prioritized in order to secure the long-term commercial and economic benefits of Germany. Secondly, Qingdao was planned to be a 'cultural city' playing the role of a public relations museum that would display German studies, science and technology, and building. Third, Qingdao was planned as a 'hygienic city' with the goal to improve the living environment by improving the roads and the water and sewage facilities. Finally, it was planned as a 'summer resort city', taking advantage of the mild climate of the Jiaozhou Bay.

One noticeable part is that Qingdao was designed as a summer resort city from the beginning. Japan, which started to rule Qingdao in 1914 following Germany, expanded the beaches and seaside parks. The Nationalist Party regime, which received the ruling power from Japan in 1924, also made many efforts to develop Qingdao as a maritime sightseeing and resort city. Therefore, Qingdao was already spotlight as the most famous summer resort city domestically and internationally.

It seems as if the development of Qingdao as a maritime sightseeing and resort city had been prepared just for Shen Cong Wen alone. Before moving to Qingdao in August 1931, Shen Cong Wen stayed in Shanghai for a few years, looking for a way to become a professional writer. However, he faced unfavorable circumstances, including the failure of the publication business, the death of his literary friend Hu Ye Pin(胡也頻), the hijacking of Ding Ling(丁玲), and the death of his father. He particularly went through economic difficulty to support his sick family members: he was forced to write in order to earn money no matter how small it was. His autobiographical writings of the time, such as "Sent it to an Editor(寄給某編輯先生)" and "Building 樓居", show that he was devastated mentally and physically even to bleeding at the nose everyday and to think about suicide from time to time. At that time, Xu Zhi Mo (徐志摩) recommended Shen Cong Wen to the position of a professor at Qingdao University, which was a precious opportunity for Shen Cong Wen to relax himself in the relatively stable job position.

After coming to Qingdao, Shen Cong Wen made the best use of Qingdao as a resort city. He particularly loved a seaside walkway linked to a mountain trail leading to his faculty accommodation. The regular walking might have contributed significantly to the recovery of his health. Shen Cong Wen recalled it later as follow.

> While I was in Qingdao, I always used to walk along the beaches and mountain

> trails, which gave me a very good impression to me. Probably because I had congenital blood shortage, I felt comfortable in my body and mind whenever I visited the beaches. My mind was clear and my body was full of energy, even thought I slept just three hours each day("Memories of Qingdao(小憶青岛)").

To Shen Cong Wen, Qingdao was an excellent resort city that 'made him feel comfortable in his body and mind.' He walked each day on a regular basis the mountain trails with a view to the sea and the endless sandy beaches. He recovered his physical strength to the point of 'having a clear mind and full physical strength even after sleeping just for three hours.'

His recovery of physical strength helped to him to be recharge himself with the creative energy that was exhausted during the Shanghai Period. For the short period of a couple of years until he left Qingdao in July 1933, Shen Cong Wen wrote his autobiography *Cong Wen's Autobiography*(從文自傳) and published about 35 novels, which include relatively well-known works, such as "Under the Moon(月下小景)", "San San(三三)", "Guizhou Scenes(黔小景)", "Tranquility(靜)", "Feng Zi(鳳子)", "Cub(虎雛)", "Hasty(躁)", "Wise(賢賢)", "Muddy Track(泥途)", "A Lady in City(都市一婦人)" and "A Black History(阿黑小史)". In addition, his representative work *Border Town*(邊城), was planned in this period. In summary, Qingdao, as a maritime resort city, played a critical role for Shen Cong Wen to recover his health, thus positively affecting his writing activities.

2) Qingdao University : Establishment of Identity as Countryman

When the Nationalist Party, which obtained the ruling power over the Shandong Province after Germany and Japan, was planning the establishment of a national university in Shandong, Cai Yuan Pei(蔡元培), one of the national university foundation committee, recommended Qingdao instead of Jinan(濟南) where the Shandong provincial government was located. He said, "Considering the topography and climate of Qingdao, the city will be a center of culture in the future, and this is closely related to the foundation of the university." In fact, around the time when the national university was established, the charming points of Qingdao, the maritime resort city with a mild climate, attracted many celebrities in the field of culture to Qingdao, which was then a barren land from a cultural point of view.

> With reference to landscape and environment, Qingdao is the top city in China, I guess. If you two are happy, please visit Qingdao and look around firstly. If you are satisfied, you can teach in Qingdao. If you are not satisfied, we will not force you to do so.

The quotation above is what Yang Zhen Sheng(楊振聲), the first president of Qingdao University, said to Liang Shi Qiu(梁實秋) and Wen Yi Duo(聞一多) to invite them as professor. This indicates that the advantages of Qingdao as a resort city played a positive role in the development of Qingdao.

However, Qingdao as a resort city might have not be appropriate for the scholars of literal arts who were accustomed to the traditional culture to settled down there permanently. In addition to the lack of traditional culture, Qingdao earned a vulgar impression as a city of pleasure with the increase of the vacationers. On the other hand, Qingdao was apart from the traditional culture and had an exotic atmosphere, and thus allowed the intellectuals to candidly expose what was inside their hearts.

> Qingdao is a good place. With a mountain in the back and a water in the front, Qingdao has warm winter and cool summer. It has clean and wide urban areas as well as one of the most beautiful beaches of Asia, being suitable for families. The only thing that I am sorry about this city is that it lacks cultural background and thus the atmosphere is slightly dry. So, in each weekend, we used to drink wine in a bar until becoming dead drunk.

According to Liang Shi Qiu(梁實秋), the people of culture who gathered at the Qingdao University called themselves the Eight Intoxicated Taoist Hermits(酒中八仙). Since most of the drinking party members were away from their families, they spent merry days in the pattern of 'A small drinking party every three days, and a big drinking bout every five days.'

The Qingdao University provided a dormitory for the single professors. Some of the professors living in there unknowingly exposed their bare-face of the intellectuals because the merry-making atmosphere of Qingdao. By observing the life of the professors, Shen Cong Wen could learn about the slick and gilded inner world of the urban intellectuals who had studied abroad. Take a look at the novel entitled "Eight-Horse Painting(八駿圖)" about his life in this period.

> When the summer came, the semester started according to the schedule. At the welcoming ceremony, the president called, seriously or humorously, the lecturers from a far distance 'Swift Horses.' The first reason why he called them so was because they all were prominent individuals. Secondly, they did not fear the fat distance. If we are all swift horses, our dormitory may be appropriately called a stable!
>
> What I feel is a little bit different from what the president said. To me, the dormitory should be called 'a natural nursing home.' Believe or not, it seems that all the people who have gathered here have a disease from a medical point of view. ("Eight-Horse Painting (八駿圖)")

"Eight-Horse Painting(八駿圖)" is a novel that describes from the viewpoint of Mr. Da Shi(達士) the perverted sexual mentality of the professors living in the dormitory at the Qingdao University. They look like saints and noble people. However, Professor A hung up a seminude painting of a beauty in his room, and Professor B is busy looking at the women in swimsuits in the beach. The quotation above sarcastically calls the dormitory of the professors a nursing home. This was a poignant sarcasm to the so-called intellectuals of the time who had studied abroad.

The sarcasm shows the complicated psychological state of Shen Cong Wen. He had undergone almost no formal school education, but he was able to teach in the university with his literary accomplishments alone. As many scholars have pointed out, Shen Cong Wen had a sense of inferiority to the intellectuals of the time who had studied abroad. His novel "Visitor(來客)" reveals that he was always conscious of the intellectuals who had studied abroad and he was used to console himself through the sarcasm toward their poor internal world.

However, Shen Cong Wen was not devoted to finding the bad things of such intellectuals. He indiscriminately read books that were popular among the intellectuals and paid attention to the issues among them, even conducting a study project about the issues. In addition, he made efforts to find out his own strengths in comparison with them. In other words, he was making efforts to establish his unique identity that was differentiated from that of others through long contemplation.

Shen Cong Wen's process of finding his own identity through the comparison with the professor who had studied abroad was, roughly speaking, a collision between the maritime culture and the continent culture. Most of the professors teaching at the Qingdao University were the intellectuals who had studied in foreign countries across the oceans, and they sought their mental values on the basis of the Western culture. Shen Cong Wen, who did not have an opportunity to receive the school education, not to mention the opportunity to study abroad, had to find his own cultural ground that was different from them. What he found was the traditional culture of Xiangxi(湘西), his hometown located in the innermost part of the Chinese continent. That culture was not an elite traditional culture but the culture of the folks. Shen Cong Wen tried to establish his identity on the grounds of China, tradition, interior continent, and folk culture, which were contrasted to the West, modernity, ocean and intellectual culture. This is often found in many parts of his writings where he declared himself to be a countryman.

> I am a countryman. Wherever I go, I have my own measures and scales, which are always inconsistent with the common ideas of the society. With regard to all the occurrences and things that I face within my destiny, I estimate the values and meanings of life according to my own dimensions and weight. I don't need the things that are created by what you call 'society.' I hate uniform standards ("Water and Cloud (水雲)").

He herein declared that a countryman estimates the values and meaning of life by using his own measures and scales. A countryman measures and scales that he mentioned were not the 'knowledge' of the intellectuals but the 'wisdom' of the folk. Shen Cong Wen compared the knowledge system of the intellectuals of the time with the wisdom of the common people in the area of Xiangxi(湘西). Through the comparison, he became confident that the wisdom of the common people that he experienced in Xiangxi(湘西) was as valuable as the knowledge of the intellectuals who had studied abroad. His allegorical novel "Knowledge(知識)", published in 1934, well demonstrates his attitude toward the knowledge that the intellectuals of the time possessed. On his way home after finishing his study in a foreign country, the main character of the novel, Zhang Liu Ji(張六吉), encounters a group of farmers in a mountainous region, and acquires a great lesson through the meeting with them. The first thing that he did after arriving at his hometown was to write a letter to his advisor, the prominent foreign professor in his graduate school:

> You are an impostor worth dying. You taught me for ten years, but you are not smarter than the illiterate country people in our town. You are legal impostor. What you know is what is unnecessary in human life. What you don't know is what a man must know. I am assured that you are a large impostor. ("Knowledge (知識)")

Then, Zhang Liu Ji(張六吉) put all his books into a fire. The novel "Knowledge(知識)" plains shows how Shen Cong Wen viewed the intellectuals who had studied abroad and their new knowledge. It is quite surprising that Shen Cong Wen, who had been almost brainwashed by the May 4th New Culture Movement before he started his literary career, had such as simple and radical idea. However, that is partially understandable if it is considered that the novel was published immediately after Shen Cong Wen's Qingdao Period. In other words, because the novel "Knowledge(知識)" was an outcome of his process of forming his own identity as a countryman in the middle of the meetings with the professors of the Qingdao University, he exposed his standing in such an outright manner.

In conclusion, Qingdao helped Shen Cong Wen to recover his health and regain the vitality for creative works, and allowed him to recognize his own continent culture-based identity through the meeting with the professors who were familiar with the Western maritime culture. Ironically, the maritime literary arts environment of Qingdao awakened Shen Cong Wen to be a folk novelist who was rich in the rural culture of the continent.

3. Natural Maritime Environment of Qingdao and Shen Cong Wen's Creative Works

When Shen Cong Wen resided in Qingdao, his accommodation was near to Huiquan(匯泉) beach, which was very famous in China. He walked along the beach every day, and was able to see half-naked women wearing swimsuits, which was an exceptional experience in China at that time. According to the relevant records, the women were of the high social class who were rich in terms of economic status and time. They were objects of envy as well as those of voyeurism.

To Shen Cong Wen, the women in the beach were not the objects of voyeurism. Unlike the professors described in "Eight-Horse Painting(八駿

圖)", he did not objectified the women from man's point of view. Then, how was Shen Cong Wen able to be freed from the male-centered viewpoint and view the women just as they were? That is closely related to his contemplation and imagination about the 'sea.' This chapter will discuss how the variety of the literary imaginations found in Shen Cong Wen's works and the imagery of women were related to the sea of Qingdao, the natural maritime environmental.

1) Sea : Source of Deep and Wide Imagination

Shen Cong Wen mentioned a few times that his writings were related to water. His autobiography states as follows.

> My emotions could be freely moving without being hardened, because the rolling waves of clear water has given me a considerable effect on me. My beautiful life in may young ages were mostly attached to water. I can tell that my schools were everything that was near to water. My knowledge about beauty and contemplation on it are significantly related to water *Cong Wen's Autobiography*(從文自傳).

Shen Cong Wen words, quoted above, are considerably consistent with what Bachelard asserted in his book *Water and Dreams*. He said, 'Human dreams are essentially materialistic. Our dreams are materialized in our young ages in our places of birth. The region we call home is less expanse than matter. In a person who is born in a place with a stream or a river, his unconsciousness is governed by water.' This description well fits to the relationship between Shen Cong Wen and water. Bachelard also commented, 'To understand the deep imaginative world of human beliefs, passions, ideals and philosophy, they should be regarded an attribute of the matter that governs them.'

Qingdao had the sea, which as the mother of all waters, governing Shen Cong Wen's 'deep imaginative world of human beliefs, passions, ideals and philosophy.' To Shen Cong Wen who was familiar with the rivers of the mountainous areas of Xiangxi(湘西), the sea of Qingdao must have been a novel experience. To the eyes of Shen Cong Wen having a sensitive soul, the sea was more than the 'physical space to which all the waters of the rivers are collected.' In other words, the sea was neither a national border or a wall nor a mediator of new culture. The sea was a source of art where the water that governed Shen Cong Wen's unconsciousness awakened his unlimited materialistic imagination.

In 1942, Shen Cong Wen published the prose entitled "Water and Cloud (水雲)", recalling about two decades of his literary career. The title "Water and Cloud(水雲)" draws attention. In fact, the water cycle generally starts from a sea and ends at a sea. The sea receives the solar energy, evaporates water, and the water vapor is turned into a cloud. The cloud is then converted into rain that falls on the land, and goes back to the sea. The sea is at the center of the water cycle. Therefore, the sea has various stories of water and cloud that wander the world. What is interesting is that his recollection begins with his memory of the sea in the Qingdao Period, ten years ago, just as water and cloud begin the water cycle from the sea, as the title implies.

> On one hand, I acquired the heat and power that were necessary to my life while basking in the sun at my shoulders, back, hands and feet. On the other hand, I dredged up my life from the deep by allowing the boundless sea in front of me teach me("Water and Cloud(水雲)").

To Shen Cong Wen, the sea of Qingdao was so special that it awakened his internal awareness of life. Then, how could the sea awaken his internal awareness of life? And, what impact did the awakened awareness of life had on the creative works by Shen Cong Wen? Bachelard is referred to once again to find the answers. Bachelard mentioned 'material imagination', emphasizing quietly gazing at matters that arouse imagination, such as water or fire. Through the quiet gazing, "matters may be given value in two ways: by deepening or by elevating. Deepening makes it seem unfathomable, like a mystery. Elevation makes it appear to be an inexhaustible force, like a miracle. In both cases, meditation on matter cultivates an 'open imagination.'" Similarly, Shen Cong Wen quietly gazed at the sea while walking along the beach each day, and he was able to awaken his internal awareness of life with the power of the 'open imagination.' This process is well illustrated in his autobiographical novel "Feng Zi(鳳子)".

Where the young man stayed was not too far from the sea. (······) Because the great sea was rolling regularly, he was able to regulate his breathing. As the sandy beach was very flat, the tidings left numerous glittering things on the wet sand. Since everything was so beautiful, he went to there almost everyday and left a long line of footprints. The boundless ocean expanded his scope of meditation, and help him to cultivate the habit of looking at a far distant part of life. (······) Therefore, his heart was always soft like the sea and peaceful like the sandy beach ("Feng Zi (鳳子)").

"Feng Zi(鳳子)" was Shen Cong Wen's autobiographical novel based on his experiences in Qingdao. The novel was unfinished even though he worked on it for five years from 1933 to 1937. The story and form of the novel are very unique: the writer directly appears in the novel to tell what he wants to tell the readers or an agent of the writer appears in the frame story to lead the story in the way he wants. Therefore, the young man who walked along the sea every day was none other than Shen Cong Wen himself. Young Shen Cong Wen gazed at the sea quite to synchronize his breathing with the sea that was 'rolling regularly.' His comment "The boundless ocean expanded his scope of meditation, and help him to cultivate the habit of looking at a far distant part of life" means that Shen Cong Wen himself entered into a realm that is hardly experienced by common people by means of the power of the open imagination related to the sea. This is confirmed by the author's comments, "Because I felt the wisdom and power of life in the process of realizing in my heart the high and distant ideals, I was not sad although being lonely". Shen Cong Wen learned from his experiences the prototype image of the sea, which was formed by humankind, in the space of imagination provided by the primitive matter of the sea, for thousands of years through the survival in the sea, and he was able to realize the meaning of the image. As if he was providing evidence to the comment, "The novel was what the water told me", in his autobiographical novel "Visitor(來客)", Shen Cong Wen planned and wrote numerous literary works while he was walking along the beach each day.

2) Sea : Birthplace of Goddess

Most of the main characters appearing in Shen Cong Wen's novels are women, all of whom are described as better than the men. The stories included in *Under the Moon*(月下小景), written in the Qingdao Period, well show this feature. In the story "The Woman", the king and the good-looking man abandon their thrones and possessions and set out on a journey to find out the "genuine reason why women are respected". The story "Love and Lust(愛慾)" says, "Women conquer everything so easily". The story "'Break the Mountain (扇陀)" describes a woman who makes a man a lump of clay with formidable power. In some cases, women are described as a goddess who is in charge of love and death, the essential elements of the circle of life.

This feature of Shen Cong Wen's novels was further developed through the Qingdao Period. What in Qingdao intensified such a feature? The clue is that the space of imagination that the primitive matter of the sea provides is closely related to woman. The original gender of the sea is female, and the sea symbolizes both birth and death. Shen Cong Wen elevated women to the position of goddess through his imagination, rather than objectifying them, because he was able to combine his imagination about the sea with his view of womanhood. The general symbolism of the sea may be appropriately mentioned herein.

> The sea is often associated with the image of "low ocean". Therefore, the sea is recognized as a mediator between intangible existences, such as flowing water and air, and tangible existences, such as the earth. Based on this, the sea has the image of a mediator between death and life. The seawater is considered as not only the source of life but also as the goal of life. "Returning to sea" means "returning to mother", which also means 'going back to death.'

Among the symbolisms of the sea, what draws out attention is the part that "The seawater is considered as not only the source of life but also as the goal of life". Life herein refers to maintenance of life. The source of life means the birth of life, while the goal of life refers to the end of life, which is death. An important point is that life consists of the endless cycle of death and birth, and that 'the goddess of the earth — woman' is indispensable in the cycle. The sea, symbolizing the source and goal of life, shares a common feature with woman in the sense that they administer both birth and death.

Shen Cong Wen, who was near to the sea, naturally deepened his meditation on the source of life, which is birth, and the goal of life, which is death. The figure of woman created in this Period is described to have both birth and death. The following example shows how the sea, woman and death are closely related with each other:

> A sudden shower was pouring upon the head, and the thunder was rumbling. What was around her was only the dark furious sea. She thought in her mind, "This is not a bad experience". She felt no fear and believed that she would be able to endure it with her abilities and that no misfortune would occur to her. She continued swimming forward joyfully. (……) However, when just about 200 meters remained before the coast, her power remaining in her could not help her any longer. She just gave her own body to the huge rolling waves. She felt exhausted and thought that she would be sinking down to the bottom of the sea, failing to reach the beach. She was drifting on the waves. ("Ru Rui(如蕤)")

The quotation is from the short novel "Ru Rui(如蕤)" published in 1933. The women named as Ru Rui(如蕤), looked up as a goddess by all men, was enjoying a boat ride in the sea of Qingdao, but she was sinking into the sea by a storm. What is intriguing is that she felt no fear even though she fell into the stormy sea. She was neither embarrassed nor fearful even when she was exhausted and sinking down to the deep sea in the state of faint. She is described as willingly accepting the death brought by the sea while giving herself to the rolling waves. Why? It is because the sea, woman and death are correlated with each other.

The figuration of woman, representing the attribute of the sea, is sometimes described as one that guides a man to death or that watches a man dying. The girl in *Under the Moon*(月下小景) sings a song to her lover: "Water can flow to anywhere; and fire can be built anywhere. The moon can shine anywhere; and love can be made anywhere". She guides the man to death, giving the assurance about a love after death. In "Mei Jin, Bao Zi and Na Yang(美金・豹子・與那羊)", Mei Jin guides Bao Zi to death by firstly stabbing into her own chest. In *Border Town*(邊城), Cui Cui(翠翠) and Tian Bao(天保) have to tolerate the death of the grandfather. San San(三三) in "San San(三三)" must accept the death of the young man from the city, and Hei Mao(黑猫) in "The Inn(旅店)" must accept the death of the man with whom she has become intimate.

The following example shows how the sea, woman and birth are closely associated :

The woman still looked like smiling, and soon stood up on the sandy land. It was very close to her, and she was wearing a white cloth. Her body silhouette in the dark was very slender. — Her back was truly attractive, and her walking was so beautiful. The young man suddenly felt indescribable sadness. Changing his plan, he was standing still on the dark side of the street to let the two people pass by. Even after coming back to his hotel, he, a fugitive of the world, could not remove the appearance of the woman out of his mind due to an unknown reason ("Feng

Zi(鳳子)").

The quotation above, a paragraph in "Feng Zi(鳳子)", describes a young man who firstly encountered a woman, whose name is Feng Zi(鳳子), in the sandy beach at twilight, and became unable to forget her. The young man just saw her back, but he felt mysterious awe as well as strong curiosity. Eventually, to learn who the woman is, the young man visits the house of the old gentleman who was with Feng Zi(鳳子). The unfinished work "Feng Zi(鳳子)" ends when the young man does not know who Feng Zi(鳳子) is yet. However, the frame story of the novel lets the readers guess that the woman named as Feng Zi(鳳子) is the personification of nature and beauty. One interesting point is that the author designed the place of his first encountering of Feng Zi(鳳子) to be the sandy beach at twilight. The beauty of the woman was fantastically described in comparison with the beauty of the seashore aglow with the sunset. The young writer in the novel considers the woman, Feng Zi(鳳子), as the beauty of the nature itself. The appearance of Feng Zi(鳳子) recalls that of Aphrodite just born from the foams in the seashore. It is a rendezvous between the attributes of woman and the sea.

The figuration of women, manifesting the attribute of the sea as the birth of life, was described as the very personification of the vitality and beauty of the nature. Cui Cui(翠翠) in *Border Town*(邊城) is compared to a little animal in the forest, such as baby deer. San San(三三) in "San San(三三)", considering himself as the owner of the reservoir and Xiao Xiao(蕭蕭) in "Xiao Xiao(蕭蕭)",

enjoying ultimate freedom in the mountain, have the characters of the sprits of the reservoir and the mountain, respectively.

Therefore, the great nature of woman is recovered when combined with the sea. The half-naked women in the beach of Qingdao might be simply the objects of voyeurism to most men who considered the sea just as a background. However, they were different to Shen Cong Wen who viewed women with the 'open imagination' brought by the sea. As described above, he created the figuration of woman being freed from life and death and appearing in the image of goddess. Therefore, the sea of Qingdao had a profound effect on the literary works by Shen Cong Wen, especially in creating the figuration of woman.

> "I already agreed to your thought ten years before that (writing of novels: comment by translator) may be accomplished by giving everything to 'coincidence' and 'feeling.' I think I have to accept the control by another 'coincidence.' When I approached her, I could discover God from her smiles and worries. When I parted from her, I could discover from the colors and lusters of all forms of nature. As you said before, this may be because I believe nothing but 'life.' (……) I think I have to go back to the seaside, I mean, to the seaside of the 'past.' To other people? I am sure that what she needs is the seaside of 'abstraction.' Both have a good landscape. The difference is that one is the resting place of the lonely heart, and the other is a house where passion and dream work together to let 'coincidence' convert from 'God' to 'human.' ("Water and cloud(水雲)")

The text is slightly difficult to understand, but it clearly shows that 'coincidence', 'she', 'God' and 'seaside' are associated with each other. In the entire context, the 'coincidence' represents a woman who can arouse Shen Cong Wen's passion for creative works or the meeting with such a woman, 'she' denotes a specific woman that lets him be immersed in creative works, and 'God' refers to the attributes of all women, corresponding to divinity. Hence, to Shen Cong Wen, woman is a divine existence, like Muse, that arouses his passion for creative works. In addition, Shen Cong Wen mentioned 'the seaside of abstraction' as the house where 'coincidence' is converted from 'God' to 'human.' This clearly shows that her birth as a divine existence originates with the sea. Therefore, recalling his creative works over a decade, Shen Cong Wen was firstly reminded of the sea of Qingdao. So, he confessed that he felt the need to go back to the sea, the birthplace of the goddess Muse, for new creative works.

4. Conclusions

Qingdao became an international maritime city when Germany built in 1898 a colonial city as a bridgehead toward the interior continent. This paper shows that the unique maritime environment and maritime culture of the maritime city Qingdao had a profound effect on the novels written by Shen

Cong Wen. The following conclusions are made from the review of his texts.

First, the unique maritime and literary environment of Qingdao, constructed as a resort city, helped him to recover his physical strength and provided the environment where he could focus on his writing. Before moving to Qingdao, Shen Cong Wen was devastated mentally and physically for various reasons, including the failure of his publication business, pressure of supporting his family financially, and frustration in his efforts to win love. By walking the walkway along the beach of Qingdao every day, Shen Cong Wen was able to recover his health and fill himself again with creative energy.

Second, through the association with the professors at the Qingdao University, he could establish his own identity as a writer. In various aspects, the northeastern maritime city Qingdao was different from the southwestern inland Xiangxi(湘西) area, Shen Cong Wen's hometown. Shen Cong Wen, who was familiar to the traditional inland culture, could contact as a stranger the modern maritime culture. In the middle of the collision between the traditional inland culture and the modern maritime culture, Shen Cong Wen established his identity as a 'countryman.'

Third, the natural maritime environment of Qingdao, the sea itself, was a source of wide and deep imagination to Shen Cong Wen. While walking along the beach every day, he gazed at the sea and positively accepted the 'material imagination' that the sea provided. He learned by experiences the prototype image of the sea, which humankind have accumulated for thousands of years through the survival in the sea, and realized its meaning.

Fourth, the sea of Qingdao configured the prototype characteristics of the 'figuration of woman' and the 'life ideology', which are the features of Shen Cong Wen's novels. He combined the symbolism of the sea, which is 'The sea is considered as not only the source of life but also the goal of life', with the femininity to deepen his contemplation of life. This enabled him to develop the figuration of woman that is closely related to the cycle of life consisting of birth and death, not considering the women of the beach as simply the objects of voyeurism.

In conclusion, the unique maritime environment and maritime culture of Qingdao played a profound role for Shen Cong Wen to recharge himself with creative energy, explore his own identity, enrich his literary imagination and create the figuration of woman with deep implication about life. The investigation from the viewpoint of the maritime environment and maritime culture of Qingdao reveals the profound reason why Shen Cong Wen's level of literary works could be elevated and his literary individuality could be more distinctive through the Qingdao Period.

A Study on the Introduction of Modern Western Languages to Japan

a Focus on Loan Words from the Dutch Language

Minho Yang

1. Introduction

Historically, foreign culture has been introduced to East Asia through the sea region. In the case of the neighboring country, Japan, a number of Western powers sought to enter Japan through the sea regional areas in Kyushu. The Nagasaki areas, in particular, served as an entrance for foreign culture, which makes it pivotal to focus on this region when examining the introduction of foreign culture into the sea regional areas in Northeast Asia. This paper focuses on Nagasaki, Japan, among the sea regional areas in Northeast Asia, to study the loan words from the Dutch language which were introduced through Nagasaki.

Japan's geographical characteristic as an island had a great influence on Japan's history and culture. As an island country, Japan is surrounded by the ocean and is separated from the world. Due to this geographic condition, Japan was not affected by foreign invasions or the rule of other nations but was able to absorb the culture and technology from its neighbors and reconcile them within the "island" to build its own unique culture. Being separated from foreign nations by the sea, it was difficult for Japan to diffuse its culture, which was why it actively and voluntarily accepted the foreign culture. Reception is at the center of Japanese culture. While Japan was the best in the world in receiving foreign culture, its own culture was rarely sent to other countries. Japan was not only selective in choosing which foreign culture to accept, but it was also adept in skillfully infusing the received foreign culture and to Japanize them. Japan infused the Chinese characters or religious ideologies such as Confucianism, Buddhism, and Taoism, which were imported from ancient Joseon and China and absorbed the newly introduced the products of the Western civilization and endeavored to meld such elements with its national situations. One characteristic of receptive cultures is that they have options from which to choose. Since the sea prevented foreign powers from attacking Japan and further prevented any ruling by foreign nations, Japan rarely experienced any enforced reception of foreign culture with any disregard of the receiver's consciousness and situations. In fact, it was able to adopt Western culture without any reservations. It, therefore, would be appropriate to focus on the introduction of new cultures and the ensuing changes in the language by examining the formation of the cultural network in the sea regional areas in Northeast Asia. This paper thus attempted to verify the spread and survival of words in accordance with historical facts found on "Japan in Northeast Asia" and "Nagasaki in Japan".

2. The Introduction of Foreign Culture to the sea regions of Northeast Asia

1) Nagasaki as a Window to Foreign Culture

The sea as an open space serves as an entrance of human and material resources. When people and goods move, it is natural that the languages the people use are also introduced. The reason why Western loan words were introduced during this era is in a sense extremely simple.

A country first accepts Western loan words to fill in the linguistic gap. In other words, if a new product or concept is newly introduced to a country but the word could not be replaced, the concerned country will adopt the word in accordance with the phonological system of the country's own language. Second, Western loan words are adopted out of an interest in the words used by foreigners. Such type of words could be used temporarily and disappear like buzzwords but could take root and be used by the general public. However, since such expressions share the meanings with existing expressions, they could thrive for a while but could simultaneously be in decline.

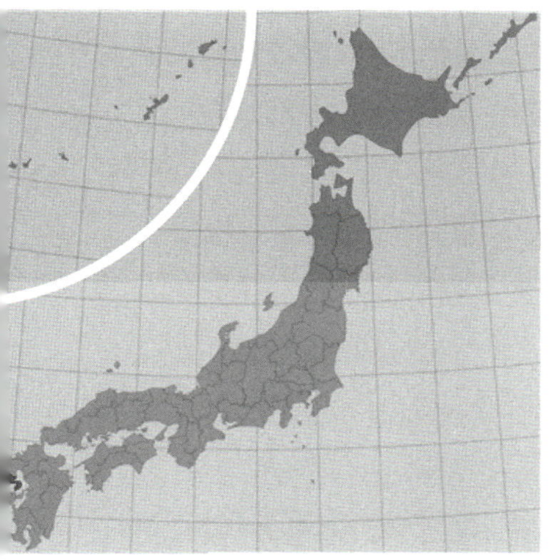

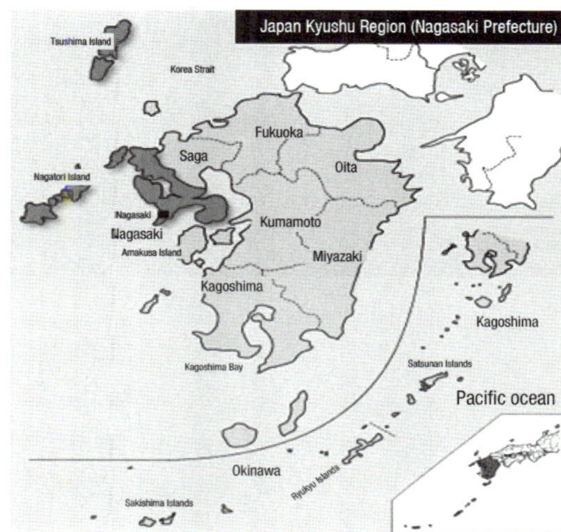

ge 1〉 Location of Nagasaki, Japan's Treaty Port

Such introduction of new Western loan words, especially the introduction of Dutch words into the Japanese language, could not be separated from the city of Nagasaki. This city, which was the only city that opened its doors while the country closed its doors, needs to be introduced.

As shown in 〈Image 1〉, Nagasaki is situated in the West of Kyushu and became a trade port as it began to trade with Portugal in 1571. Nagasaki also began to trade with the United Kingdom and the Netherlands as Christianity found its roots in this area. However, it made it an exception with the Netherlands, which did not engage in any missionary activities in Joseon and China, to trade until Japan opened its door, which served as an opportunity for Japan to accept the advanced culture from Europe. The trade was stopped in

1641 when Christianity was banned and Japan rejected foreign trade.

Afterward, through modernization, Nagasaki became one of the leading fishery cities and base for the deep-sea fishery in Japan. It became an international culture and tourism city in 1977 and Oura Church, which was built in 1864, was declared a national treasure and became a well-known tourist spot along with the Twenty-Six Martyrs Museum and Monument. Since the topic of this study is the introduction of Western culture, the focus of this paper will be on the Dutch language and Nagasaki.

As the only port open when the closed-door policy was implemented in the seventeenth century, Nagasaki served as the entrance to Western culture and civilization. Nagasaki became the starting point of Japan's contact with a foreign culture, served as an open window towards the world, and became the foothold for Catholic missionaries, especially the Society of Jesus, which contributed to introducing a great number of religious terms as well as scientific terms to Japan, thanks to the Jesuit's contribution to scientific development. However, as the religion began to take roots in Japan, it experienced conflicts and disputes with the ruling class, which led to a complicated society where natural cultural negotiations and adaptation simultaneously took place. Numerous loan words from Dutch which were first introduced during this period have been deeply rooted in the everyday lives of the Japanese people and are still in use to this day. The reasons behind the words' vitality should be identified.

3. Loan Words from the Netherlands

1) Background of the Introduction of Dutch Culture to Japan

While this paper analyzed the Dutch language introduced to Japan during the Edo period, it is also important to take account of how Japan first had contact with a foreign culture and the historical trends of the era. This may reaffirm the sociolinguistic proposition that language reflects its times.

Ishino and Ishiwata posited that foreign culture actually began to be introduced to Japan when the ports were opened during the Muromachi period. Information on the introduction of foreign culture and languages by periods could be found in 〈Table 1〉.

The early culture which was introduced to Japan included the Chinese characters, which were used before the Heian period from the end of the third century until the early sixteenth century, and Sanskrit, which was used in Buddhist scriptures. However, since foreign culture is commonly understood as Western culture, this paper focuses on Nagasaki and the Western culture during the Edo period, especially on the Dutch language.

The Edo period was the age of early scientific culture when Dutch was introduced. The drifting of the Dutch ship Liefde nearby the Oita Prefecture in 1600 became a major event in the history of the introduction of foreign culture to Japan. The Netherlands soon began to trade in Japan, along with Portugal and Spain, and the competition among European merchants in 〈table 1〉

Period	Culture	Language
Heian Period (Ninth to Thirteenth Century)	Buddhist Culture	Chinese Characters, Sanskrit
Muromachi Period (Fourteenth to Sixteenth Century)	Christian Culture	Portuguese
Edo Period (Seventeenth to Eighteenth Century)	Early Science Culture	Dutch
Meiji Period (Nineteenth Century)	Early Western Culture	English, German, French, etc.
Taisho/Showa Period (First Half of the Twentieth Century)	Modern Western Culture	English, German, French, etc.
Heisei Period (Second Half of the Twentieth Century)	Various Global Culture	Various Global Languages

Japan became fierce. In 1639, Japan closed its doors as Portugal, which was struggling in the Orient, ended its 97 years of trade relations with Japan. During this period, only China and the Netherlands were allowed to trade. Western culture during this period, therefore, was limited to the Dutch culture that was imported under the closed-door policy. The Netherlands monopolized Japan's trade with Europe for 220 years, after Japan closed its doors in 1639 and until it opened them in 1859 and exclusively used Nagasaki port for trade. Although the trade with the Netherlands began in 1609, it was only after Japan implemented its closed-door policy that the Dutch culture actually was introduced. In terms of the history of foreign culture, words on Rangaku(Dutch Studies), which included knowledge on science, culture, and technology, were introduced to the Japanese language. The words introduced under the context of the early scientific culture from the Netherlands differed greatly from the words introduced under the influence of the religious culture from Portugal and Spain. Words on foreign culture introduced during this period were trade terms related to the early scientific culture and were mostly in Dutch(1609~1859), which also became the starting point of the cultural network in the Northeast Asian sea regional areas during the Edo Period. In the case of Japan, the influx of Western culture began with its encounter with the Netherlands. The Netherlands had a significant impact on modern Japanese history.

This paper, therefore, focused on the Dutch language and traced back the vestiges of the Dutch language in the Japanese language during this era. The following words are some of the Dutch-originated words which were introduced and became a part of the Japanese language.

2) Background of the Introduction of Dutch Culture to Japan

The Dutch-originated loan words referred to in this study were retrieved from the list compiled by Umegaki and Ishiwata and compiled by this researcher by web search and bibliographical data. The list of Dutch-originated loan words includes vocabulary from various fields.

> Country names, military, machine and engineering, others, physics, objects, boats and sea-related, medicinal herbs, cooking and food, clothes, medicine, chemical and pharmacy, units, etc.

Among the words in the list, this paper examined the Dutch-originated loan words on the Northeast Asian sea region and the sea. "Deck" is used to indicate planks in Korean but is pronounced as "Deki"(デッキ) in Japan. Unlike the English expression "deck", the word deki has been used in Japanese for a long time and is still pronounced in the Dutch way. The original meaning of the word in Dutch is "cover" or "roof", and since the Dutch language has the first-mover advantage, it still is used in ports and or in ships.

"Dok"(ドック) is the word which is used to describe the facilities or installations constructed to dry, fix, dock, and load or unload ships. Its pronunciation is similar to how the word "dock" is pronounced in an English accent but it is a word originated from the Netherlands and concerns boats and the sea.

"Mast"(マスト) could be defined as the perpendicular stick which is erected on the deck of a sailboat to set the sail. While the translated versions of the word are sometimes used, the Dutch word mast is the most often used version.

The flag wishing for a big catch of fish is called "Furaiki"(フライキ Vlag) and in the Hagi region in the Yamaguchi Prefecture, the fish-shaped flags which are attached to boats during the regional festivals are called "Furaiki". The flags are mostly used when ships depart or when a ship catches a great amount of fish.

Finally, the term "Matroos" is a frequently used term when explaining the sea and ships. Matroos(マドロス), which signifies a sailor, usually indicates the captain of a ship larger than ordinary fishing boats or a sailor who works for such captain. People who wear white outfits with navy hats with golden patterns and black lines indicating their positions on the wrists and who have pipes in their mouth are called matroos. This has now become a natural title for some people. In addition, the Edo period, which was represented with Rangaku, was the era of early scientific culture and many Western cultural products, as well as academic terms, were introduced to the Japanese language, which included the following words.

electriciteit(エレキテル), asbest(アスベスト), alkali(アルカリ), alcohol(アルコール), inkt(インキ-インク), ether(エーテル), extract(エキス), ontembaar(お転婆 オンテンバール), gas(ガス), catarre(カタル), kalium(カリ), kalk(カルキ), calcium(カルシウム), gom(ゴム), kurk(コルク), soda(ソーダ), nikkel(ニッケル), pistol(ストル), jodium(ヨード), retort(レトルト)

The early scientific and academic fields introduced and the influx of Western culture during the Edo period could, therefore, be related to the Japanese language. This paper further discusses the words which were introduced during the Edo period and are still used despite the competition from words from English. This paper focuses on the vitality of the Western loan words used in various academic fields, and that of the Dutch language in particular.

3) The Vitality of Dutch-originated Loan Words

Oh Sunhee(2005) discusses the advantages of the early movers in loan words. The early-mover advantage, a concept first popular in economics, was used to analyze the usage of loan words.

A number of Dutch-originated loan words which have first been introduced during the Edo period and are still used could fall into this category. When in competition with English and Japanese, quite a high percentage of the Dutch words which were introduced into the language in the Edo period could gain the upper hand because they were the first words to be used among the various alternative words. The words which have been introduced during this period and are still in use are explained in more detail below.

This paper first discusses the words "Glas"(ガラス) and "Kop"(コップ), which are two words from Dutch that are still being frequently used in the present.

(1) Glas(ガラス) and Glass(グラス)

Glas(ガラス) was introduced during the Edo period and was acknowledged as a part of the general language by the Meiji period and still occupies an important semantic domain in the Japanese language. Glass(グラス), which had been more frequently used during the Meiji and Taisho era, nearly threatened to take over the semantic domain of Glas(ガラス) but was not adopted and instead was used to indicate Western glasses, mirrors and glasses and it took some time for it to have a different meaning from Glas(ガラス). At the end of the Showa era, Glass(グラス) was finally used to indicate glass-made products among Western style glasses, which are called Kop(コップ) and could be found in 〈Image 2〉. Its use was expanded as a general term and thus the dual structure of Glas(ガラス) and Glass(グラス) was formed. The difference which aroused in the process of these two words, each from Dutch and English, being incorporated into the Japanese language was likely because of the point in time each word was introduced.

By the time Glass(グラス) was introduced, during the Meiji period, Glas(ガラス) was already popular in use. Even if one would like to replace the Dutch Glas(ガラス) with the English word, the English alternative lacked the power to replace it. Another reason the Dutch word prevailed may be because Glas(ガラス) and Glass(グラス) have similar pronunciations. Thus, there was no urgent need to replace the Dutch word with the English word.

(2) Kop(コップ, a cup without a handle) and Cup(カップ, a cup with a handle)

Another example of a Dutch word which was not replaced with an English word would be Kop(コップ), detailed in 〈Image 3〉. While there had been a number of Dutch-originated words in the Meiji period, a number of such words have been replaced by their English equivalents.

This was the case with Kop(コップ) and Cup(カップ). The reason why the word Kop(コップ), which was introduced during the Edo period along with the influx of foreign culture, still remains in Japanese to this day because the Dutch-origi-

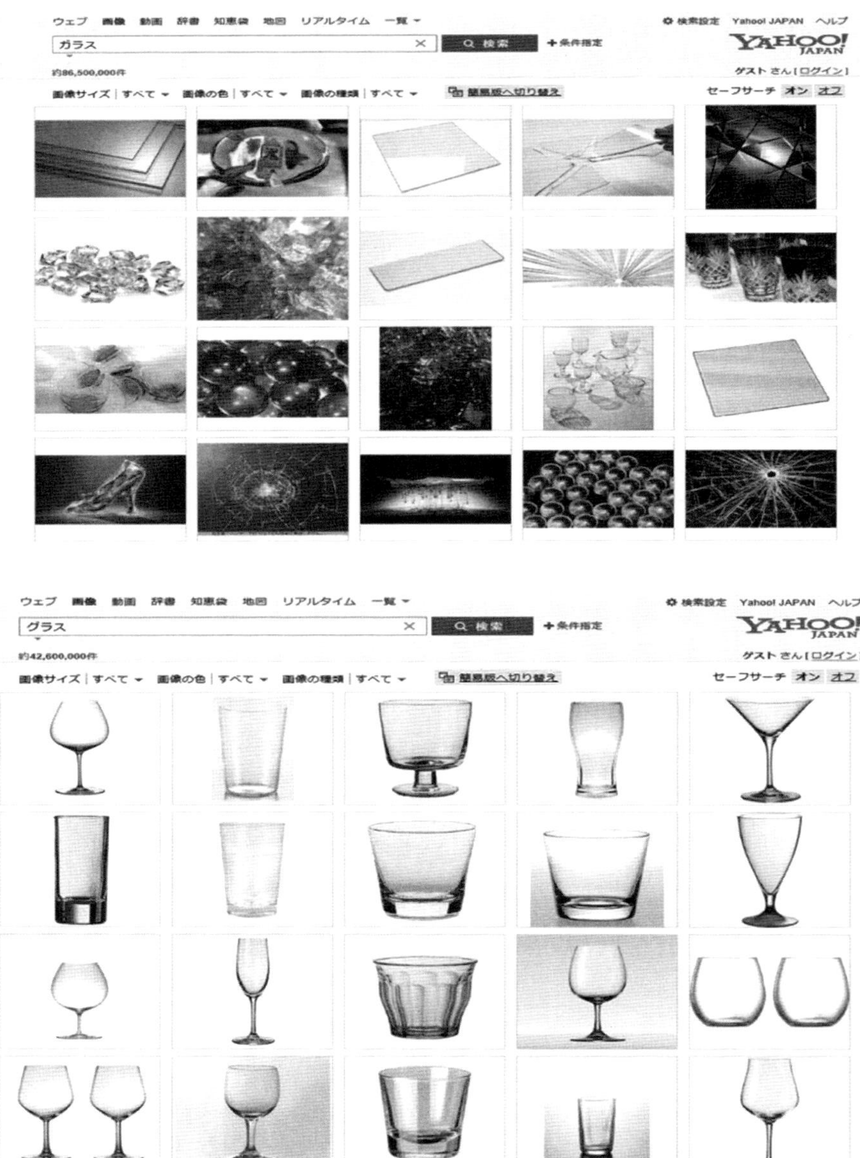

〈Image 2〉 The Difference Between Glas and Glass(Yahoo Japan Image Search)

nated word has been in the language for a longer time and did not easily give its meaning away to the English word Cup(カップ). These two words continued to be in fierce competition which caused a semantic differentiation between the two words. As of now, a cup with a handle is called a Cup(カップ) and a cup without it a Kop(コップ). George Lakoff's prototype theory may be used to explain the different semantic categories of Kop(コップ) and Cup(カップ).

The scholar Lakoff presented the "idealized cognitive model" and the "radical category". Both theories concern the existing general understanding of categories of "all categories objectively having common characteristics". Such characteristics become the necessary and sufficient condition for an attribute to be a part of a certain category. This theory criticizes and rejects the idea that all entities in a certain category take the same position. A majority of categories human beings use every day are not only defined by their objective characteristics but is reorganized around an entity representing the biggest category. Lakoff thus posited that the prototype and other entities are not equal within a certain category.

Lakoff used birds as examples to explain his theory. There is a prototype of "typical birds" including sparrows and larks which are at the center of this category, whereas penguins or ostriches exist in the category as peripheral entities. Lakoff's categorization and prototype theories suggest that not only objective characteristics of "birds" or "species of birds" but also the subjective characteristics human use to understand and categorize such birds also exist in categories(categorization).

〈Image 3〉 The Difference Between Cup and Kop (Yahoo Japan Image Search)

This theory could be used to analyze the process of how the Dutch-originated loan words were accepted and set their roots in the Japanese language. This theory could be applied to explain the division of the semantic domains between kop and cup. A kop is a round cup without any handles while a cup indicates a glass or ceramic cup with a handle. There is a strong prototype which is accepted by everyone and in the peripheries are the various entities of kops and cups, as shown in 〈Image 3〉. Since the Dutch-originated word kop existed as a prototype loan word, the English word cup was not able to trespass its domain.

In the end, the two words were established by maintaining the domains in which they could best keep their identities. The fact that the Dutch-originated words could survive without disappearing to the present day suggests that the words have functioned as prototypes and were established at an early state.

(3) Koffi and Café

While koffi became a staple during the Meiji period, café was not a generally used term which was a synonym to koffi but only used by the high collar class during the Taisho period. However, as cafés gained popularity at the end of the Meiji period, the meaning of this word changed from being a koffi store to an izakaya and thus creating a new semantic domain. This case is similar to the example of glas and glass and could be an example of a newly adopted loan word attaining a new semantic domain, in terms of synonyms. It is also important to consider that it took some time for both glass and café to be established in each of their semantic domain, which may be related to the introduction of a new language and the difference in the phonetic environment with each of the word's pair. Glass, which was phonetically similar to glas, was unable to be established until the Showa period. Café, on the other hand, benefited from its popularity and phonetically differed from koffi, which made it easier to form a separate semantic domain and helped the expression settle at a swift pace.

4. Conclusion

The analysis of the introduction of Western loan words to the Northeast Asian sea region conducted in this paper could be summarized as follows.

Japan's trade with Portugal and Spain ended as the Tokugawa shogunate banned Christianity during the Edo period. Japan thus closed its doors but a limited amount of trade continued only with the Netherlands among Western countries. The advanced Western culture during the Edo period came only from the Netherlands, as a result, and the foreign cultural words imported during this period were trade-related terms concerning the early scientific culture and word related to the sea. The cultural network in the Northeast Asian Sea began in the Edo period with the Dutch language.

Japan's interaction with Western culture began again since the Muromachi period to this day and after overcoming a series of obstacles through the process, Japan has been able to be open towards foreign countries in all fields with relatively little resistance. It was thus able to absorb and accept many loan words and has been using them ever since.

Glas and kop, in particular, are Dutch words which competed with the English words glass and cup but succeeded in maintaining each of their own semantic domains by using the first-mover's advantage.

Dutch, which was introduced to Japan during the Edo period, exists in various fields including science, technology, and culture, but its influence is noticeable in sea-related terms. Words such as dek, dok, mast, vlag, and matroos, are found intact in the Japanese language but some of the words are hidden in dialects used in the sea regional areas as a part of the sea region language(浜言葉). This could not be studied by simply looking at the flow of the language. Only when this topic is researched rationally and persistently under the grand research theme of the Northeast sea region area and the cultural network could this issue could be accurately understood and rationally resolved.

A closer look on the loan words which were introduced with the foreign culture, accompanied by on-site interviews and fieldwork, would make it possible to suggest how the new cultural contacts in the Northeast Asian sea regions took place and were changed within each society. Based on such observations, researchers may be able to identify the introductory mechanism of new culture and civilizations via the sea regions in Northeast Asia. Although the topic of this study was limited to a certain area(Japan) and a specific language(Dutch) in terms of the introduction of foreign culture through the sea region in

Northeast Asia, this researcher plans to conduct follow-up studies which will analyze the Northeast Asian sea regions in detail.

Part 3

Hybridity of Sea Area Culture

Minkyung Choi_

A Review of the Concept of 'Diaspora Space' and Busan

Focusing on the Beginning of a Movement

Sehyun Cho_

From the Chinese Concession Area(淸國租界地) to Choryang(草梁) Chinatown

History of Overseas Chinese in Busan

Mihee Kong_

A Consideration of the Characteristics and Historical Background of Japanese Fusion Cuisine Created Through Cross-cultural Exchanges with the West in Port Cities

A Review of the Concept of 'Diaspora Space' and Busan

Focusing on the Beginning of a Movement

Minkyung Choi

1. Introduction

Busan, which has developed greatly during the formation of Japanese colonial city, became the center of population migration, especially between the Korean Peninsula and Japan with the connection of railways crossing the entire country and the cross-channel liner between Busan and Shimonoseki. The migration of population between the Korean peninsula and Japan through Busan became active as Japan rapidly commissioned its vessels in order to transport necessary human and material resources for colonialization. In the early days of colonial rule, the movement of 'colonizers' from Japan to the Korean peninsula was actively carried out, while as the colonial rule progressed, the number of people moving from the Korean peninsula to Japan increased. In particular, such tendency became clear in the 1920s as farmers from collapsed rural areas moved to Japan to make money. In the late 1930s, the number of Koreans crossing into Japan in the form of forced labor increased.

This study examines the significance of diaspora space, Busan, which was at the center of population migration between the Korean peninsula and Japan. Diaspora space refers to "a place where economic, political, cultural, and psychological processes converge, where transit, boundary, and location change intersect".[1] In this space, change occurs in the mutual relationship between a person that moves and a person that does not, and the mutual relationship based on the experience of hybridity forms a space with a new meaning. Then, in what sense is Busan a diaspora space? Busan is a place where Korean diaspora has left their homeland to make life in Japan. Korean diaspora who moved through Busan and its ports is "old comer". In other words, before the 1980s, those who had already settled in Japan before the normalization of diplomatic relations between Korea and Japan were those who had a status of 'special permanent residence.' Most of them left the port of Busan to Japan between 1920s～1930s in search for jobs, or in the form of forced labor, while others went to Japan in the form of 'stowaway' through ships. Busan was a place where facilitative transportation began, but is was also a place where migration was difficult and a place where migration was stopped and had to hope for a

1 Brah, Avtar, *Cartographies of Diaspora*, New York : Routledge, 1996, p.208.

promising future. Through such process, Busan became a place for Korean diaspora to question the meaning of the movement between the Korean peninsula and Japan and the relationship between Joseon and Japan as well as its peoples. And thus Busan was born into a new place based on interrelationships.

Based on the aforementioned problems, this study examines the meaning of Busan as a diaspora space in respect to Korean diaspora. This study is organized as follows. Chapter 2 reviews previous researches related to diaspora space, critically reviews the concept, and seeks methods to implement its application to Busan. Chapters 3 and 4 analyze the significance of Busan as a diaspora space by dividing it into pre and post-war periods, respectively. In chapter 3, migration to Japan through Busan port is examined in detail and what the Korean diaspora experienced in Busan before moving to Japan is studied. Chapter 4 seeks to discuss the various aspects of 'illegal entry' or 'stowaway' to Japan from the port of Busan after the WW II. Lastly, chapter 5 will summarize the discussion of the main topic and reveal the limitations and implications of this study.

2. Literature Review

One of the most actively rediscovered concepts in the 'age of migration' is 'diaspora.' Originally rooted in the history of Jewish separatism, this concept is used in connection with international migration of various backgrounds and forms in the process of globalization, which R. Brubaker calls "the 'diaspora' diaspora".[2] However, as the denotation of a concept grows, the implications are blurred. In other words, the proliferation of the concept of diaspora rather makes it difficult to answer to question 'what, who is diaspora?' Recently, it has been argued that diaspora should be understood as a point of view and attitude rather than as an entity or specific group. Diaspora is an orientation and the possibility of overcoming "methodological nationalism" which is thinking that the nation-state is a natural unit and prevalent in social science research.[3] However, in the case of research that establishes diaspora as an attitude, study, and orientation, it tends to form an abstract discourse with "text analysis or narrative becomes mainstream, and the structural and material background is ignored", and is limited to remaining at an "intellectual consciousness".[4] Then how can these limitations be overcome? In this regard, Sangbong Lee suggests that "there is a need to specifically verify the various experiences of di-

2 Brubaker, Rogers, "The 'Diaspora' Diaspora", *Ethnic and Racial Studies* 28-1, 2005, pp.1~19.

3 Wimmer, Andreas · Nina Glick Schiller, "Methodological Nationalism, the Social Sciences, and the Study of Migration : An Essay in Historical Epistemology", *International Migration Review* 37-3, 2003, p.576.

4 Ong, Aihwa, *Flexible Citizenship : The Culture Logics of Transnationality*, Durham : Duke University Press, 1999, pp.12~13.

aspora in historical and geographical contexts by associating them with culture", and specific places must be noted.[5] In previous diaspora research, regardless of whether diaspora is recognized as the entity or as a research point of view, attitude, or orientation, the two nation-states, the homeland and host nation, has been heavily shrouded. However, by focusing on specific places, in other words, diaspora space, limitations can be overcome and new possibilities for diaspora research can be explored.

The diaspora space is a concept proposed by A. Brah, which refers to "a point at which the boundaries of inclusion and exclusion, of belonging and otherness, of 'us' and 'them' are contested".[6] This concept is characterized by the fact that not only the moving but also the non-moving are included in the field of view, and can be said to be "the place where the plurality of subjects is juxtaposed, contested, and recognized or denied".[7] In the diaspora space, the identity of 'us' is recognized in the relationship between the moving and non-moving, and the distinction of 'them' is made. This movement is constantly reproduced and transformed by the convergence of economic, political, cultural, and psychological factors.

Renowned studies applying the concept of diaspora space include the work of Julia Jiwon Shin and Sangbong Lee.[8] Julian Jiwon Shin identified Leicester

5 Lee, Sangbong, "Diaspora and Locality Studies : A New Way of Looking at the Korean Residents in Japan", *Journal of Korean-Japanese National Studies* 18, 2010, pp.118~119.

6 Brah, Avtar, *Op. cit.*, p.242.

7 *Ibid.*, p.208.

8 Shin, Julia Jiwon, 2017, "A Multicultural City's Diversity Management and 'Diaspora Space' : A Case Study of Leicester in Britain", *Journal of DIASPORA Studies* 11-1, pp.53~92; Lee,

of UK as a diaspora space and Sangbong Lee identified Osaka(大阪) and Ikuno (生野) as a diaspora space, and based on a review of the interrelationships between those who have moved to the area and the indigenous people, the value and limitations of diaspora space have been examined. Leicester city has become a multicultural city in the UK that realizes the value of diversity and integration. An interesting fact is that racism was strong in the past. Julia Jiwon Shin focused on the economic, political, and social positions and class changes of those who have moved to Leicester, and revealed how the change in interrelationships between such people and the indigenous led to the formation of diaspora space. The Ikuno district of Osaka city was an area for Korean residents, and was researched by Sangbong Lee by reviewing the process of transforming the area from a space symbolizing discrimination and exclusion into a diaspora space after the 1990s through the identity of the Korean residents and the change of the relationship with the Japanese residents.

Such existing studies have focused on a diaspora space, which is beyond abstract discourse, and evaluated diaspora in relation to their interrelationships, economic, political, cultural and psychological backgrounds, including both those who move and those who do not. However, one factor that must be taken into account is that these studies set diaspora spaces as a place of arrival and settlement. In other words, existing research using the concept of diaspora space examines the interrelationships between indigenous people and those

---

Sangbong, "Locality of Korean Town in Ikuno, Osaka as a Diasporic Space", *Journal of Korean-Japanese National Studies* 22, 2012, pp.99～133.

who have moved from their home country while examining factors of their identity transformation.

However, the aforementioned studies have a limitation to "the question of where migration originated remains silent".[9] In particular, C. Alexander criticizes that the direction of this existing study is related to the North-South problems, focusing only on the 'rich' cities where migrants arrive in the northern and western hemispheres. In other words, there is little interest in the place where movement begins, given that fact that international migration is active in the southern hemisphere and that the majority of the population around the world does not move, such research is short-sighted. Alexander points out that it is necessary to question and analyze the diaspora situation of not only the place of arrival but the place of departure, and how mobility and non-mobility are connected.[10]

In this study, based on the critical review of these existing studies, the concept of diaspora space is newly explored. The definition of Brah will be implemented, but will also consider that the diaspora space includes not only the place of arrival and settlement but also the place where movement begins. Additionally, this study will examine Busan as a diaspora space by specifically implementing the aforementioned notion. Although Koreans who had crossed over to Japan during the Japanese occupancy, for a variety of reasons,

9 Alexander, Claire, "Beyond the 'The "Diaspora" Diaspora' : A Response to Rogers Brubaker", *Ethnic and Racial Studies* 40-9, 2017, p.1548.

10 *Ibid.*, pp.1547~1549.

were expected to stay temporarily, the return to the Korean peninsula was delayed due to chaos of the Northeast Asia after the defeat of Japan. As a result, they settled in Japan and became Korean diaspora. After the defeat of Japan, before the normalization of diplomatic relations between Korea and Japan in 1965, the movement from the Korean peninsula to Japan was conducted as the form of 'stowaway', and the people who crossed to Japan settled down to form a part of the Korean diaspora. Busan is a meaningful place where the movement of the Korean diaspora that settled in Japan started, and is an example that can complement the limitations of the preceding studies that have been critically reviewed.

3. The Formation of Korean Diaspora and Busan

1) Korean Migration to Japan Through Busan

Busan port was developed and established as a gateway to continental advancement for Japan, thus the movement of population from Japan to the Korean peninsula was very active. However, as colonization progressed, migration from the Korean peninsula to Japan gradually increased. The main reason for the increase in migration from the Korean peninsula to Japan was the downfall of farming areas. Through the land survey project and increasing rice production policy, most Joseon farm lands were turned over to Japanese landlords and a large number of farmers were reduced to peasants. Furthermore, as the detainment of landowners worsened, more and more Joseon peasants abandoned farming and wandered in search of new means of livelihood, among others one of them was moving to Japan. Meanwhile, in Japan, many workers were needed as the construction of various social overhead capital was actively built in the midst of the expansion of power as an empire and the boom of WWI. In other words, the migration from the Korean peninsula to Japan has been active since late 1910 due to the combination of the downfall of farm lands, which is a push factor in Joseon, and the lack of labor force, which is a pull factor in Japan.

Nearly half of the Koreans who went to Japan during this period were from Gyeongsangnam-do, followed by Gyeonsangbuk-do and Jeollanam-do; farmers had to pass through Busan to go to Japan. The fact that most of the movement from the Korean peninsula to Japan were through Busan can be found in a fragmentary indication through the *Annals of Higher Police*(高等警察報) issued by the Japanese government general of Korea in 1934. In August 1933, 76.2%, 12%, and 8.9% Koreans migrated to Japan used ports in Busan, Jeju, and Yeosu, respectively, showing Busan port to be significantly higher for migration. Sukyung Park explained that in the 1920s, Busan had low settlement and high mobility. One of the main reasons for this was that the number of members per was low household, indicating that there were many short-term migrants staying to go to Japan.[11] Of course, the fact that fewer members per household does not directly support mobility, but what should not be overlooked is that some of the short-term migrants who entered Busan with the intention of moving to Japan had temporary residence which can be identified by statistical analysis.

Then, how can this temporary settlement be understood? If the farmers who moved to Busan from Gyeonsangnam-do, Gyeongsangbuk-do, and Jeollanam-do went to Japan through the Busan port seamlessly, they would not have shown up in statistics. The fact that they were identified by statistics indicates that they were not able to move to Japan seamlessly and they were forced to stay in Busan, most notably in Busan port, for more than a certain period of time, largely because of the foreign voyage regulation system. The labor shortage in Japan led to the rise of Japanese companies recruiting and arranging workers in Joseon. As the number of workers that were migrated to Japan surged due to reckless recruitment, the Japanese government general of Korea promulgated and enforced the 'regulation on recruitment of workers(労働者募集取締規則).' The main purpose of this rule was to have a licensed Japanese company get permission, and to let workers who go to Japan to report their identity at the residence police station and to the police station at the origin.

In 1919, regulations on foreign voyage to Japan were strengthened by the March 1st movement. Concerned about the spread of the independence

11 Park, Sukyung, "A Study of Mobility in Colonial City, Busan", *The Japanese Language and Literature Association of Daehan* 55, 2012, p.398.

movement, Japan took full control of the influx of Koreans, and the system introduced for this purpose is the so-called travel certification system. The travel certification system was a measure for Koreans who wanted to move out of Joseon, including Japan, to receive travel certificates that included travel purposes and reasons from their residence police station and submit them to the police station of departure port, and had do the same after returning home. This system caused complaints from many Koreans and was abolished soon after the March 1st independence movement because it did not conform to the policy direction of the Japanese government general of Korea, who was in charge of cultural rule. However, in September 1923, after the Great Kanto earthquake, Koreans, specifically workers among them, were more strictly controlled than when the existing travel certificate system was implemented. Among Koreans, only those who had previous experience working in Japan, had considerable travel expenses, and had a definite place to work were able to receive a certificate of travel from the police station and go to Japan.

The problem was that these regulations were not implemented consistently, but were arbitrarily carried out under the cooperation of the Home Ministry and the Japanese government general of Korea. After the introduction and abolishment of the travel certificate system in 1919 and 1922, respectively, traffic regulations were enacted without an official system. Migration to Japan was banned for months immediately after the Great Kanto earthquake, and after the ban was lifted in December 1923, a copy of family register issued from the resident police was requested from June 1924. A while after, conditions for limiting travel, for instance, Japanese proficiency, travel expenses, and etc. were added arbitrarily. In 1928, the family register and letter of introduction issued by the local police station should be reviewed by the Busan Maritime Police. Such frequent fluctuations caused significant confusion to the Korean people who wanted to migrate to Japan, and Busan was the place where confusion and chaos was compressively shown. The collapse of the rural economy, which began in the 1910s, overlapped with various natural disasters, prompted farmers to become laborers. However, there was not enough industrial base in Joseon to absorb the increased number of workers, and as a result, the number of Korean who wanted to go to Japan increased despite the tightening of regulations. The important fact is that more people in Busan tried to migrate to Japan than the actual number of people who actually went to Japan, and their presence began to be recognized as a social problem in Busan. Busan, specifically the Busan port was an "open road to Japan, at the same time, a road that is blocked".[12] In May of 1924, nearly 10,000~20,000 workers were inundated in Busan, waiting to go to Japan, and the situation deteriorates further. The economic situation worsened as most could not find a job during a period trying to figure out a way to migrate to Japan, which lasted a few days to several months. And the experience in Busan port during such situation could be said to be the experience in the last place of stay in the home country, the experience of departure for diaspora.

12 *Ibid.*, p.401.

2) Busan as a space of frustration and identity recognition

The Great Kanto earthquake has led to a strict control of the voyage to Japan, but since the provision of the travel certificate has been abolished and an official system has not been established, expectations for crossing over were raised and was highly expressed in Busan. As mentioned earlier, Busan and Busan port were contradictory spaces that were opened and closed to Japan, and were a place of chaos "where workers could not stay or leave and went through great hardship",(*Dong-A Ilbo*, 1925.10.22) and "where it felt like war"(*Sidae Ilbo*, 1926.3.7). Also, among others, one that deepened this chaos was the travel agency that was made up of government service groups. The reason Koreans who wanted to go to Japan were in Busan was not just because the port of entry was controlled, but because of the expectation that there was a way to overcome the control. In the case of Korean residents who did not receive certificate of travel from their residence police station, in other words, a copy of the family register and a letter of introduction, they were able to go to Japan by receiving a certificate of travel from the Busan maritime police. As a result, Busan was a place of both frustration and expectation for crossing over to Japan.

However, in order to obtain a certificate from the Busan maritime police, they had to go through travel agencies such as Sangaehoe(相愛會) and Busan labor union. They demanded entry, travel, job placement fees and bibes to bet a certificate of travel from Busan Maritime Police, therefore Korean laborers were greatly damaged. Such "collaborators" adjoining created more chaos in Busan(*Sidae Ilbo*,

1926.3.19). On May 22, 1924, Dong-A Ilbo reported on the situation of Korean workers at the time.

> [Travel agency][13] After a bribe of some money or goods to the executives, the worker is barely able to cross over with minute expenses, which creates the dilemma of wanting to go or staying along with alienation thus making the entirety of such choice difficult (……) Sustaining life with such little wage and deciding to stay or crossing over is nearly impossible as it is the scheme of a parasitic being (……).

Receiving the travel certificate at the Busan maritime police was the only hope for the Korean laborers who had left their hometowns. However, as the aforementioned article describes it as "parasitic", the travel agency received money in all kinds of pretexts, and rarely succeeded in actual travel to Japan.

As a result, the time spent in Busan to get a travel certificate was extended, and if money was all spent and returning home was not an option, many got involved with day labor and crimes. The most common crime was fraud, targeting those with high hopes of stowing away, the following is a stowaway fraud article regarding an inn keeper.

> The 30-won travel expenses was taken in advance by the inn keeper, Byeong-ok

13 In the quotation of this study, '[ ]' is added by the author to help understanding.

> Kwon, telling me I will be able to stowaway soon but kept delaying, and keeping me in a room on the second floor for seventeen days as if I was in prison. (*Dong-A Ilbo*, 1930.3.2)

In the midst of such situation, Korean workers in Busan became a social problem in the mid-1930s. Those who could not go to Japan and could not return home remained in Busan, causing problems regarding the poor. The following article in Dong-A Ilbo, dated September 12, 1938, depicts a Korean worker who failed to cross over to Japan and lived in Busan.

> The huts and houses at the foot of the mountain in Busan express how miserable the low-class families. This causes the viewer to sigh (⋯⋯) all of these low-class families came to Busan seeking passage, and now are forced to huddle at the foot of the mountain not being able to stay nor leave (⋯⋯).

As such, Busan was a space that ultimately brought frustration to Koreans wishing to move to Japan. The expectations of getting a travel certificate at the Busan maritime police became "false hope", even the means and methods of coping with such situation was lost as the economic and psychological difficulties were already challenging. Sukyung Park expresses the situation of Busan port as "the field of bare life".[14] According to G. Agambem, "bare life"

14 Park, Sukyung, *Op. cit.*, p.404.

is contradictory in that it is included in the community by being excluded by sovereign power, allowing them to die by ignorance, thereby maintaining the order of life in society. [15] Sukyung Park claims that the Koreans, who are thwarted by crossing over to Japan and left in Busan eventually becoming poor are the "bare lives".[16] The Busan maritime police determined that moving to Japan could be done arbitrarily, and in most cases, moving to Japan failed, and in the process people were reduced to being unemployed and poor, abandoned by the power, specifically by Busan and Gyeongsamnam-do, leading to social "death". Busan was a place where these "bare lives" accumulated.

Furthermore, Busan, which was the "the field of bare life", was a space of diaspora, once again giving recognition to Korean diaspora to their own identity, in other words, carving in the meaning of living as a Korean laborer. This can be explained through two major dimensions, the first being the ethnic identity felt as a Korean, and second being a hierarchical identity felt as a low-class worker. In the former case, it was engraved in comparison with the Japanese who freely migrated via the Busan-Shimonoseki liner without travel certifications, and in the latter case, it was engraved in comparison with Korean students and merchants who could easily obtain a certificate of travel. From this regard, the port of Busan for Korean diaspora was a space where economic, political, cultural and psychological elements converge, recognizing the identity of "us" and make ethnic and hierarchical distinctions of "them", thus was a diaspora space.

15 Agamben, Giorgio, trans. Park Jinwoo, *Homo Sacer*, Seoul : Saemulgyul, 2008, pp.45~52.
16 Park, Sukyung, *Op. cit.*, pp.408~412.

4. Stowaway and Korean Diaspora, and Busan

1) Stowing Away to Japan

At the time of Japanese defeat in 1945, the number of Koreans living in Japan reached nearly 2 million as a result of population migration from Joseon to Japan in the 1920s and 1930s. Additionally, the collapse of the Japanese empire promoted a new form of migration; the return to their homeland. Koreans who lived in Japan as colonized, especially those who were 'coerced' to move to Japan to work in the form of forced labor after the 1930s, gathered at the port of Kyushu(九州) to return to the Korean peninsula immediately after the Japanese defeat. They returned to the Korean peninsula by 'conversely' using a salvage ship that had been set up to bring the Japanese residing in Joseon back to Japan. The number reached about 1.3 million by March 1946. Then what was the condition like for the remaining 700,000 Koreans living in Japan? In most cases, they expressed their intention to return home through registration of returnee conducted by the General Headquarter(GHQ), which had occupied and ruled Japan. However, the number of Koreans returning home was greatly reduced by measures that limited the assets that could be taken out of Japan. As mentioned earlier, most of the people who hurried to return after the defeat of Japan were those who were forced to go to Japan to work. On the other hand, those who remained in Japan even after March 1946 were people who moved to Japan in the 1920s and were able to lay a foundation of living. In their cases, their return was delayed due to the necessity of organizing their property, but when the measure of limiting the amount of assets when leaving Japan was implemented, they once again 'put off' going home and stayed in Japan. This is how the prototype of Korean diaspora living is Japan is made.

However, the movement of Koreans due to the collapse of the Japanese empire was mainly directed toward the Korean peninsula from Japan, there was also a reverse trend, namely a movement from the Korean peninsula to Japan. 'Stowaway' is a point where "the life of an individual and a nation collide and antagonize, making it possible to clearly witness and prospectively look back".[17] In the late 1940s, most of the people who became the subject of 'stowaway' from the Korean peninsula to Japan were Koreans who had lived in Japan in the past. Soon after the defeat of Japan, those who returned to their homeland were 're-migrating to Japan' and chose to 'stowaway' in order to escape from economic difficulties as the situation on the Korean peninsula was unstable. In other words, 'stowing away' existed due to "life- an opportunity of choice that darkened and permeated outward beyond the state territory, neglecting moral values at the national level".[18]

The important fact is that the movement of the Koreans from the Korean peninsula to Japan was 'created' in the form of 'stowaways.' After the defeat of Japan, the legal status of Koreans living in Japan was unclear until the San

---

17 Kim, Yerim, "Affect of Hyunhaetan: The Nation as the Structure of 'Sadness' and Stowing Away", *Journal of Sokdang Academic Research of Traditional Culture* 49, 2011, p.313.

18 *Ibid.*, p.311.

Francisco Peace Treaty was signed in 1952. In other words, it was a situation that "Japan could not decide which nation Koreans should belong to".[19] GHQ and the Japanese government arbitrarily established them as foreigners (= Koreans) or Japanese, depending on the situation. Therefore, dealing with Koreans who have returned to their homeland and re-migrated to Japan was always at a state of flux and could not conclude the situation as being a 'stowaway'. However, the occurrence of cholera in the southern region of the Korean peninsula in May 1946 became a decisive moment, changing the situation and 're-migration to Japan' became the same as 'stowing away'. As a result of the cholera outbreak, the GHQ and the Japanese government banned the re-entry of 'non-Japanese' who had returned to their homeland to Japan, and the 're-migration to Japan' of Koreans became 'illegal' in an instant.

In 1946, the GHQ sent a letter to the Japanese government entitled 'Restraining illegal entry to Japan' on the grounds of cholera in the southern region of the Korean peninsula. This memorandum required the Japanese government to take effective measures to find vessels illegally entering Japanese ports and if such were found, it had to be escorted to the US military stationed in Sasebo including the crew, passengers, and cargo. According to the GHQ memorandum, the Japanese local government actively started the seizure and repatriation of stowaways. More specifically, since the late 1946, intensive control

19 Park, Sarah, "Identify Koreans: On the definition of 'Koreans' and 'illegal entry' during occupational period", Heoktae Kwon·Jungeun Lee·Kyunghee Choi, *Frontiers of Sovereignty : Korean Border-Crossing and Deportation Camps in Post-Empire Japan*, Seoul : Hanul Academy, 2017, p.79.

of 'stowaways' was carried out in cooperation with civilians, including the occupying forces, police, and fishery associations in the neighboring areas of the Korean peninsula including Nagasaki(長崎), Kumamoto(熊本), Saga(佐賀), Shimane(島根), and Tottori(鳥取). As a result, about 19,000 Koreans were arrested for 'illegal entry' in 1946, and the number significantly reduced in 1947 due to the enforcement action. However, the number increased again, and in 1949, 8,302 stowaways were arrested. In addition, it is anticipated that there was considerable amount of cases where stowaways were not discovered and 'non-regular routes'[20] from the Korean peninsula to Japan in the late 1940s were more actively operated than those shown in statistics.

It was the political and economic instability as well as the macroeconomic background that led to the stimulation of 'stowing away'. However, the micro factor that enabled 'stowing away' was the presence of the Korean diaspora living in Japan.[21] Normally, one among many factors that triggers and facilitates international migration is the existence of human network, particularly families, relatives, and acquaintances in the host country for early-stage support. Furthermore, using an 'illegal' method such as 'stowing away' requires a network of family and friends to secure safety upon arrival. Consequently, in the late 1940s, the movement through 'non-regular routes' from the Korean peninsula to Japan was promoted by those who have 'delayed' returning to Korea,

20 Tonomura, Masaru, trans. Yuwon Shin · Induck Kim, *A Historical Study of Korean Society in Japan : Formation, Structure, Transformation*, Seoul : Nonhyung, 2010, p.394.

21 *Ibid.*, pp.394~396.

the Korean diaspora, more specifically, family members, relatives, and acquaintances residing in Japan.

2) Busan as a Wandering and 'Boarder Crossing' Space

Busan was the center of 'illegal' migration to Japan from the Korean peninsula in the late 1940s, consisting of the aforementioned methods and forms. According to Sarah Park, the center of 'stowing away' to Japan by Koreans during this period was the southeastern region of the Korean peninsula and the northern region of Tsushima and Kyushu, centering on the Genkai sea. This, of course, is natural considering geographical proximity, but simultaneously, it is a result of social grounds. In particular, after the defeat of Japan, Busan was one of the first lands of the homeland that Koreans, who lived under the Japanese empire's sphere of influence including Japan, set foot on. However, some Koreans who returned to the Korean peninsula through Busan port failed to decide on their next destination due to the lack of news from their families and thus stayed in Busan.

> The people who flocked away in search of a way to live are now liberated, and are returning home through the port of Busan (……) As the population in Busan is rapidly increasing, the port of Busan is in chaos amid various social problems including housing shortages, food shortages, food prices, illegal trade with Japan, public security, disease, unemployment, and etc. all of which must be solved

urgently (*Joseon Ilbo*, 1946.2.11)

As previously seen, Busan experienced a phenomena of population buildup and consequent chaos during the Korean diaspora formation in the 1920s and 1930s. This situation was reproduced very similarly in the late 1940s, and the difference was that it was caused, unlike in the past, by the collapse of personal life not by state control such as regulations regarding the migration to Japan. In this regard, an article titled "Social Realities Reflected on the Busan Employment Agency" was published on July 9, 1949, and according to this article, most of the unemployed were "compatriots of war" and only 1 in 20 could find jobs through the employment agency while only 1 in 100 could find jobs when encompassing Busan as a whole. As such, Busan was a place where those who returned had to face unemployment, poverty, and wandering not a welcoming homeland.

Of course, such wandering does not go neglected but exists as an object that must be overcome, and one among others was going back to Japan. In order to overcome the situation of unemployment and poverty, the movement across the Genkai sea increased, despite the situation in Japan which was hardly satisfactory objectively as the Japanese economy had been devastated through their defeat. However, the experience of getting jobs and having an income in Japan in the past, and the presence of family members, relatives, and acquaintances residing was enough to convince them to move. In second half of 1946, however, GHQ and the Japanese government began to strictly control the entry of "non-Japanese" to Japan due to the vague legal status of Korean living in Japan, and migrations from the Korean peninsula to Japan became "illegal" for most cases. It may be called the birth of 'stowaway', but the important fact is that 'stowing away' is a movement that has enabled the only influx of new population into the Korean community residing in Japan, since the defeat of Japan to the normalization of diplomatic relations between Korean and Japan. In other words, after the collapse of the Japanese empire, the Korean diaspora, which was formed by the Koreans residing in Japan, was established as a social group through the influx of people from the Korean peninsula via 'stowaway' in the late 1940s.

Then, what meaning could Busan have for those who became Korean diaspora through 'stowing away?' In order to answer this question, it is necessary to look at how society viewed 'stowing away' at that time. Originally, 'stowing away' meant an 'unavoidable choice' for those who have returned home but had economic hardship. Therefore as the following news article suggests, stowaways were also a subject of sympathy.

> Even if you cover your eyes from them, the cries of your people crossing the waves of the dark sea will be heard by your ears, no matter if you close your eyes, the pale faces of those who have been estranged by this land and chose to stowaway will come to mind. (*Seoul News*, 1946.8.20)

However, with the division of the Korean peninsula entrenched and political situation unstable, the public opinion on 'stowaways' changes drastically.

> Stowing away! Why has this predicate that which came from the tyranny of Japanese resurrected on this liberated land, when it must be gone forever. Why must our people once again go through the thorny path of stowing away when we all should gather the capabilities of the entire nation and march forward in constructing a democratic nation that is fully independent.(*Seoul News*, 1948.6.23)

As mentioned above, in 1948, 'stowaway' began to contain negative nuances like leaving the nation and national task behind, and after the outbreak of the Korean war, it was regarded as an act of having a "dream of self-absorbed complacency and vanity, turning away from the reality of war". (*Seoul News*, 1952.9.11).

In the midst of such shift in social perspective on 'stowaways', Busan, the center of which, has become a space with a meaning that crosses the boundaries of national borders. During this period, 'stowing away' was a "'danger' chosen by those whose possibility of life was damaged by the empire and by the nation".[22] After the collapse of the empire, the formation of the nation-state was violent, ignoring the various aspects of an individual life, and the method against such violence was bound to be 'illegal.' 'Stowaway' was an act to overcoming the border building of a violent nation, and Busan was the place where

22 Kim, Yerim, *Op. cit.*, p.314.

this border of violence and dynamic of crossing such boundaries was most evident. In other words, Busan existed as a place for Koreans who were trying to 'stowaway' —including Korean diaspora- to feel, act, and overcome the boundary of Joseon and Japan; the border of Korea and Japan must be rejected for the survival and life of an individual. From this respect, it can be said that Busan has be reborn as a diaspora space thorough the 'movement' of different forms and meanings to the Korean diaspora in the 1920s and 1930s. Specifically, it was a space beyond the boundaries of recognizing how the borders between "us" and "them" diverged from personal life in the amalgamation of economic, political, cultural, and psychological factors.

5. Conclusion

In this study, the meaning of "diaspora space" was applied to Busan, which was the center of Korean diaspora's movement to Japan. Busan is now known as the starting point of the movement to Japan for Korean diaspora commonly called 'old comers.' In the 1920s, farmers who had become laborers from the collapse of rural areas began to move to Japan, and by 1930s, many Koreans crossed the Genkai sea from Busan in the form of forced labor. In the postwar period, mainly in the late 1940s, the move to Japan was carried out in the form of 'stowaway' in Busan.

From such movement, Busan is now meaningful as a 'diaspora space' where various elements such as politics, economy, society, and culture converge and identified by those who do not move, those who move, and the boundaries between nations are dismantled and reorganized. Considering that the movement by coerced recruitment in the 1930s was completely an involuntary movement, the meaning of 'diaspora space' in Busan in the 1920s and the late 1940s is as follows. First, Busan in the 1920s, as an open and closed contradictory space for those moving to the Japanese empire, once again confirmed the meaning of living as a Korean laborer. Particularly, the meaning of the travel certification, essential for crossing the Genkai sea, was elucidated in Busan. This system gave the realization of ethnic and hierarchical identity to Korean laborers in contrast to Japanese, and merchants and students, respectively. Moreover, in the late 1940s, Busan was a space where the Korean people who returned to their homeland, with the collapse of the empire, attempted to cross the border by 'stowing away', an 'illegal' manner during times of extreme confusion and frustration. As the boundaries of the nation-state were being reset violently, irrespective of the life of individuals, 'stowing away' was created, and Busan as the center of stowing away became a diaspora space, where the boundaries of Joseon and Japan, and the boundaries Korea and Japan competed and overcame their conflict.

The discussions made in this study are intended to reflect on the concept of diaspora space through Busan and examine its potential. Diaspora space is a concept that gives concreteness to the tendency of research; allows for the understanding of diaspora as a point of view, away from methodological nationalism, and examining the boundaries between 'us' and 'them' focusing on experience in a specific place. However, most previous researches regarding the concept of diaspora space only pays attention to the end of movement, in other words, to the place of settlement, and is thus limited. Nonetheless, it is clear that the boundaries of 'us' and 'them' are confirmed, reconstruction, and destroyed at the beginning of the movement as well as throughout the movement. Busan is a space where the Korean diaspora began their movement, and it is meaningful as an example for understanding the limitations and reviewing the concept of previous researches related to such diaspora space. Of course, this study deals only with Busan at a particular time, thus comparative analysis of domestic and international studies is necessary for a more comprehensive review of the concept of diaspora space. Specifically, it is necessary to accumulate a review of the diaspora space where diaspora movements in the Northeast Asia including Incheon, Yokohama(横浜) and Kobe(神戸), Guangzhou(广州), and Xiamen(廈門) began.

From the Chinese Concession Area(淸國租界地) to Choryang(草梁) Chinatown

History of Overseas Chinese in Busan

Sehyun Cho

1. Introduction

There is a saying, "There are overseas Chinese in any place touching sea-water". There are many ongoing studies on overseas Chinese' cultural and/or economic network all over the world. This is true even in Korea, the "exceptional country without a Chinese town". Korean scholars only started their research on expatriate Chinese in Korea in the beginning of this century. Before that, there are some reports written by Japanese during the Japanese occupation or by the Taiwanese government on expatriate Chinese in Korea. Even though the expatriate Chinese have not resided in Korea as long as those in Southeast Asian countries or in the USA or Japan, the Chinese in Incheon or Seoul have lived there long enough to form and maintain a small

Chinatown due to those cities' proximity to Shandong Province of China. The overseas Chinese in Korea formed their own community since the 19th century when China was strongly invaded by powerful western countries and therefore their sense of nationalism grew, not only the strong perception of China as their own country but also the strong identity of themselves as Chinese. The Qing Empire opened its port for foreign trade and protected and promoted Qing merchants. Also, it established Chinese settlements at open ports in Incheon, Busan and Wonsan. Therefore, the difference about the expatriate Chinese in Korea is that they settled down relatively easily with their government's support, unlike other expatriate Chinese.

The Choryang alley at Busan's Chinatown was the pathway to Waekwan(倭館) in the late Chosun period, where the Chinese Concession Area was established during the period of opening ports and was called Sinamajji(支那町) during the Japanese colonial period. Named as the post-liberation Cheonggwan street, it once became the Texas street of the US Army. Here, Cheonggwan street was a corresponding name to the Japanese Waekwan street that was near Yongdu Mountain. Such Choryang Chinatown maintained its geographical position without change, however, but the origins of the overseas Chinese as the owners of Cheonggwan street changed with the times. Furthermore, the transformation process of the US Army's Texas street after liberation, foreign shopping street of the Russians, Shanghai street, and the recent Choryang Chinatown that transformed into a multicultural space is an interesting example of history.

2. The Chinese Settlement and Qing merchants in Busan during its opening of the Port of Busan

First of all, we must take a brief look at the history of the initial settlement of Chinese in Busan in this section. Busan embarked on its full development as a port city in the 1880s. During this decade in particular, not only Busan but also Incheon and Wonsan, opened their ports and these two newly emerged cities took away Busan's exclusive position in foreign trade. On the other hand, the Qing empire became involved in foreign trade, adding one more major trade partner to the scene.

1) Setting up the Chinese settlement in the area of Busan

(1) The signing of *The China-Korea Treaty of 1882*(朝淸商民水陸貿易章程) and Qing merchants' entry to Korea

After the Imo Incident in Joseon in July, 1882, the admiral Wu Changqing (吳長慶) from Qing dynasty arrived at the gulf of Namyangju(Masanpo) leading 3 warships, 2 merchant ships from China Merchants Steam Navigation Company and approximately 3 thousand troops all the way from the regiment in Shandong province(Dengzhou) to repress the revolt. He dispatched 40 Qing merchants along with Qing military at that time. These merchants were expected to trade with the Qing soldiers but they ended up dealing with Koreans too, as the Qing force was stationing longer than expected, and thus they are known as the very first Chinese merchants in Korea.

It is clear in *The China - Korea Treaty of 1882* signed on the 4th of October of 1882 that those merchants during the era of port opening were protected and promoted by the Qing dynasty. After concluding this treaty, some fundamental changes started occurring not only in traces between the Joseon dynasty and Qing dynasty but also in many other aspects. As is well known, this treaty was composed of 8 articles, and established in its first article that the Joseon dynasty was a subordinate state of the Qing dynasty, and on this basis, the Qing would set up its settlements, open Seoul for trades, dispatch committee members to help Qing merchants and protect them with extraterritoriality. Therefore, it had every element of an unequal treaty. This was one of the most unfortunate incidents in modern history of relations between China and Korea, since China at that time was suffering itself from unequal treaties with western powers and had forced the same suffering upon its closet friendly nation. This treaty opened the door to Korea for Qing merchants more widely than ever before.

(2) The incident of the Deokheungho(德興號)

It is interesting how the so-called incident of the Deokheungho has much to do with the initiative to build up Chinese settlements in Korea, starting from Incheon in particular. The incident occurred in Busan in October 1883, right after the Qing consul Chen Shoutang(陳壽棠) started his term. It is interesting especially because the Deokheungho is known to be the beginning of the expatriate Chinese history in Korea. From related sources, such as a memoir written by Qin Yuguang(秦裕光), a Chinese living in Korea at the time, we know the full story of what happened to the Deokheungho.

In November 1883, a Qing merchant from Kobe, Huang Yaodong(黃曜東), tried to send two of his employees, the brothers Zheng Yizhi(鄭翼之) and Zheng Weisheng(鄭渭生), to Busan to open a shop in the Japanese Concession there. They entered the port of Busan on a Japanese boat in Kobe, and they wanted to rent a house owned by a Japanese, Danaka Heitaro(田中平太郎), and through a connection with a British, to open a shop called "Deokheungho". However, they got into a conflict with the Japanese while they were preparing for the shop opening, because the place they wanted to open their shop — now called Jungangdong — was a Japanese settlement in Busan. The Japanese consul interrogated the Zheng brothers, and insisted that Busan, being a Japanese base, was off limits to Chinese traders. The consul insisted that they leave the settlement but they refused to leave. Other Japanese started to impede the opening of the Deokheungho, which complicated the situation. On the other side, the Qing merchants of Deokheungho wanted Chen Shoutang to intervene and solve the problem, and thus it became a diplomatic problem between China and Japan.

The remarkable fact about this occurrence was that the Qing merchant Huang Yaodong was actually not from the Qing Dynasty but from Kobe in Japan and ran a shop called Gongheungho(公興號) there. The Gongheungho was a company with a capital of more than 10,000 yuan — calculated in 1888 standard — in Kobe, Japan. This implies the probability that the majority of Qing merchants that arrived first in Korea might have come from Japan. It is probable that the Qing merchants residing in places like Nagasaki, Yokohama, and Kobe in Japan might have wanted to come to Busan along with Japanese merchants who came here in the early period.

③ Forming the Chinese Concession Area

The Qing dynasty decided to build a Qing Consulate in May of 1884, in the area now called Choryang, and in July of the same year, Chen Weikun(陳爲焜), a member of the Standing Committee in Busan, discussed a settlement section with the Supervisor of Dongrae. When an agreement was reached, boundary stones were laid and residents lived with autonomy under the supervision of the Qing consul. However, contrary to what the Qing expected, the government of Joseon continued to reject the construction of Qing settlements in Busan and Wonsan during the term of Chen Shoudang. Afterward, Yuan Shikai(袁世凱) took over that role in Korea and succeeded in forcing Busan to accept the settlement in 1887. Yuan Shikai was much more willing to support and protect Qing merchants. This means that, although the Chinese settlement in Busan was officially authorized in 1887, the stone post indicating the boundary of the settlement was installed in 1884. In the same year, attempts to bring sewage and a police force to the place assigned for the settlement were initiated, and therefore it is reasonable to believe that the establishment of a Chinese settlement in Busan actually began in 1884.

At that time, the area nearby current Yongdusan Park in Jung-gu in Busan was Choryang Waekwan — the biggest Japanese settlment to house the Japanese diplomatic mission and traders in Korea. The Qing Consulate in Choryang, Donggu, was built after that, so consequently, it was named 'Cheongkwan(清館)', and the street where it was located became Cheongkwan street.

2) Activities of Qing merchants in Busan

(1) Before the Sino-Japanese War

Beginning in May 1884, the Busan Consulate started to register some Chinese. During that year, a Cantonese family of 4 opened up a shoe shop. This was likely the aforementioned Deokheungho. The total number of merchants who moved back and forth was 87, and among them there were 29 Cantonese merchants, and thus, the majority, taking up about one third. The next year, in 1885, the registration documents list 17 Qing merchants in total, among them were 5 Cantonese, 3 Jiangxinese, 4 from Jiangsu, 4 Fujianese, and 1 from Shandong. Moreover, there was a fair amount of merchants who came to Busan for their commercial activities from Hunchun through Incheon and Wonsan.

Statistics show that there were 90 traders based in Busan, among whom 39% were Cantonese, 28% were from Zhejiang, and 21% from Shandong. The other merchants were from Hebei, Tianjin, Jilin, and Jiangxi, etc. Those merchants who moved back and forth from China to Busan travelled through seaports at Hunchun, Wonsan, Busan, Nagasaki, and Incheon. In particular, many traders from Hunchun migrated to Busan. That is to say, most of the early Qing merchants who came to Busan did not stay long term to pursue their commercial activities, since they were only stopping by on their way to Hunchun or Shanghai in China, Seoul(Hanseong at that time) or Wonsan in Korea, or other cities in Japan. This is why in Busan there were only 15 residing Qing merchants, among whom 3 were workers at the maritime customs, 2 were British consulate, and several were merchants from Deokheung shoe store. The other Qing merchants were transitory. In short, Busan, just like Wonsan, was a stopover place for merchants travelling with itineraries including Hunchun, Busan, Incheon, and Shanghai.

(2) After the Sino-Japanese War

After the Sino-Japanese War, the diplomatic relations between Joseon and Qing were severed for about 5 years, and thus, the Qing settlements in Busan, Wonsan, and Incheon were stalled. The Qing promoted Tang Shaoyi(唐紹儀) to take Yuan Shikai's place as the Qing diplomat in Busan. However the Great Korean Empire which was newly established on October 12, 1897, did not officially recognize him as a diplomat.

It was not until September 11, 1899, when these two countries created in *The Korea-China Trade Treaty*(韓淸通商條約) consisting of 15 articles after a year of negotiations, that the diplomatic relations of the two countries normalized. The China - Korea Treaty of 1882 had fixed a dominant-subordinate relationship between the two countries but this new treaty established an equal relationship between them. Both countries recognized the extraterritoriality of the other, and rights for each other's people to stay at each seaport for the same amount of time, making the treaty as equal as possible.

After the foundation of the Qing Consulate in 1899, the Qing merchants started selling their products at stores set up in their residences, on both sides on the Qing Consulate street. Most of their products were convenience goods such as silk, cloth, mirrors, thread, towels, and cosmetics, etc. Their customers were not only people from Busan but also women from Kimhae, Yangsan, Ulsan, Milyang looking for goods for their marriage. As their sales went well, more shops opened. The Qing Consulate in Busan also covered the issues related to Qing people(淸人) in Masan, whose port was opened in 1899. Perhaps this means that the Qing who migrated to Masan were from Busan, since Masan is quite far from Chinese coasts and close to Busan, and the appearance of Qing merchants in Masan was merely a reflection of the prosperity of the business of the Qing merchants in Busan.

In the end, the Qing settlement in Busan, which was a hub for area Qing merchants, was shut down and transferred to the local administration of the Governor-General of Korea. Although the Qing settlement in Busan was abolished and therefore its privileges were revoked, the Qing properties were recognized, which allowed the Qing communities and their residences to remain. Despite political turmoil, Qing shops in Qing Consulate street were full of goods such as silk, cloth, mirrors, and shoes, etc. These goods were from China, in particular from Shanghai, and they were not only for retail but also for wholesale to local merchants. The Japanese there would call that street "Sinamajji" meaning Chinese street.

3. The Sinamajji(支那町) and Overseas Chinese in Busan in colonial time

Next, we will take a look at the history of the Qing in Busan in colonial time in this chapter. During the Japanese colonial period, due to the lack of labor, many Qing workers from Shandong came over to Busan as well as other places in Joseon, making the majority of the next generation of Qing people in Busan from Shandong.

The Qing people in Busan up until 1920 seemed to work as part of a trade route in East Asia. However, though Busan was relatively close to Japan and yet Japan restricted the Qing people business, during the colonial period, Qing society in Busan could not expand as it did in Incheon, Seoul or North Korea.

1) The everyday life of Overseas Chinese in Busan under Japanese occupation

(1) Census on demography and profession

'Three knives(三把刀)' is a well known expression in China. The three knives are: the kitchen knife, scissors and the shaving knife. These knives are for cooking, tailoring and haircutting, respectively. Overseas Chinese usually take up one of these three skills to make a living. The majority of the Qing in Korea were also involved in cooking, textile shops and barbershops. Over time, more restaurants than textile shops or barbershops opened, and eventually, Chinese restaurants were common across the country.

According to research done by the Japanese Governor-General of Korea in late 1923, the following are the major professions held by the Qing in Busan at that time. From 333 Qing people — 310 men and 22 women — 19 families owned textile shops, 23 families owned restaurants, 11 families owned dumpling(Chinese pancake) shops, and 15 families worked on a farm. We can see that, as in other cities, the textile shops and restaurants were the majority of commercial activities of the Qing in Busan. Since there is no mention of Qing workers among the statistics, the workers who moved seasonally must have been excluded. From these records, it is also difficult to know about Qing-run barbershops in Busan at that time. So, of the three knives, the cooking knife and the tailoring knife were in wider use, as is reflected in a record written in 1912. The *Busan booklet*(釜山要覽) shows that the 30 Qing shops in Busan were mostly textile shops and restaurants. Therefore, the textile industry and restaurant industry were still the Qing people main businesses in Busan. Going forward, we will take a look at how the Qing in Busan were led their lives by looking at first the Qing merchants who worked at textile shops and restaurants and secondly Qing workers and finally Qing farmers.

(2) Qing merchants 1(textile shops)

Among the Qing-run textile shops in Busan, Seotaeho(owned by Du Shuxin杜樹新), Deokchwihwa(owned by Ding Shoushan丁壽山), and Dongsoonheung (owned by Zhao Xiumei趙修美) were the most representative. In particular, it appears that Du Shuxin of Seotaeho was the most prosperous, since he was paying the most business and housing taxes. However, it is uncertain whether he was from Canton or Shandong. If Du was actually Cantonese, that would mean that the Qing people from southern China who had been in Busan during the open port era had remained there.

Exports and imports to and from China were still ongoing using the network between Korea. China and Japan. The imported goods were mostly textiles, convenience goods and some farm products, and most likely Qing merchants traded these goods with other Qing merchants in China, Seoul or Incheon. Most customers of textiles were Korean and most customers of convenience goods and groceries were Japanese. Most of the goods that Qing merchants exported were seafood, such as sea cucumber. Koreans of that period did not consume sea cucumber so the Qing merchants bought them at low cost and sold them to Chinese restaurants. The Qing people in Busan in the 1920s mostly lived in the Choryang-dong and Joongang-dong areas, and most of them did not own houses, but instead lived in Japanese-owned housing.

(3) Qing merchants 2(restaurant)

The Qing people in Sinamajji in Busan, or Cheongkwan(淸館) street, were mostly from Shandong or Hebei and they came due to connections with their fellow citizens. They stayed not only in the Qing Consulate street, but also spread into places like Changseondong, Bupyungdong, Dongkwangdong, and Youngdo to open up Chinese restaurants. In 1923, all over Busan, 23 Chinese families were running both high class and regular Chinese restaurants. The high class establishments were places like Inhwaroo(仁和樓) in Seojeong(西町), Youngkiho(永記號), Dongseungroo(東昇樓), Joonghwawon(中華園) in Choryang(草梁), and Euiseongkwan(義盛館) in Nokjeong(綠町). According to the standard value of tax imposition, Inhwaroo and Youngkiho each paid 3,000 won, Dongseungroo paid 2,500 won, and Joonghwawon and Euiseongkwan each paid 1,800, so it stands to reason that Inhwaroo and Youngkiho were the largest establishments. Initially they had mainly Chinese and Korean customers but over time, their Japanese customer base grew.

Regular restaurants were taxed at a rate of 1,000 to 1,500 won. Since Chinese restaurants were relatively cheap, many of their customers were Chinese and Korean workers. In particular, the 11 existing dumpling or Chinese pancake shops usually paid less than 1,000 won in taxes and their usual customers were both Chinese and Korean. It is said that Qing food in Busan was characterized by its abundance of Shandong-style dumpling shops. Cantonese people must have brought their hometown favourite with them and it must have been well received, since many dumpling places opened up in the Choryang area, similarly to how Jajangmyeon (noodles with black soybean sauce) became popular in Incheon where it was the specialty of the Qing people there, and it grew in popularity in local restaurants.

There is a story about a Chinese restaurant in Busan at that time. Cui Yonghai(崔鏞海), a medical doctor, built the biggest western style building in Busan in the Choryang area and turned it into the Baekjae Hospital(百濟病院). However, the building was difficult to maintain, so the hospital was closed and sold to a Chinese person named Yang Moumin(楊牟民), who turned it into a high-class Chinese restaurant called Bongraekak(蓬萊閣). Bongrekak was the biggest Chinese restaurant and home to many Korean and Chinese kisaeng and held splendid banquets daily. However, since the Sino-Japanese War was now expanding into the Pacific War, the owner husband and wife of Bongraegak were unjustly arrested and detained by the police and they began to be pressured from all directions. Eventually, Bongraegak closed in 1942 and the owner couple went back to China. After that, Japanese officers lodged at the building until liberation.

(4) Qing workers

An analysis of ID cards recorded in the Chinese Residents' Association in Busan shows a sharp influx of Chinese into Busan in the 1920s and 1940s because of the political conflict of the Chinese military government and the economic crisis in the 1920s. Then, in the 1940s, many Chinese from Shandong came to Korea to escape the Civil War in China many of whom migrated all the way down to Busan, changing the Chinese demography in Busan. In 1930s, on the other hand, the Wanpaoshan Incident and the Sino-Japanese War caused most overseas Chinese to return to their country, not due to the situations in China but to those in inner East Asia.

Initially, all the workers in Busan were Korean, but, in late November of 1919, the Korean workers from Busan Mail Shipping Line working with sampans went on strike, demanding a raise in salary, and the company was forced to hire 30 Chinese workers who had been fired from Gabsandongsan(甲山銅山) mine in Northern Hamkyeong Province. These are said to be the first Chinese workers in Busan. The next year, in 1920, the extensive Busan port reclamation work began, and therefore workers with patience and strength were needed for the intense labor of collecting and carrying stones. The civil engineering branch office in charge hired about 50 Chinese people to because the Qing workers were generally reputed to be patient. They judged the Qing workers to be very efficient, and so they continued to hire more. In 1922, when the second Busan Port construction work was undertaken, hundreds of workers from Shandong, China came to Busan, increasing the entire Chinese population in Busan. Some among these Chinese workers died from fatigue and disease, and a Chinese cemetery was created in the southeast part of the reservoir near the current 16th Street of Chorayng.

(5) Qing farmers

Agriculture became an important profession in Qing society in the 1920s. As more Qing moved across the country, some started farming around Seoul, particularly in the Youngdeungpo area and the outskirts of Incheon to provide the Chinese in Korea with farm produce. It is said that the first Chinese vegetables in Korea were planted in Dajoomyeon, Bucheongun of Kyunggi province, from seeds brought into the country in 1887 by two sailors, one surnamed Wang(王), and the other surnamed Jiang(姜) from Shandong. Chinese vegetables are mostly cultivated in the suburbs, and much of the products of these farms are sold commercially to Chinese restaurants in the nearby cities. At first, the produce was only intended for the Chinese but their unique agricultural skills and excellent sales attracted Korean and Japanese customers as well, and thus their farming industry as a whole increased rapidly.

The Chinese farmers in Busan growing vegetables numbered 18 families and 32 people in total in 1923, and all of them were from Shandong. Most of them did not own property, so they lived in the suburb areas and grew vegetables on others' properties mostly that of Japanese or Koreans. Their way of their growing and selling vegetables was no different from Chinese farmers in other areas in the country. However, after the Sino-Japanese War, all the

Chinese farmers returned to their country, and the remaining Chinese had to import their vegetables from inland Japan. Unfortunately, the vegetable farming in Japan was insufficient and the transportation was limited so a supply imbalance occurred in the market. There is a story of how this was overcome.

The chief officer of the Busan Police at that time had served for some time in Sinuiju, so he knew that the Chinese farmers there were highly skilled. He called the Consulate in Sinuiju and requested that some of the Chinese farmers there come and farm in Korea. On June 20 of that year, several Chinese farmers came to Busan and cultivated the land with cabbage on a trial basis. However, their report to the Consulate in Busan was that it would at least ten days longer in Busan than in Sinuiju to grow the cabbages and that there were too many vermin. They tried several more times, with unsuccessful results. The Busan Police Office refused to give up, however, and found an investor to hire the farmers for a monthly payment of 50 won for living expenses, and 50% of any profit from the vegetable sales. This shows the importance of Chinese farmers, especially the vegetable growers in Korea.

2) Overseas Chinese in Busan during riot and war

(1) Wanpaoshan(萬寶山) Incident

In Kyeongnam province, a boycott movement against Chinese residents started gaining strength, first in Busan, and then spreading to Ulsan and Masan. Around 9pm on July 8 of the same year, a riot broke out in which two people were severely injured and property losses of approximately 14,791 won to 300,000 won were sustained. The Consulate in Busan took about 160 Chinese under their protection, and contacted the Masan Police Office to urge them to protect local Chinese residents. However, Kyungnam Province and Busan had less conflict with their Chinese residents since there were relatively fewer Chinese workers there than in other major cities in the country. Consequently, the Chinese residents in these areas did not experience as much damage as those in places such as Pyungyang, Wonsan, Sinuiji, Incheon, Seoul, and Jinnampo, but the pressure and hostility towards them forced many of them to go back to their country.

In the 1930s, strengthening nationalism and political pressure compelled many Chinese residing in Busan go back to their country, as it did in other places in Korea, but the Wanpaoshan Incident caused even more to flee. This time, the Chinese had become an enemy of the Japanese, so the relationship between Joseon and China was restricted. The Chinese experienced political oppression, but this only served to strengthen the local community in unity and solidarity. Chinese residents in Busan were no exception.

(2) The Sino-Japanese War

In December 1941, when the Sino-Japanese War was expanding into the Pacific War, the Chinese residents in Busan started supporting Japan as requested by their Consulate in Busan. One example of this support was that the Chinese residents in Busan raised funds for Japan to purchase an airplane on

January 8, 1944, urging their fellow Chinese to support the cause and asking the Consulate to lead the fund raising. In the end, they raised 4,500 won and donated 3,000 won to Japan so they could buy an airplane and donated the other 1,500 won to the government of Wang Jingwei. The fund raising was held nationwide and under the leadership of the regional Consulates. However, the Japanese did not cease their hostility against or interrogation of the Chinese.

The alleged Pyeonghwaroo(平和樓) incident in 1944 near the end of the Pacific War, when the Japanese persecuted the Chinese, was representative of this hostility. If the Pyeonghwaroo incident did indeed occur, it signifies that the Japanese at that time still considered the Chinese their enemy. In recent times, China had gone through many changes of government, such as from Namkyeong National Government, to Pukkyeong Temporary Government, to the government of Wang Jingwei. It was a risk for the overseas Chinese to switch from supporting the government of Chiang Kai-shek to Wang Jingwei and keep changing their position from anti-Japan to pro-Japan.

4. Reconstruction of the Cheongkwan street directly after liberation

As the economy of the overseas Chinese became active, old buildings were brought down and replaced with new ones in the Cheonggwan street of Busan. On the Cheonggwan street, Chinese restaurants stretched to ten places, along with stores for Chinese food materials, Chinese pharmacies and Chinese stationeries expanding throughout the area. The situation was in contrast to the oppressive Japanese colonial period. However, such renaissance was only temporary with the majority of overseas Chinese in Busan acquiring their nationality from the Republic of China through the consulate of the Nationalist government, blocking the passageway towards trade with China. Furthermore, the mainland People's Republic of China was hit hard with its hostile relations with Korea where anti-communism was promoted. A significant number of Chinese fled to Korea for a while to avoid the vortex during the Chinese Civil War, however, never returned due to severance of diplomatic relations between the two countries. Among the retrospections of overseas Chinese in Busan, it is noteworthy that the majority of the current overseas Chinese are those who have entered the border in-between 1945 and 1947 and never went back due to the Korean War.

Among the interview data of overseas Chinese in Busan published in Kim Taeman and Ahn Mijung's research, ten cases were classified depending on whether the settlement process either of the interviewees themselves or their ancestors in Korea was traceable. Most of them originated from the Shandong area. Seven were cases whose grandparents and parents had already settled in Korea during the Japanese colonial period, and three were whose parents settled in Korea during the Chinese Civil War period. Although most Chinese had ties with Korea overall since the Japanese colonial period, unconfined to Busan in specific, it was confirmed that there were considerable number of Chinese who came over to Korea during the Chinese Civil War period. For example, Mr.L recalled that "my relatives came over and settled down between 1945 and 1947 in the midst of the Chinese Civil War", while Mr.Y remembers that he came over to Korea as "his army unit boss asked to go to Korea", or due to his "dislike towards the Communist Party".

Moreover, sorting the process of settlement in Busan of oneself or their parents, only one case was recorded to have resided in Busan since the Japanese Colonial period, whereas nine settled down in Busan due to the Korean War, which indicates that their settlement was arranged after seeking refuge during the Korean War. Mr.X recalled, for example, that he "came down to Busan after escaping from the army unit where he used to interpret captives during the Korean war". Mr.C retrospect that his parents "evacuated to Jeju Island during the Korean war, and came back to Busan to live in Choryangdong" where he was born. Ms. K recalled that her husband just settled "after the Korean War broke out soon after he arrived at the hot spring to meet his brother".

In general, overseas Chinese in Busan are mostly those who migrated and settled down in Busan to avoid the chaos of the post-liberation Chinese Civil War and the Korean War, rather than people who steadily resided in the city since the Japanese Colonial period. This indicates that new migrants were filling in the Cheonggwan street in place of the small number of overseas Chinese who lived in Busan during the colonial period. In particular, the Korean War was an incident large enough to make fundamental change in the ethnic structure of overseas Chinese in Busan.

5. Korean war and overseas Chinese refugees

1) Overseas Chinese in Busan during the War

During the war, the population in Busan exploded with overseas Chinese refugees coming in from all over the country. Although the exact number is not known, a rough estimate is possible with the overseas Chinese population remaining by region for the years of 1948 and 1952. Prior to the war in 1948, Busan had an overseas Chinese population of 593, while according to the statistics, 4,182 overseas Chinese resided in Busan in October 1952. As a simple figure, approximately 3,600 overseas Chinese refugees came to Busan, a little less than ten times of its original population. There were many overseas Chinese refugees also in Daegu. The overseas Chinese population recorded

600 in 1948, which increased to 1,300 by 1952, though falling short of the population in Busan.

During the war, Busan operated a wartime autonomy system to take measures against overseas Chinese refugees. During the wartime situation, the Korean government recognized the overseas Chinese autonomous district as a type of self-governing government, thereby enabling autonomous adjustment of internal conflicts and disputes. In overseas Chinese autonomous district, some overseas Chinese legally owned and managed guns. The most famous place within the autonomous district was originally the Baekje Hospital site as mentioned in the above retrospection, which was formerly a Chinese restaurant called Bongraegak. The place was used as the Embassy of the Republic of China during the war, which was once a symbol where the overseas Chinese around the Cheongkwan street area were concentrated.

2) Construction of the refugee camp

In the winter of 1950, when the Communist Chinese army crossed the Han River once again, the overseas Chinese of Seoul and Incheon fled further south and gathered in Busan. A total of 500 all lived inside an old Busan Consulate. Rooms were made with wooden planks or thick paper with a very poor environment. Ambassador Wang Dongyuan(王同原) decided to arrange and establish an overseas Chinese middle school on the back garden of the former consulate at the end of 1952. For this reason, refugees at the former consulate were migrated to a separate village that was newly formed. A cemetery owned by the overseas Chinese firms existed behind the Choryang Cheongkwan street in Yeongjudong, which was unable to be used as a cemetery due to regulations of the Busan city. Here, the Korean refugees have been increasing day by day and have already occupied approximately half of the cemetery. With the help of Busan City, the Chinese Embassy decided to build a new village on the 1,300 pyeong area of the cemetery in order to settle overseas Chinese refugees. Under the support of the Korean government and the temporary public office of the Embassy of the Republic of China, the new village began construction from July 1952 and completed in October. It was named as Chunghyo-chon(忠孝村), where over 1,000 overseas Chinese refugee households were migrated.

After the war in addition to Chunghyo-chon, the overseas Chinese Relief Committee again rented 1,500 pyeong of land owned by Koreans of Geojeri in the form of 50-year long-term lease for overseas Chinese refugees residing in the Hwangnyeongsan Mountain area, and established a group residence of overseas Chinese called Inae-chon(仁愛村). This new village is known as being built for those arriving in Busan, by overseas Chinese who migrated from Wonsan to Geoje Island. Approximately 150 refugees in Geoje Island during that time faced a livelihood crisis after losing support that they were living on for several years from the Korean society and the overseas Chinese Relief Committee. As Inaechon was a mountainous area with uneven ground, flattening work was done with support from the Korean troops and help from many overseas Chinese in Busan. It was built in December 1955 and completed in May 1956, which was a large-scale construction project since Chunghyo-chon.

Moreover, an overseas Chinese village called Shinui-chon(信義村) was also formed around areas of Seo-myeon that was owned by overseas Chinese. Likewise, there were a total of three group residence of overseas Chinese refugees in Busan. Population of Cheonggwan street did not surge as the overseas Chinese Relief Committee dispersed overseas Chinese refugees, nevertheless, the Cheonggwan street emerged as the center of overseas Chinese across the country during the war.

6. Formation of Texas village and the rise and fall of Cheonggwan street

1) From Cheonggwan street to Texas street

Jang Sehoon 's work well-describes Cheonggwan street in the 1950s. To summarize, Busan during this period of time was a place where smuggling was rampant centrally around the Gukje Market. With connection to Chinese capital, the economic activities of overseas Chinese were more active compared to other cities. However, the Cheongkwan street in Choryang did not become the economic center of overseas Chinese capital. This is because all the customs where goods were brought in through ships for customs clearance were located in Jungangdong, thus all the then large trade firms nested specifically in Jungangdong. Foreign foods that came in through such process was handed over to the overseas Chinese wholesale dealers of Bupyeong Market, located near the Gukje Market. Indeed, the Choryang Chinatown also had some trade firms and general stores, along with dozens of entering Chinese restaurants. However, the majority of these stores were merely small shops for overseas Chinese, and all of the large Chinese restaurants were located in downtown Jungangdong. Busan's largest Chinese restaurants of the times were Dongabanjum and Hwagokbanjum, which were located in Donggwangdong and Jungangdong. This is mainly due to the fact that Cheongkwan street was neither the center of economy nor was it sufficiently equipped with urban infrastructure such as parking lots and roads. The wealthy class among overseas Chinese not only made their economic activities outside the Cheongkwan street, but also moved their residential area as well. Nevertheless, overseas Chinese always gathered at Cheongkwan street in the evening, for various information exchange and networking that was all made in Choryang. Diverse business information were exchanged at Choryang Chinatown, which was a basis for carrying out external economic activities. As the Cheongkwan street was frequented by overseas Chinese as if it was their living area, nearby residents mistook most overseas Chinese as actual residents of Cheonggwan street.

It was the Jungangdong area around Busan Station back alley where the UN

Forces centered on US Army, who took part in the Korean War, enjoyed their nightlife. Here, red-light districts for the US Army sprang up and people called the area as the Texas village. The Cheonggwan street emerged as a newly-rising hub as the train station moved to the opposite side of Choryangdong towards the Cheongkwan street, after the disappearance of the Busan Station in Jungangdong on November 27, 1953 with a disastrous fire. The name Cheongkwan street was forgotten and started to be called as the 'Texas street', as entertainment establishments and stores for the US Army began to enter the area with economic vitality revived with influx of American dollars. Although it is unknown who named it as Texas, but perhaps it was because "the US Army often reminded people of scenes from western action movies with guns". As the surrounding shopping streets were turned into entertainment establishments, lights were brightened up and American popular music prevailed. Around the time of the Vietnam War in the 1970s, there were a total of 19 entertainment establishments and 450 female employees. Aspects of a slum were somewhat found with clubs and bars for foreigners banning entrance of the underaged and locals, still, the entertainment district flourished with influx of foreign currency.

The Cheongkwan street gained mutual growth with the Texas village with its commonality as a foreigner street. The economy shrank significantly with the US President Nixon announcing the Guam Doctrine, and withdrawal of the US Forces in Korea. Still yet, foreign exclusive stores selling goods to foreigners began to enter the area with increase in international trade through

Port Busan and frequent in and outs of foreign crewman and soldiers of the US warships with increase in the number of foreign warships entering Busan. With its commonality as a foreigner street, the Texas village added strength to the economic vitality of nearby Chinatown. In the 1970s, changes in the domestic and international situation brought about a downturn in Chinatown streets and foreigner shopping areas. The voice of criticism insisting the relocation of the entertainment establishments located in front of the Busan Station increased, pointing out the fact that it was a shame as the station was the gateway into the city.

2) Overseas Chinese discrimination policy and remigration

The Korean government's discrimination policy against the overseas Chinese since the 1960s is notoriously well-known. Constraints and discrimination in the Korean society led to remigration of overseas Chinese. The number of overseas Chinese in Busan reached its peak in the early 1970s, but its population suddenly began to shrink when they felt there was no chance of success in Korea. In particular, the decline of Texas village in Busan and the generation conflict among overseas Chinese were main factors that affected their leaving from the Cheongkwan street, such as immigration. Generational conflicts among overseas Chinese surfaced within the Busan local community in the 1970s. Conflicts over the overseas Chinese Association president election also caused a crack in the overseas Chinese community. In addition, most businesses were going down with lower level of foreign crewman visits and with decreasing number of US Army stationed in Busan, who were the main customers of the Texas village. As a result, the Texas village as a foreign bar street disappeared with the restriction on access of locals lifted during the late 1980s. In the process, vacant houses in the Choryang Cheonggwan street increased, and the Texas village rapidly became a slum.

In the mid-1970s, a large number of overseas Chinese including overseas Chinese in Busan moved to Longhua(龍華) in Taiwan, where they lived as peddlers in group residence. With the establishment of the People's Republic of China, the only country that overseas Chinese traders could rely on was the Republic of China, Taiwan. This was due to the fact that Taiwan was not only in alliance relations with Korea, but also since overseas Chinese in Korea held a Taiwanese nationality.

Since the 1960s, the Korean government imposed strong regulations against the economic activities of overseas Chinese. The 'Foreign Immigration Control Act', the 'Foreign Land Ownership Restriction Act', and the 'Ban on White Rice Sales' were typical examples. In particular, the one house one store per household policy imposed on the overseas Chinese was fatal. Alike other overseas Chinese, overseas Chinese in Busan were subject to strict legal control, and resultingly, the number of overseas migrants increased since the 1970s. Due to the Korean government's discrimination policy against overseas Chinese, the barrier built between Koreans and overseas Chinese did not disappeared for a long time.

7. Conclusion

After the Imo Incident, the Joseon and Qing Empires signed *The China - Korea Treaty of 1882* and the Chinese began to reside in Busan. In the early 1880s, it appears that the Chinese residents in port cities in Japan settled in Busan along with Japanese migrants. However, since Busan was already dominated by Japanese merchants, there were not as many Chinese merchants in Busan as in Incheon, and most of them were individuals without family.

The Deokheungho incident in the end of 1883 has various symbolic meanings in the history of Chinese residents in Busan. This incident had a direct impact on the decision to make a Chinese settlement in Busan and unlike the Japanese Waekwan, the center of Qing community can generally be traced back. Before the Sino-Japanese War, the Qing Dynasty stopped Japanese merchants from coming to Korea by controlling the maritime customs and opening more maritime routes. This also occurred in Busan. However, after the Sino-Japanese War, the Qing merchants in Busan and other places in Korea no longer needed the same level of support and protection from their country to actively to continue their international commerce.

How was the life of Chinese residents in Busan during the of Japanese occupation? At that time, the Japanese called the Qing settlement in Choryang "Sinamajji" because of the many resident "Sina" people. In this presentation, I described the life led by the Chinese residing in Busan during the Japanese occupation by first looking at the lives of Qing merchants who worked in the textile and restaurant industries, and then at Qing workers and Qing farmers. After that, I discussed the circumstances at that time, in particular, the Wanpaoshan Incident and the Sino-Japanese War.

During the Japanese occupation, the labor force in Korea was not big enough, so a new generation of Chinese workers came from Shandong, forming a majority among Chinese in Busan. During the Japanese occupation, unlike in North Korea, Incheon or Kyungseong(Seoul at that time) where the Chinese population grew continuously, the number of Chinese in Busan did not increase much. In the 1930s, due to the strengthening of nationalism and political pressure in China, the total number of Chinese in Korea fell when many went back to their country. In particular, the Wanpaoshan Incident and Sino-Japanese War forced the overseas Chinese to return to China, after which, only a minority of Chinese residents in Busan remained in Choryangdong and Joongangdong waiting for the liberation.

Liberation gave joy and hope not only to Koreans but also to Chinese-Koreans. Soon after, Chinese-Koreans faced major changes due to the division of Korea and the Chinese civil war. The number of Chinese ethnic groups in Busan increased as other cities did due to those who have escaped the civil war in China. The Korean war can be considered to be the most influential event for Chinese-Koreans who resided in Busan. The number of Chinese ethnic groups increased at an unprecedented rate due to the refugees flocking to Busan. As the capacity of the Chengkwan street reached its limit, three

Chinatowns were built during the war. 3 years after the war, Busan had the largest number of Chinese-Koreans nationwide and a surprising number of people stayed.

After the war, Chengkwan street, which was somewhat a fractious space, was brought about a great change when the so called Texas-town moved to Chengkwan street after the Busan station in Joongangdong was destroyed by a fire in 1953. Although there was a slum-like appearance within the city, it thrived as it was a district with entertainment flowing with foreign currencies. However, in the 1960s, the Korean government implemented various regulations regarding economic activities of Chinese-Koreans. Chinese-Koreans in Busan, like others, were no exceptions to such regulations and were stagnated for quite some time. However, due to the diplomatic relations between Korea and China, they were revived.

However, such dynamic change of Choryang Chinatown was not always pleasant. Even today, they are treated as Chinese in Korea, as Koreans in Taiwan, and even as Taiwanese in Mainland China, which shows the unfortunate lives of overseas Chinese as the third wheel in a word. The need for us to understand the sad history of the overseas Chinese as a minority, could be a process of self-reflection that must be undertaken in order to aim for a better community as a whole.

A Consideration of the Characteristics and Historical Background of Japanese Fusion Cuisine Created Through Cross-cultural Exchanges with the West in Port Cities

Mihee Kong

1. Introduction

It was during the 17th-century Edo period under the Tokugawa Shogunate that Western cuisine was first introduced in the process of exchange with Westerners in the foreign settlements at Hirado and Dejima in the port city of Nagasaki. Before the Meiji era, in 1862, steamed beef started to be sold at Irifune-cho(横浜入船町), a foreign settlement in Yokohama, a port city. When the demand for beef increased, the first gyu nabe restaurant opened at Shibatsuyutsuki-cho(芝露月町) early in the Meiji Era. In 1869, a Sukiyaki restaurant started a business at Motomachi(元町), Kobe. Prior to the announcement of the Meiji government's lifting of the ban on meat eating(1872), a food culture of consuming beef had already being formed around foreign settlements in port cities.

The Meiji government and intellectuals implemented a policy to spread a meat-eating culture to the common people in the process of carrying out a policy for national prosperity and military power enhancement under the perception that they gained while exchanging with Westerners: The Japanese had a smaller build and weaker physical strength.

As part of the process of spreading a meat-eating culture, the Meiji government promoted the popularization of Western cuisine, absorbing Western food culture and modern civilizations. The imperialist policies aiming at modernization based on the acceptance of Western culture and the enhancement of national prosperity and military power that had been implemented since the Meiji era were further strengthened after the Sino-Japanese War. As beef was supplied to the military for soldiers' meals, there was a shortage of beef in the market. Consequently, pork became popular as a substitute, which brought about a food culture related to pork and the birth of Tonkatsu, another Japanese-Western fusion dish.

The consideration of the meat-eating culture of Japan that seemingly has no relation to its history of invasion leads to the recognition of many aspects of the history of Japan and Korea that the latter should have been vigilant about. The fusion cuisine and meat-eating culture spread all over Japan through military meal service. Therefore, if Koreans had had insight and wisdom to understand the relationship between Japan's military expansion and its imperialist policies and ambition of the invasion of Korea and to proactively respond to it, Korea could have avoided the colonialization by Japan. This kind of insight and wisdom is still needed for Koreans to lead their country in the future. Okada Tetsu(岡田 哲), the author of "The Beginning of the Meiji Era Western Cuisine History: The Birth of Tonkatsu"(明治洋食事始め — とんかつの誕生, 2012), writes that the Meiji government lifted the ban on meat consumption as part of its policy to make its country and military wealthy and strong, thus introducing its praise for beef to promote Western cuisine and the contribution of the common people to the birth of gyu nabe, Sukiyaki, anpan (a sweet roll filled with red bean paste), and Tonkatsu.

Kosuge Keiko(小菅桂子), a Japanese cooking researcher, explains in "Stories about Japanese Western-style Food"(にっぽん洋食物語大全, 1994) how the Japanese introduced Western food and developed it into its own food culture from the invention of various dishes such as Tonkatsu, korokke(a Japanese-style croquette), and kare raisu(curry with rice), to the establishment of table manners. Also, in "The Birth of Kare Raisu"(カレーライスの誕生, 2013), she insists that the introduction of curry and its application to this Japanese-Western fusion dish serves as a historical basis for the acceptance and Japanese-style transformation of Western civilizations in modern Japanese society.

Hashimoto Naoki(橋本直樹) mentions in "What is Japanese Traditional Culture"(日本食の伝統文化とは何か—明日の日本食を語るために, 2013) that the Chinese continent served as a channel for the introduction of foreign food cultures to Japan and that the Japanese established their own culture by accepting advanced cultures through exchanges with China and Korea. In addition, the author discusses the Japanese-Western fusion dishes such as gyu nabe, kare raisu, korokke, and Tonkatsu, which are the results of the Japanese-style transformation of the Western dishes introduced to Japan during the Meiji era.

Cwiertka(2006) focuses on the changes in Japanese cuisine since Japan's opening of its ports in the 19th century and considers how Japan's national cuisine developed. These aspects are illustrated in her discussion of the influx of Western culture, urban cuisine, wars, and high economic growth before and after the rise of imperialism and militarism during this period. Against this background, the author investigates the impact of Japanese militarism and the wars and imperialism based on its influence on the modernization of Japanese dining.

Majima Ayu(真嶋亜有) examines the changes in the discourse on meat eating and the development of the livestock industry through military expansion during the Meiji era in "The Modernity of Meat Eating: The Military Demand for Meat and the Characteristics of Viewpoints toward Meat Eating in the Meiji Japan"(肉食という近代一明治期日本における食肉軍事需要と肉食観の特徴一, 2002).

Most Japanese literature pertaining to the topic of these fusion dishes only introduce the development process of the dishes regardless of the historical background such as the then Japanese government's policy for the enhancement of national prosperity and military power and its imperialist policy. This study, however, intends to maintain its focus on the fact that Sukiyaki and Tonkatsu were invented and developed into representative Japanese-Western fusion dishes in a very systematic and intentional way in accordance with these policies.

Therefore, this study examines the historical facts about the emergence of gyu nabe and Sukiyaki around the foreign settlements of Japanese port cities, which were formed in the wake of the government's policy for increasing national prosperity and strong military power and the opening of ports based on the consideration of the circumstances of the times. This study also looks at the conflicts that the Japanese society experienced in the process where Western cuisine was popularized among the common people in accordance with the government's policy after the lifting of the ban on meat consumption of Emperor Meiji. Furthermore, the study examines the birth of Tonkatsu through the spread and acceptance of Western cuisine among the commoners in the course of cross-cultural exchanges.

2. Policies to Enhance National Prosperity and Military Power and Promote a Meat-Eating Culture

The Meiji government embraced Western cultures to recreate Japan into a modern country similar to the Western powers. The state longed to overcome the country's physical inferiority complex and be on a par with the Westerners in terms of physical stature and condition by promoting meat consumption. Popularizing Western cuisine as part of its policy to spread a meat-eating culture, the Meiji government sought to absorb the Western food culture, along with modern civilization, colonialist, and imperialist policies. The Japanese had maintained a food culture of prohibiting meat consumption for 1,200 years since Emperor Tenmu's ban on eating meat in 675 under the influence of traditional Buddhist culture. However, in 1872, with the removal of the ban by Emperor Meiji, the government and intellectuals began actively promoting meat consumption to enhance national prosperity and military power.

The meat-eating habit that failed to penetrate Japanese society after the introduction of Buddhism revived during the Sengoku period. At that time, soldiers who were unable to obtain food on the battlefields would steal cattle from farmhouses and eat the meat by seasoning it with the soybean paste that they carried with them(Horio and Yokoyama, 2016).

Also, the Nanban(Portuguese and Spanish) trade and Western missionaries influenced the meat-eating culture of the time. From the mid-16th century, Portuguese missionaries entered Japan to spread Christianity, which led to the rapid increase in the number of Christians in the country. People who converted to Christianity were freed from the taboo against meat eating and started to enjoy European-style meat dishes(Ishige, 2017).

The preference for the Nanban cuisine spread around Kyushu, by Christians, contributing to the spread of meat eating. There is a historical record that the Shimazu Army of Satsuma moved live pigs to battlefields to provide pork to soldiers. Later, however, meat eating was banned again by Toyotomi(Horio and Yokoyama, 2016)

Meanwhile, although the Japanese had raised chickens from ancient times, they had rarely eaten chicken and eggs. Also, as horses had been used as a means of transportation by the upper class and cattle had been indispensable in the lives of farmers, the Japanese generally had not considered procuring meat from them. However, as cattle had not been regarded as significant, as compared to the farmers, by the upper class, they had practiced a conditional meat-eating habit to replenish nutrition, which violated the ban on meat consumption. To consume beef, a Western ingredient, they had cooked it in a Japanese style, seasoning it with soybean paste. Based on the recipes of cooking meat with soybean paste, the gyu nabe was later invented in the Kanto region.

One of the biggest changes in the diet of the Japanese during the Meiji era was the lifting of the ban on the use of four-legged livestock such as cattle and hogs for meat, and the introduction of a meat-eating culture that re-shaped their everyday food culture.

The Meiji government actively absorbed the cultures of the advanced civilizations of Europe and America as part of its movement for the enlightenment of the nation. The movement, which spurred modernization and promoted the development of industries and the growth of production, further sought national prosperity and strong military power. In addition, the Meiji government promoted a meat diet through nutrition education, cooking practice education, and media such as newspapers and magazines for women in order to establish a meat-eating culture in Japanese society. The meat diet was also introduced to the military. The Imperial Army actively introduced a diet combining traditional Japanese foods that the Japanese had been accustomed to before the war period and Western foods and meat, such as cutlets and croquettes, etc.

In 1869, the beef Sukiyaki restaurant Gekkatei(月下亭) opened in Motomachi, a foreign settlement in Kobe, but it did not earn a good reputation. As the commoners lacked recipes for beef, which was introduced to them through the government's policy to increase national prosperity and military power, they began consuming beef by cooking it using traditional condiments such as soybean paste. As the demand for beef soared and its supply was insufficient, pork, which was cheaper than beef, began to be supplied to the market. In 1900, the Japanese government launched a project to foster hog raising. Subsequently, the Russo-Japanese War, which broke out in 1904, contributed to the popularization of pork. Because beef was in short supply as it was supplied to the military, pork drew attention as a substitute. In the middle of the Meiji era, pork food culture was widely spread in the society and people became acquainted with Western pork cuisine as the pork food culture was created and the fusion dish Tonkatsu was invented.

From the Meiji era, the Japanese government strengthened its imperialist policies implemented since the start of the period aiming at modernization and the enhancement of national prosperity and military power based on the

〈Image 1〉 At the beginning of the Meiji era, along with the trend of civilization opening up, gyu nabe shops and beef shops prospered to a great extent.
『東京開化繁昌誌』萩原乙彦著 1874年刊 国立国会図書館所蔵
"Monograph of the Enlightenment and Thriving of Tokyo" written by Otohiko Hagiwara(1874, National Diet Library)

embracement of Western culture after the Sino-Japanese War(Nishikawa, 2010).

However, in the 1860s, the Japanese colonialist militarists came up with a definite theory. In 1875, Japan, which had been involved in the Unyoho issue, entered into the Korean-Japanese Treaty of Friendship February 27, 1876. It can be considered that it has begun to appear in earnest. After the failure in 1884, the Japanese, who favored Joseon, had a definite view, and Fukuzawa published 'Datsu-A Ron(Theory of Escaping from Asia)' on Jiji Shinpo's news on

March 16, 1885.

In addition, based on his imperialist ideas(Mitani, 2018), he urged the introduction of policies for increasing national wealth and promoting the progress of civilization(Suzuki, 2009) and emphasized the importance of balanced diet including meat and milk, pointing out that the traditional Japanese diet makes people prone to various diseases.

The removal of the existing ban on meat by Emperor Meiji in 1872 brought about arguments for and against meat eating while the upper class welcomed the lifting of the ban. However, the discourse on the meat diet turned to a political issue through the changes in the social conditions, such as the increased demand for meat from the military in the wake of the Sino-Japanese and Russo-Japanese Wars. In order to secure large quantities of meat in accordance with the increase in armaments, Japan began importing cattle from Korea. The Meiji government placed not only the import of Korean cattle, but also the Korean livestock industry under its administration.

So, the policies related to the import of Korean cattle were actively promoted during the Russo-Japanese War, and the number of imported Korean cattle surged after Japan's annexation of Korea. In 1910, Japan imported about 0.7 million cattle from Korea, but the number rose to about 0.9 million in 1911, to 1.04 million in 1912, and to 1.2 million in 1923. In short, the number increased by 0.2 million per year(See <Image 2>).

That is, in the process of controlling and developing the Korean livestock industry for food supply to Japan, meat eating gained a symbolic meaning of

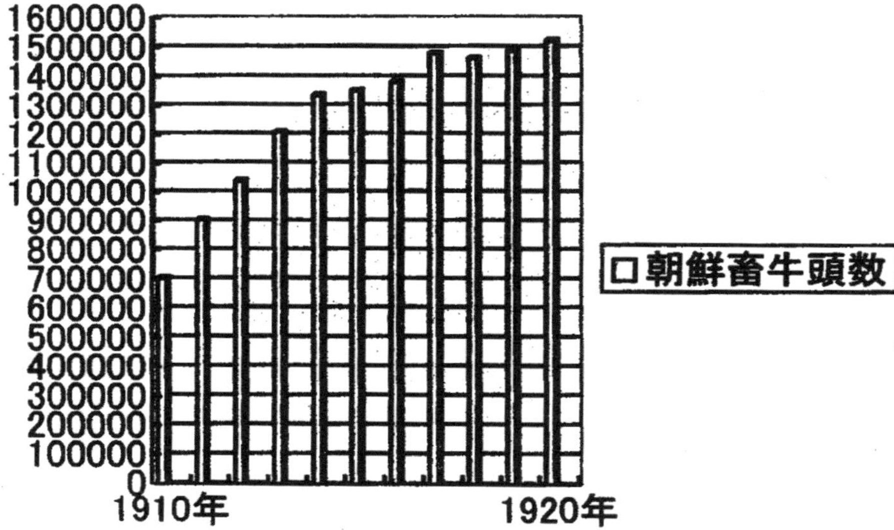

〈Image 2〉 The number of Korean cattle exported to Japan from 1910 to 1920(excerpted from the Korean Government's "Livestock of Korea")(Majima, 2002)

modernity as a product of colonialism(Majima, 2002). With these Japanese historical and political backgrounds taken into consideration, gyu nabe, Sukiyaki, and Tonkatsu can be regarded as Japanese-Western fusion dishes that were born and developed in accordance with the Japanese government's policy to increase national prosperity and military power during the Meiji era that marked the onset of the imperialist period.

〈table 1〉 The Changing Process of the Japanese Policy for National Prosperity and Strong Military Power and its Meat-Eating Culture

Year	Key Changes	Details
The 1860's	The rise of the Seikanron	The Seikanron (Debate on the Invasion of Korea) debate started by the Japanese militarists who sought the enhancement of the national prosperity and military power
1869	Thick sirloin used for Sukiyaki	The Sukiyaki restaurant Gekkatei(月下亭) opened in Motomachi, a foreign settlement in Kobe
1872	The lifting of the existing ban on meat eating and the promotion of meat consumption	The removal of the ban on meat eating by Emperor Meiji, which led to the active promotion of meat consumption by the government and intellectuals
1876	The signing of an unequal treaty	The US-Japan Treaty of 1876, which was an unequal treaty, concluded between the two countries on February 27; the launching of imperialist policies
1884	The expansion of the Seikanron	After the failure of the Gapsin Coup in Korea, the Seikanron spread among the Japanese who were favorable to Korea
1885	The rise of the Datsu-A Ron	The imperialist Fukuzawa Yukichi(福澤諭吉) published "Datsu-A Ron(Theory of Escaping from Asia) in Jiji Shinpo(時事新報) on March 16, in which he urged the policy for the improvement of the national prosperity and military power, emphasizing the need for increased meat consumption
1900	The launching of nationwide pig-raising project	A nationwide pig-raising project launched by the Japanese government as part of its policy to increase the national wealth and military power
After 1904	The supply of pork to the military for meal service	The outbreak of the Russo-Japanese War; Meal service in the military greatly affected the popularization of pork.
After 1910	Meat eating culture as a product of colonialism	The symbolic meaning of modernity attached to meat eating in the process of controlling and developing the Korean livestock industry for food supply to Japan

3. The Birth of Fusion Cuisine through Cross-Cultural Exchanges with Westerners in Port Cities

1) The Birth of Sukiyaki

In the 17th century under the Tokugawa Shogunate, the Japanese were exposed to opportunities to experience Western cuisine, including Portuguese and Spanish(Nanban) cuisine and Dutch(Komo) cuisine,[1] in foreign settlements at Hirado and Dejima in the port city of Nagasaki. The Nanban and Komo cuisine is regarded as the first Western cuisine introduced to Japan. Western dishes such as cocido[2] and picado[3] that used both meat and vegetables started to spread among the upper class and merchants of Nagasaki. At this time, onions, potatoes, carrots, pumpkins, red peppers, corn, pomegranates, and strawberries were also introduced to Japan, allowing the Japanese to experience various dishes. Three Japanese cooks called "Dejima kuzuneri"(出島くずねり) were dispatched from the Nagasaki Bugyosho(Magistrate's Office) to the Dejima Dutch Trading Post. The Dejima kuzuneri had played the role of pro-

---

1 Dutch(*Komo*) cuisine : cuisine introduced by the Dutch

2 Cocido : a dish made by seasoning poultry, fish, beef or boar meat and roundly cut white radish with green onions, garlics, whole peppers and then boiling them until they are fully cooked and cut only with chopsticks; It is served with a little vinegar added at the end.

3 Picado: Nagasaki's local food thought to have been originated from Japanese-style stew and made by boiling sliced tuna, pork and various vegetables such as radishes, carrots and sweet potatoes together; The name came from the Portuguese word "picado" meaning "to slice".

curing and preparing food since the Edo period and was the first to introduce Western cuisine to Japan. They learned Western cuisine while performing the job of dishwasher at the Dejima Dutch Trading Post. In 1863, Kusano Joukichi(草野丈吉), one of these cooks, opened Japan's first western restaurant in Nagasaki(Hiroma, 2014). Kusano received culinary training under the supervision of the Dutch consul general and named his restaurant Ryorintei(良林亭). These cooks who worked in Dejima laid the foundation for the development of Western cuisine in Japan since the Meiji era.

With the opening of ports after the US-Japan Treaty of 1858, Japan began to actively exchange with the US, the UK, France, the Netherlands, Russia, and other Western countries. The cross-cultural exchanges centering on foreign settlements in port cities also created opportunities for Japanese interpreters and government officials who often visited the areas to taste beef. The increase in trade and exchange with foreigners led to a surge in demand for beef, mainly in foreign settlements, resulting in a shortage of beef. At that time, as the cattle-raising livestock industry was not developed in Japan, cattle were imported from Europe, the US, China, and Korea, and was butchered on board ships(Nakazato, 1990). In 1865, beef processing facilities for foreigners were installed in the port city of Yokohama, and in 1866, beef produced in the port city of Kobe began to be supplied to Yokohama and Tokyo. Sukiyaki restaurant was opened in 1869 by Kobe Motomachi, a foreign-born settlement, and the beef Sukiyaki house Gekkatei opened its shop, but its reputation was not good. The Meiji government and intellectuals, thinking that the Japanese were inferior to Westerners in terms of physique and strength, implemented a policy to spread the meat-eating culture to the common people as part of their efforts to enhance the country's prosperity and military power.

The Japanese government believed that it was necessary to embrace the Western culture and cuisine in order to develop Japan into a modern nation like those of the Western powers and to achieve national prosperity and strong military power. Therefore, the state praised Western cuisine and promoted it nationwide. Western food culture spread among the upper class who first accepted Western foods through cross-cultural exchanges with the West. However, the commoners were still unfamiliar with the meat-eating culture, mainly because of the antipathy against Western culture caused by the Meiji government's radical reform, the influence of Buddhist culture, and the low preference for beef dishes. Repulsion towards eating beef was still felt among the common people.

Kanagaki Robun(假名垣魯文), a journalist from the late Edo period to the early Meiji era who was greatly influenced by Fukuzawa Yukichi(福澤諭吉), promoted meat eating in "Aguranabe(The Beef Eater, 牛店雑談 安愚楽鍋) (Okada, 2012)".

Also, Kato Yuichi(加藤祐一), an enlightenment reformer, emphasized the significance of the consumption of meat such as beef and pork.

Under the influence of the government's policies to establish a wealthy country and strong military power, and promote enlightenment and reform, the early Meiji era(around 1873) saw the increased interest in incorporating beef

◀「安愚楽鍋」(仮名垣魯文)〈挿絵〉1871～72年刊行。①ざんぎり頭②すそが出たワイシャツ③新聞④シルクハット⑤洋傘⑥牛鍋(すき焼き)など，文明開化のようすがわかる。魯文は，「牛肉食わねば開化不進奴」と記述。

〈Image 3〉 Published between 1871 and 1972, this book shows the appearance of the civilization and enlightenment, such as ① Cut one's hair short head ② Shirt from which the skirt appeared ③ Newspaper ④ Silk hat ⑤ Western Umbrella ⑥ beef pots(Sukiyaki). Robun wrote, 'If you don't eat beef, you'll never make a good enlightenment.
(『新詳日本史』浜島書店 2006.10 p.201)
("New Advanced Japanese History" Hamajima Bookstore 2006.10 p.201)

into Japanese cuisine, such as gyu nabe(the Kanto region) and Sukiyaki(the Kansai region), among the commoners.

In the Kanto region, beef restaurants used venison, wild boar meat, and horse-meat as well as beef. Since the beef at that time was tough and had a strong smell of fat, it was often boiled down using the traditional Japanese condiment soybean paste to remove the odor. That is, gyu nabe was a fusion dish that cooked beef, which had been introduced from Western cuisine, with traditional Japanese condiments such as soybean paste. As the meat quality was improved and various ingredients such as green onions, tofu, and pine mushrooms were added, and the *warishita*[4](割り下) broth, made with soybean sauce, sugar, anchovy broth, and mirim started to be used to simmer the beef, gyu nabe was further enhanced.

On the other hand, residents in the Kansai region employed a different method to prepare Sukiyaki. They first cooked the beef in a pan and seasoned it with sugar and soy sauce. The seasoned meat was then boiled and added to the other ingredients in order, starting from the vegetables as they had the highest moisture content. Sukiyaki was different from gyu nabe, which was made by boiling meat and vegetables at the same time after placing the ingredients in the warishita broth. However, in that the Sukiyaki incorporated beef, a Western ingredient, and was cooked with traditional Japanese condiments, it can be also classified as a fusion dish. It has been presumed that Sukiyaki originated from the Edo period farmers' habit of cooking fish or tofu on the metal parts of their farming tools such as plows when they got hungry while working. It has been also argued that the farmers used cedar wood boards instead of farming tools to cook their meals. However, it has been widely known that Sukiyaki originated from uosuk i,[5] a dish that was popular in the Kansai region. The fish of uoski was replaced by meat and the name of the dish also changed to Sukiyaki.

Japanese-Western fusion cuisine, not authentic Western cuisine, emerged from the middle to the late Meiji era. Kawabata Shoko, an authority on culinary arts, states that Japan's unique fusion cuisine greatly influenced the birth of Western-style Japanese cuisine in "The Development of Western Cuisine(Western-style Japanese Cuisine, or Fusion Cuisine)". From around 1897, the term

4 Warishita : broth prepared by mixing and boiling soy sauce, anchovy broth, sugar, mirim, etc. together to use it for hot pot or nabe dishes

5 Uosuki : a dish using seasonal fresh marine seafood such as bream, sea urchins, shellfish, seaweeds and various vegetables and served with broth seasoned with various spices

〈table 2〉 The Historical Development of Sukiyaki

Year	Key Changes	Details
1866	The supply of beef	Beef produced in the port city of Kobe started to be supplied to Yokohama, Tokyo and other regions
1869	The opening of the first Sukiyaki restaurant	The Sukiyaki restaurant Gekkatei(月下亭) opened in Motomachi, a foreign settlement in Kobe
1871～1872	Sukiyaki found on the menus of restaurants	Sukiyaki mentioned in "Aguranabe"(The Beef Eater, 牛店雑談安愚楽鍋) by Kanagaki Robun(假名垣魯文), a journalist from the late Edo period to the early Meiji era who was greatly influenced by Fukuzawa Yukichi
Around 1873	Increased interest in gyu nabe(the Kanto region) and Sukiyaki(the Kansai region)	Increased interest in gyu nabe(the Kanto region) and Sukiyaki(the Kansai region), which are the Japanese dishes using beef, among commoners
Around 1897	The coinage of the term "Japanese-Western fusion cuisine"	The term "Japanese-Western fusion cuisine" popularized in Japanese society
Around 1923	The integration of "gyu nabe" into "Sukiyaki"	The closing of most gyu nabe restaurants in Tokyo due to the Kanto Earthquake in 1923; The entrance of Sukiyaki restaurants into the Kanto region, leading to the integration of "gyu nabe" into "Sukiyaki"

"Japanese-Western fusion cuisine" began gaining popularity, referring to the cuisine between Japanese cuisine completed during the Edo period and authentic Western cuisine. In 1886, Western cuisine was included in the curriculum of the girls' schools in Tokyo and culinary education grew more active in these schools at the request of the parents who wanted their daughters to be acquainted with fusion cuisine. When Western cuisine was first introduced to Japan, the Japanese were mainly influenced by cross-cultural exchanges as they learned recipes from Westerners. However, it was the influence of internal exchanges rather than that of cross-cultural exchanges that greatly contributed to the birth of fusion cuisine. Many of Tokyo's gyu nabe restaurants that were severely devastated by the Kanto Earthquake in 1923 were forced to close. Subsequently, as the Sukiyaki restaurants in the Kansai region were expanded to the Kanto region, the term “gyu nabe” was integrated into “Sukiyaki”. Since then, Sukiyaki has been known as a representative dish of Japanese-Western fusion cuisine around the world.

2) The Birth of Tonkatsu

In the early Edo period, pigs were introduced to Satsuma[6] from China via Ryukyu(the present Okinawa). Satsuma soup(Satsuma jiru), which used pork as the main ingredient, gained popularity among Japanese swordsmen and Rangaku(Dutch or Western Learning) scholars and medical practitioners in the port city of Kyushu, despite the ban on the slaughter of livestock, and even spread to Edo. As the Chinese people living in Nagasaki started to raise pigs, Dejima's Dutch people processed pork into ham and sausages. Therefore, in Nagasaki and Satsuma, the custom of eating pork was preserved from earlier times.

After the Meiji Restoration, Tsunoda Yonesaburo(角田米三郎) founded the Kyokyusha(協救社) in 1869, and sought to improve the national prosperity and military power by fostering school establishment and railroad construction through pig farming, which promoted the consumption of

6 Satsuma : present Kagoshima, southernmost of mainland Japan

pork(Tokyo Metropolitan Museum of Public Library. 2003). With the popularization of pork in the middle of the Meiji era, the Japanese became acquainted with the Western cuisine for pork, and a food culture related to pork was created. With the soaring demand for beef, which is an essential ingredient of Western cuisine, it became difficult to secure beef due to insufficient supply. Therefore, pork, which was cheaper than beef and the primary ingredient of Tonkatsu, began to be supplied to the market. In 1900, the Japanese government actively fostered pig raising by importing breeding pigs from the US and the UK in order to respond to the shortage of beef, which was supplied to the military for the soldiers' meals. At the same time, meat eating was promoted as part of the country's policy for national prosperity and military power increase, which led to the active popularization of pork. Steadily, the common people became more familiar with pork through the spread of Western cuisine, and from 1882 to 1883, demand for pork began to soar in Tokyo. Also, as exchanges with foreigners from different countries increased during this period, the Japanese people began to pay more attention to pork, which established the foundation for the invention of Tonkatsu. Tonkatsu was first made in Japan approximately 60 years after the recipe for horu katsuretsu(ホールクコツトレツ) was introduced to the country in 1872 through "The Western Cuisine Expert"(西洋料理通) written by Kanagaki Robun(仮名垣魯文). "Horuku" means pork and "katsuretsu" means cutlet, which is pork meat attached to the ribs or sirloin covered with flour, not breadcrumbs, and then fried in a frying pan with a small amount of oil. The term "pork katsuretsu", which has the same meaning as "horuku katsuretsu", is a combination of "pork" and "katsuretsu", the Japanese pronunciation of "cutlet". Pork katsuretsu, the predecessor of Tonkatsu, began to be sold in 1895 at Rengatei(煉瓦亭) in Ginza, Tokyo, and was served with cabbage. Ginza, where this restaurant was located, was close to a foreign settlement in Tsukiji Akashi-cho and the Tonkatsu of this restaurant was popular among regular foreign customers as it was a Western-style dish that they could not taste in their countries. During this time, a number of fusion cuisine restaurants began to open. These restaurants used more than half of the pork that they secured for Western dishes such as pork katsuretsu. The historical records on Tonkatsu and the restaurants that served the dish are as follows.

Nagai Kafu(永井荷風)'s essay "Ginza"(銀座, 1911) refers to the Japanese Tonkatsu served by street vendors(Nagai, 1986). It also writes that new fusion dishes called "Tonkatsu kare"(カツカレー, curry rice with a pork cutlet) and katsudon(カツ丼, rice topped with a pork cutlet) were invented and started to be served in local restaurants in 1918 and in 1921, respectively. Also, in 1921, the Tonkatsu specialty restaurant Oroji(王ろじ) in Shinjuku began to sell the Tonkatsu made by frying thick pork sirloin that was then cut into bite-sized pieces. In 1929, Shimada Shinjiro(島田信二郎), who was working at Ponchiken(ぽんち軒) in Okachimachi(御徒町), Ueno, Tokyo, invented a new type of Tonkatsu. Instead of roasting pork on a Western frying pan with a small amount of oil, he applied a deep frying method in fat, soaking the pork in oil and frying it until it was cooked deep inside. This method made it possible to fully cook 2.5cm-3cm thick meat. Gradually, the pork meat used for Tonkatsu was replaced by the boneless variety that could be eaten with chopsticks, and breadcrumbs were used instead of flour for the batter. In addition, cutlets began to be served cut into small pieces to allow customers to eat the Tonkatsu with chopsticks without knives or forks reminiscent to when they ate Japanese dishes. With the addition of chopped cabbage to the dish, the present Japanese Tonkatsu was completed.

Since then, Tonkatsu was accompanied by the side dish of chopped cabbage, which went well with soybean paste soup and rice. In addition, the chopped cabbage removed the smell of fat, adding freshness to the dish. In 1932, restaurants claiming to be Tonkatsu-specialty restaurants(楽天, 喜田八, 井泉, etc). opened one by one in Ueno and Asakusa, creating a Tonkatsu craze in Downtown Tokyo. By this time the term "Tonkatsuretsu" was often found in cookbooks and menus. The term "Tonkatsu" was established through the naming evolution from horuku katsuretsu → pork katsuretsu → Tonkatsuretsu → Tonkatsu.

The difference between the whole cutlet and the Japanese Pork Cutlet can be seen in the following in 〈table 3〉.

Tonkatsu, a Japanese fusion dish, was born and developed under the influence of Western cuisine during the time when pig raising was fostered nation-

〈table 3〉 The difference between the whole cutlet and the Japanese Pork Cutlet

Whole cutlet	Japanese Pork Cutlet
The Western Cuisine Expert: pork	First: beef, chicken Later: pork
Meat on bone	Bone-free meat that can be eaten with chopsticks
Only flour on the surface and no bread crumbs	Use flour and bread crumbs.

〈table 4〉 The Historical Development of Tonkatsu

Year	Key Changes	Details
1895	The birth of pork katsuretsu	Pork katsuretsu, the predecessor of Tonkatsu, started to be sold at Rengatei(煉瓦亭) in Ginza, Tokyo, served with chopped cabbage
1921	Thick sirloin used for Tonkatsu	The Tonkatsu specialty restaurant Oroji(王ろじ) in Shinjuku began to sell the Tonkatsu made by frying thick pork sirloin and then cut into bite-sized pieces.
Around 1929	The establishment of the current Japanese Tonkatsu style	Ponchiken(ぽんち軒) in Okachimachi, Ueno, Tokyo, invented and started to sell a new type of Tonkatsu. Deep fat frying method 2.5 to 3cm thick meat Boneless meat Bread crumbs used instead of flour for batter Served cut into small pieces to allow customers to eat it only with chopsticks, without knives or forks Accompanied by chopped cabbage Established as the style of the current Tonkatsu
1932	OpenINGpork cutlet shops in Ueno(上野) and Asakusa(浅草), such as 楽天, 喜田八, 井泉	- A series of shops that specialize in pork cutlet, such as "楽天" "喜田八" and "井泉" in Ueno(上野) or Asakusa(浅草), have opened, booming for pork cutlet in downtown Tokyo. - Popular restaurants dealing with various Japanese, Western and Chinese dishes, including the Sudacho(須田町) restaurants and large department stores, have become famous, contributing to the spread of pork cutlet.
1941～1948	Booming for pork cutlet temporarily disappears	The pork cut boom temporarily disappears due to control of supplies by World War II.
1958	Opening of the first store in Wako, a pork cutlet chain	- A way to keep frying clothes covered with pork cutlet crunchy is for barbed wire. - New service offensive, including additional shredded cabbage and soybean paste soup, will intensify competition among pork cutlet stores

wide as part of the Japanese government's policy for promoting national prosperity and a strong military. The spread of pork as a food for the Japanese military greatly influenced the popularization of Tonkatsu, and the present Tonkatsu was completed in the age of Japanese imperialism. In 1958, after the defeat of Japan, the first store of Wako(和幸), a Japanese chain of Tonkatsu restaurants, was opened. This restaurant used a wire net when frying pork to prevent the batter from becoming soggy and to keep it crispy. It also provided new services, offering free refills of chopped cabbage and soybean paste soup, which intensified competition among Tonkatsu-specialty restaurants.

4. Conclusions

This study examined the historical facts about the emergence and development process of Sukiyaki and Tonkatsu in Japan around the foreign settlements formed by the then Japanese government's policies to enhance national prosperity and military power and promote a meat-eating culture and the opening of ports, based on the circumstances of the times. It also investigated the historical facts about the birth and evolution of Tonkatsu, a fusion dish created by using pork during the time of beef shortage due to its soaring demand in Japan and in response, the supply of pork to the market as a substitute. The results of the analysis can be summarized as follows.

① The Japanese meat-eating culture was formed based on the government's policy for increasing national prosperity and strong military power, and it is a culture born when the tradition of banning meat eating changed to the meat-eating promotion policy.

② The meat-eating culture was promoted by the Japanese government to overcome the nation's physical inferiority complex based on cross-cultural exchanges with Westerners. This was closely related to the government-led embracement of the food culture, scientific knowledge, and the imperialist policies of the West.

③ The Japanese common people initially expressed repulsion towards the meat diet and the government policy that promoted meat-eating was initially not very successful. However, the introduction of the meat diet to the military played a major role in spreading the meat-eating culture.

④ Sukiyaki, a well-known fusion dish that combines Japanese traditional cuisine and Western food culture, was developed with the introduction of the beef-eating culture through cross-cultural exchanges with the West since the 17th-century Edo period. Sukiyaki is a dish that harmonizes traditional Japanese condiments and beef, the main ingredient of Western cuisine. In the past, it was known as "Sukiyaki" in the Kansai region, and as "gyu nabe" in the Kanto region. Both recipes incorporated similar ingredients but differed in the cooking process and methods. Under the influence of the Kanto Earthquake in 1923, the two terms were integrated into "Sukiyaki". Today, this type of dish is collectively called "Sukiyaki".

⑤ Another Japanese fusion dish, Tonkatsu, was invented as the difficulty in procuring beef increased due to its surge in demand as well as its shortage. In response, pork, which was cheaper than beef and a main ingredient of Tonkatsu, began to be supplied to the market under the Japanese government's policy to enhance the national prosperity and military power and to promote meat eating. The spread of pork as food for the Japanese military greatly influenced the popularization of Tonkatsu, and the present Tonkatsu was completed in the age of Japanese imperialism.

⑥ This study shows that the historical background, which entailed the Japanese government's policy to enhance the national prosperity and strengthen its military power, the embracement of Western culture, the promotion of a meat-eating culture, imperialist policies, and the aggressive wars, are closely related to the birth and development of beef dishes such as Sukiyaki and pork dishes such as Tonkatsu.

⑦ It is not fair to consider that the common people of Japan, who invented and developed Sukiyaki and Tonkatsu, were also closely related to the policies of the Japanese government. They succeeded in creating and developing the internationally known Japanese fusion dishes because they made great efforts to invent their own delicious dishes through research and much trial and error. Their efforts and attitudes provide a good model for Korean cuisine.

This study analyzed the historical backgrounds of Sukiyaki and Tonkatsu, the fusion dishes created through cross-cultural exchanges with Western countries in the port cities of Japan. It was proved that the food culture, which seems to have no relation to the historical facts of the aggressive wars waged by Japan, was closely related to the country's policy for the promoting national prosperity and strong military power and imperialist policy. However, the successful cases of the invention and development of new and unique fusion cuisine by combining traditional Japanese and Western food cultures through cross-cultural exchanges with the West can serve as a model for Korean cuisine. It is expected that Korea also develops fusion cuisine and products preferred by the world through the acceptance of these models.

Contributors

This paper was published in

Sehyun Cho, *From the Sea of the Tianxia(天下) to the Sea of the Nation(國家)*, *Ilchogak*, 2016.
Sukyong Kwak, *The Journal of Humanities and Social Sciences* 19-1, 2018.
Moonkee Kim, *DAEGUSAHAK* 115, 2014.
Kwangdeok Seo, *The Journal of Humanities* 40-3, 2019.
Bogo Lee, *The Journal of Chinese Languaue and Literature(JCLL)* 110, 2018.
Seungwoong Ahn, *Journal of North-east Asian Cultures* 52, 2017.
Minho Yang, *The Journal of Humanities and Social Sciences* 19-3, 2018.
Minkyung Choi, *The Journal of Humanities and Social sciences*, 19-4, 2018.
Sehyun Cho, *Overseas Chinese History in Busan, Sanjini,* 2013.
Mihee Kong, *Journal of Marine and Island Cultures* 7-2, 2018.